The
FANTASY
and
NECESSITY
of
SOLIDARITY

ALSO BY SARAH SCHULMAN

PLAYS (PUBLISHED)

Carson McCullers

Mercy

PLAYS (PRODUCED BUT NOT PUBLISHED)

Manic Flight Reaction

Enemies, A Love Story
(adapted from the novel by I. B. Singer)

The Lady Hamlet

FILMS (COWRITER AND/OR COPRODUCER)

The Owls

Mommy Is Coming

United in Anger: A History of ACT UP

Jason and Shirley

BOOKS ABOUT THE AUTHOR

*Queer Kinship in Sarah Schulman's
AIDS Novels* by Jarosław Milewski

Conversations with Sarah Schulman
by Will Brantley, ed.

The
FANTASY
and
NECESSITY
of
SOLIDARITY

SARAH SCHULMAN

THESIS

THESIS

An imprint of Penguin Random House LLC
1745 Broadway, New York, NY 10019
penguinrandomhouse.com

For details on special quantity discounts for bulk purchases,
contact specialmarkets@penguinrandomhouse.com.

BOOK DESIGN BY TANYA MAIBORODA

Grateful acknowledgment is made for permission to reprint the following:

English translation of "Resist Them" published with permission of Dareen Tatour.

"When Solidarity Fails: The Death of Bryn Kelly" by Morgan M. Page and Sarah Schulman first published as "Queer Suicidality, Conflict, and Repair" and first appeared in *QED: A Journal in GLBTQ Worldmaking—Project MUSE* in 2017. Used with permission of Morgan M. Page and the University of Michigan State Press.

"Carson McCullers, White Writer and Her Attitude Toward Life" adapted with permission from the piece "White Writer" that originally appeared in *The New Yorker* (2016).

The following essays have been previously published, sometimes in different form: "European Abortion Underground Railroad" first published as "Secret History of an Underground Abortion Network" in *Harper's Bazaar* (2021); "Jean Genet in Palestine" first published as "Edmund White's Jean Genet in Palestine" in *Crashing Cathedrals* (2019); "Jeremy O. Harris and the Plight of Women Playwrights" first published as "Sure, Resolve to Stage More Plays by Women. It Still Won't Make Up for All We've Lost" in *The Los Angeles Times* (2021); portions of "New Strategies for Abortion Rights" first appeared in *The New Republic* (2022); "Joey Soloway, *Transparent*, and the Boycott of Israel" first appeared as "How the BDS Movement Convinced *Transparent* Creator Jill Soloway to Shoot in L.A. Instead of Israel" in *Mondoweiss* (2018); "Testifying Before the City University of New York Task Force on Antisemitism" first appeared in *Mondoweiss* (2016); "Pinkwashing" first appeared as "A Documentary Guide to 'Brand Israel' and the Art of Pinkwashing" in *Mondoweiss* (2011); an excerpt in "An American Jew in Solidarity with Gaza" first appeared as "Explanations Are Not Excuses" in *Intelligencer/New York Magazine* (2023).

LIBRARY OF CONGRESS CONTROL NUMBER: 2024055409

ISBN 9780593854259 (hardcover)
ISBN 9780593854266 (ebook)

Printed in the United States of America
1 3 5 7 9 10 8 6 4 2

The authorized representative in the EU for product safety and compliance is Penguin Random House Ireland, Morrison Chambers, 32 Nassau Street, Dublin D02 YH68, Ireland, https://eu-contact.penguin.ie.

Dedicated to Matt Brim, a great friend

Ask what you can do, not what you can lose.

—GHADIR SHAFIE,
Palestinian queer activist

Contents

The
FANTASY
and
NECESSITY
of
SOLIDARITY

1

Solidarity:
Fantasy and Necessity

WHEN SOLIDARITY IS ROOTED IN INEQUALITY

Perhaps I am a novelist because I have always been fascinated by how people understand their own lives—not how we wish they would or think they should, but how they actually do. So, I wasn't surprised that one snowy night in 2023, I had my mind opened by a conversation with a brilliant woman. Not just anyone. That evening, I had the great fortune to have dinner with the American writer, intellectual, and consummate New Yorker Vivian Gornick. Author of *The Romance of American Communism* and the writers' bible, *The Situation and the Story*, Vivian is a wise woman who has lived through some of the eras of American radicalism that have most inspired me. After a fascinating conversation about her historic experiences of the American left and of second wave feminism, Vivian asked what I was working on.

"A book on solidarity."

"What are you saying about it?"

"Well . . ." It was early in the project, and I hadn't found a summary sentence yet, but . . . I just jumped in. "Since solidarity is a relationship rooted in inequality, it is by definition fraught. And so—"

"Wait a minute." Vivian was confused. "Inequality?" Solidarity, she explained clearly, is a relationship of equals joining together to create a powerful force for change.

And suddenly I realized how much my grappling reflected a different world than the traditional and perhaps original concept of people in similar conditions joining together: Workers striking for better wages, safer conditions, and meaningful labor. Tenants uniting to extend rent restrictions and for more affordable, supportive housing. Black people defying white supremacy to win access and autonomy. Women standing up to men, doctors, and government toward the goal of safe, legal, and affordable abortion. People with HIV fighting for treatment and against stigma. All these different kinds of communities unite internally to oppose and thereby transform the forces that oppress them. And of course, Vivian was right, sometimes this horizontal unity is enough to move forward toward justice. After all, if people living in shared conditions can muster enough cooperation with one another, they often have the strength to better their lives.

But in our age of globalized capital and its manifestations in government, we can't stand up to conglomerated power by ourselves. We live in a country with a court system that often defies the Constitution and leaders who don't abide by their stated values. Americans are in a time of a co-opted press, and a class-stratified educational system accountable to congressional committees. Our lives take place within complex structures of illegitimate power that are both entrenched and invisible. Starbucks workers can organize, but not if the Supreme Court undermines the National Labor Relations Board. University presidents, faculty, and students have academic freedom unless they speak out against mass murder of Palestinians and other people the system sees as disposable. Black people can vote until they live in a state whose rulers use their power to obstruct them. Everywhere we look, social control is consolidated into fewer and fewer hands. Counterculture, where the imagination of freedom is perpetually conjured, now must hide from marketing, branding, and monetization to influence the center from the margins.

By holding solid control of public discourse and relying on police violence, the machinery of dominance can make it impossible for the afflicted to win justice on their own steam. At that point, the collaboration and fellowship of people at other levels of power becomes necessary to create more justice for all. That is the idea of solidarity that I engage in this book. Recognition, by bystanders and conflicted perpetrators, of injustice against others, followed by creative and risk-taking acts of correction to the vast differences in comfort and safety among us, creates the people power necessary to reach the tipping point that transforms lives and, in the most extreme conditions of brutality, actually saves lives.

The opposite of oppression is not only freedom but also belonging. It is the construction of a listening and acting body around the suffering person that creates a context for transformation. The standard wisdom is that we can't change other people, but other people change me all the time, for better and for worse. Both committing and allowing injustice imposes tragic change. Stopping or reducing it creates the paradigm shift, building the people power needed to realize the necessity of positive new beginnings. And participating in this kind of change is among the most meaningful uses of our one and only life. Solidarity is the essential human process of recognizing that other people are real and their experiences matter. It is based in learning to evaluate the state of the world by the collective and not only by our own, individual experience. Solidarity is the action behind the revelation that each of us, individually, are not the only people with dreams.

FANTASY: FROM BYSTANDER TO FRIEND

Because I am not religious, my point of view is that heaven and hell take place on earth. Therefore, our destinies are created by mortals, not by gods, and are in our hands. While it is impossible for every part of every life to be heavenly, hell is too often a humanly imposed reality, the direct impact or long-term consequence of being overwhelmed by someone else's abused power. So, when we are trapped by other people's actions, we dream of relief. When we are being violently attacked and can't make it stop on our own, we dream of someone else physically removing the bully, underminer, police officer, soldier, father, rapist, or false accuser. We dream of a literal person driving them away, or even better, holding them down and making them understand their crime. We dream of change, of the end of pain and the beginning of amends.

When the actual bombs fall, human beings wish to survive, for their loved ones to survive, for their world to remain intact or recoverable, and this imagining includes some outside force—other people—stopping the planes from taking off. It could be the citizens of the aggressor nation refusing to serve in their military. Perhaps the obstruction will come from employees at corporations or students and teachers at corporate and public universities disrupting financial and cultural investments in the oppressing forces. It can be writers and artists refusing to prop up cultural institutions that normalize perpetrators and the values that uphold them. It can be union members refusing to ship arms, or clergy refusing to be complicit in the name of prayer.

As the helpless hide in flimsy corners, braving the violence to speak the truth, to report the facts, to teach the reality, those under attack imagine others they do not know coming to conscious awareness, risking their own safety in turn—for strangers they may have been raised to despise or ignore. The afflicted courageously risk their remaining freedom, status, and very lives in hopes that someone out there will listen, hear, and act. And occasionally, long after peace or equality should have been achieved, long after unknown numbers of lives have been wasted, talents ignored, futures obstructed and destroyed, these others may become effective in helping to create a condition in which the pendulum may swing.

Because the kind of solidarity addressed here is rooted in inequality, it is by definition fraught. The experience of reaching—or asking others to reach—from a place of protection to the reality of the vulnerable can therefore never be heroic or perfect. That false expectation too often makes solidarity impossible to imagine and therefore to enact.

Part of the fantasy of being in solidarity is a magical combination of pure motive, clean action, and predictably victorious outcome. Part of the fantasy is that we will do everything right and give up nothing and the afflicted will love us, as we will love each other and ourselves. The bystander is often so used to being powerful without effort that they fantasize a simple change in attitude fixing the pain of the victim. The delusion is that we are *so* entitled, we only have to intercede and the desired change will occur. The expectation can be that this new solidarity-fueled reality will produce the deepest of human relationships: friendship, with gratitude as the icing.

Well, it is not that way.

Even while making progress, so much can go wrong expressly *because* of the inequality. Those offering the solidarity can fail once or over and over again. They can even inflict more damage, or new damage. They can earn the legitimate wrath of those they struggled to identify with for underestimating their pain and urgency, for speaking for them, for complicating loyalties. At the same time, offering solidarity can make one an undeserved object of the anger, frustration, and pain of the suffering that the person in solidarity has not caused. Blame and resentment can replace the inaccessibility of power. And it is also possible that at some point in the long journey of standing beside another person in a deeper state of oppression, we can make ourselves feel better about our own supremacy for simply trying, even if we are unable to achieve full impact. As I will show in many different arenas and with varied nuances, *motive* for joining in solidarity can be murky, individual, filled with contradiction, and psychologically complex. Yet, if some kind of positive outcome is achieved, the lack of pure motive may actually not really matter.

Simultaneously, the threats that accompany solidarity can be very real. Whether we are effective or not, often the intervener will pay a price in the process. It is rarely equivalent to the price the oppressed must pay, but it can make a difference. The consequence can be a symbol, a stigma, a badge of honor, or much, much more. Joining with the oppressed can produce active disapproval, anger, and the desire to punish on the part of family, government, employer, clique, or milieu. The mirror created by defection from privilege reveals more truth than many left behind can bear. This defiance of the social expectation to conform to brutality, or at least be silent about it, can be very costly. It can cost you your job, your friends, your dreams, and it can cost you your life.

I often think about the Americans in the 1930s who opposed the fascism that was rising in Spain under the leadership of Francisco Franco. Our government stood silently by, but these individuals did not. They formed the Abraham Lincoln Brigade and raised funds to go to Spain to fight, filled with the fantasy of the independent actor triumphing over evil, of human beings reaching across difference to connect and embrace. Yet, because Republican forces did not have US state backing, many of the volunteers were killed or wounded as Franco triumphed into a dictatorship lasting forty years. Of course, almost a decade later, the US finally did enter the global war against German, Italian, and Spanish fascism, and Japanese Imperial monarchy. By that time, being "anti-fascist" was the US fallback position. In the 1940s the average American thought of himself as anti-fascist, meaning pro–United States. But later in their lives, the US survivors of the Spanish Civil War were highly stigmatized in America, as post–World War Two anti-communist McCarthyism swept the national consciousness. The Spanish Civil War veterans and their supporters found themselves excluded from participation and advancement, shunned and punished under the charge of being "prematurely anti-fascist."

I have always been fascinated by the accusation of opposing oppression *too soon*, before it is acceptable. The immense power of conformity, perhaps originating in early colonial American racial and religious domination, furthered by corporate cultures of marketing and branding, has always made innovators into outsiders. This includes those who innovate visions of freedom. The first person to have an idea that identifies and threatens power structures is an unlucky individual; much better to be the fifth, to come along when the waters have already been warmed and the politics of repetition have made the idea vaguely familiar. When solidarity movements finally pop through the surface of repressed ideas, it is often because preexisting insights have already been expressed by those desperate to transform their own condition outside of trend or fashion, joined by the handful who actually heed their call.

For years, decades, centuries, these developing but marginalized freedom visions may have no impact, may be mocked, and their creators punished. But then when the zeitgeist hits, these traditions become the actual infrastructure upon which movements can finally stand. The visions of the dreamer can come true, usually for someone else, but it is the fantasies of the prematurely anti-fascist that are necessary for the subsequent real transformation to take hold. The unveiling of human acts of injustice, calls to end violence or inequality, and exposés of structures of domination are unwelcome at first, when they are the most difficult to articulate and illustrate and therefore most matter. Tragically, this is especially true when the people directly hurt by unbridled power are the only voices calling for change. As they repeat and repeat and repeat their pleas for a new way to live together, they begin to be heard by a small group that starts to—unpopularly—join them by rebelling against the stagnancy of their own society. The innovator makes something rough-hewn, and because it is new, it is unrecognizable, unfamiliar, and uncomfortable. The derivator makes it smooth, conformed, and familiar in a world where familiarity—telling people what they already know—is so often confused with quality. The innovator makes the greater contribution and pays the higher price. And though they rarely are victorious, their examples are great lessons in courage and ingenuity that make the future possible.

NECESSITY: FROM BYSTANDER TO PEOPLE POWER

The purpose of this book is to make solidarity doable. My approach is to juxtapose many resonant examples of different kinds of solidarities—from individuals and communities—to reveal their complexities. I want to listen to and hear the people who are asking for solidarity in order to understand their needs, strategies, and values. And to confront the obstacles and confusion faced by those who join them. As long as we think of solidarity as saintly, we will not be able to fulfill it. But when our sense of possibility is guided by anticipation of error and contradiction interspersed with great leaps, solidarity becomes at first a realistic possibility and then eventually can be real. In this book I will look at a range of imperfect individuals and collectives from estranged contexts who stumble and rise to build the complex relationships essential to balance power. I believe and express in all my work—novels, plays, screenplays, journalism, and nonfiction—that healing occurs in relationship in both the personal and global spheres.

Framed throughout by the international call to solidarity with Palestine that defines our times, I contextualize many examples within the decades of Palestinian experience of displacement, incarceration, murder, and cultural erasure that have occurred in the face of much apathy, until now. The acknowledgment that this global abandonment, as of summer 2024, produced the deliberate slaughter of over forty thousand people in Gaza by Israel, their forced starvation and imposed thirst, and Israel's planned destruction of millions of people's homes, schools, and hospitals is essential to any contemporary ideas about solidarity in general. That this depraved consequence of Israeli supremacy ideology and Palestinian marginalization finally provokes a massive global rise of support—and that this grassroots protest has not yet achieved a tipping point—is the world we are now in. History is happening.

As I write this in 2024, millions of people literally take to the streets because they cannot stand by and passively watch the brutality. How the once-marginal Palestinian demand for BDS (Boycott, Divestment, Sanctions) and for an academic and cultural boycott of Israel have become the common parlance of the conscious of the world who are horrified by Israeli brutality is a lesson in incremental movement building. This is a process, and we are in the midst. Divestment, the *D* of BDS, is now the demand of tens of thousands of US students and the broader community who are protesting the complicity of their institutions. People are being arrested on the streets of our cities and students are getting arrested on campus, being denied graduation, being suspended or expelled, and facing the hostility of the police in their opposition to US funding of the mass murder of Palestinians, Lebanese, and others. American artists and writers increasingly stand for cultural boycott and demand it of our presenting organizations. Churches, unions, social justice organizations, and nonprofits are all facing internal staff and membership demands for BDS. In many cases it is the boards of directors that obstruct the constituency's will. For others it is the reverse. The insistence on not normalizing systematic violence is the topic of conversation at many tables, and in many corners previously solely preoccupied with personal ambition. This energy for change is coming from the grassroots as corporate media and elected officials deny what people everywhere increasingly understand to be true.

And yet this book also traverses the Palestinian example to explore a wide range of separations and creative alliances in order to understand solidarity as a phenomenon larger than any single milieu. Regardless of specificity, solidarity always requires awareness, self-criticism, consciousness, the decision to act, and the need to create strategy, to build alliances, and to listen. It always requires taking chances, making mistakes, and trying again. For this reason, I include examples from a European abortion underground railroad, the New York Prostitutes Collective, and trans life, and I provide an intense focus on the function of the culture industry in creating consensus through exclusion. I look at the role of standards in education and art that are used to justify discrediting large numbers of people, their experiences, and their points of view. I visit complex but inspiring iconoclasts like Jean Genet, Alice Neel, Wilmette Brown, and Carson McCullers to see how their motives in their reaches to connect were personal more than ideological, and yet produced valuable outcomes. I want to examine, question, celebrate, and learn from many kinds of solidarities across communities and realms, their flawed innovations and successful achievements. All, I believe, resonating to affirm the recognition that more, somehow, is possible.

2

An American Jew
in Solidarity with Gaza

IT WAS NOT UNTIL 2009 that I made the decision to face and
learn the reality of the Israeli occupation and consequences of
its force on Palestinian lives. This turning point began a lifelong
process of change whose origin is described in my book *Israel/
Palestine and the Queer International*. Although I am embarrassed
and ashamed that it took me so long to make this commitment to
understanding reality, it was one of the most influential and enriching decisions of my life. Not only did I come to face what was
actually occurring in the world, but I was able to criticize my own
self-concept in relationship to others, and thereby transform it into
action. In this way I learned who I was, relationally, and awoke to
the fact that my responsibility to myself cannot be different from
my responsibility to others. I saw these two elements become more
cohered into one life.

Up until that moment of decision, I was so voluntarily ignorant
that I did not even know that the Nakba—the Palestinian name

for literally the "catastrophe" of the murder and military expulsion of Palestinians by Israelis in 1948—was exactly the same event as the one celebrated by Israeli Independence Day marchers up Fifth Avenue that my grandmother cheered on every year, waving an Israeli flag. The idea that one reality had two entirely different impacts on two entirely different groups of people eluded me. And I had to do the emotional, intellectual, and political work to understand that how events impact everyone is inherent to their real meaning. One person's feeling of triumph and justification does not describe the totality of their actions. The suffering we impose and then—as Jews and Americans—continued to rationalize and uphold defines us because all human beings, by virtue of being born, deserve equal recognition, opportunity, access, and possibility. Anything that disrupts this is unjust.

COMING TO THIS MOMENT

Looking honestly at my past and the impact of my experiences on the formation of my character, I can now see that I was prepared to ask these questions by three earlier personal and simultaneously structural events.

First, I had already learned to question nationalism and patriotism precisely through the lens of my secular Jewish history and the alienation of my first-generation parents from American norms. I am a native and lifelong New Yorker born thirteen years after the end of the Holocaust, raised with four Yiddish-speaking, accented refugee grandparents. I have always been in possession of the names and photographs of my aunts and uncles exterminated by Nazis and their Polish fascist allies. These were: Mina, Odellah, Shmul, and Solomon Leibling, my beloved maternal grandmother Dora Yevish's brothers and sisters. We now know that some of them were shot in the town square of their city of Rohatyn, originally the Polish sector of the Austro-Hungarian Empire, part of Poland during the Holocaust, and now in Ukraine. And Anna Fuchs, the Soviet physician sister of my laundry-worker maternal grandfather, Charles Yevish. Anna was murdered, we believe, by Nazis at Babyn Yar. It was only in my sixties that I finally learned by watching Ken Burns's six-hour documentary, *The U.S. and the Holocaust*, how directly American antisemitism facilitated the Holocaust. This information helped me draw a parallel to the US role in the mass murder of Palestinians.

I was not raised to be an Americanist, but rather as a person deeply constructed by diasporic identification. In many ways, America was a mystery to my parents. Christians rarely entered our apartment, and when they did my parents were uncomfortable, as they feared the majority. My childhood took place in the 1960s, and as a beneficiary of the free rein that defined urban childhood before helicopter parenting, I had a subway pass. The normal daily background of my growing up was the war in Vietnam juxtaposed against revolutionary and countercultural New York. This dynamic dominated the public sphere for my first fifteen years of life. I came of age in a swirling sea of change, far away from both the small town and the suburb of the average American, and I thought that this adventure of vision and revelation was just the way life was, and was supposed to be.

Every week *Life* magazine would arrive in our apartment, and I would see photographs of murdered Vietnamese, burned civilians, screaming children, overwhelmed chaos, piles of bodies slaughtered by US soldiers. These images return to me daily now, as I rely on Twitter (X) and Al Jazeera to find screaming, burning Palestinians starving in Gaza, parents caressing their children's corpses, murdered journalists, murdered doctors, decimated universities and hospitals, and murdered poets like Refaat Alareer, whose targeted destruction was followed months later by the additional murder of his daughter, son-in-law, and grandson by Israeli bombs. Using the Vietnam War, with napalm and carpet-bombing, as the foundational referent, the systematic transformation of Gaza into rubble and the endless torture of its inhabitants is even more extreme. The severed feet of children, the stacks of corpses, entire families and communities crushed under decimated buildings deliberately destroyed by Israelis with American money. Even mainstream NBC News, on April 27, 2024, reported "mass graves in southern Gaza's Nasser Hospital," of adults and children executed with their hands tied behind their backs.

It does not escape me that when it comes to Palestine, contemporary images of these crimes are not available in mainstream publications like those ancient editions of *Life*. American journalists like Jazmine Hughes at *The New York Times* and David Velasco at *Artforum* were forced to resign or were fired for merely signing letters against these atrocities, not even for showing them. Television journalist Mehdi Hasan was pushed out of MSNBC (which is to the Democratic Party what Fox News is to the Republicans) for actually covering events accurately. As of July 2024, according to journalist Steven Thrasher over 150 Palestinian and Lebanese journalists and bloggers had been murdered by Israeli forces—often with their families—and eighty are currently imprisoned without due process, events ignored by the star-studded White House correspondents' roast of President Biden, who has funded these killings. Past and present images repeatedly connect.

As a ten-year-old, I went to demonstrations against the war in Vietnam with my mother, riding down to Washington, D.C., on buses organized by the National Association of Social Workers. I have spent my life marching in the avenues of New York and Washington for an end to killing, demanding help for people with AIDS, for women needing abortions, for Black lives, against police violence, for my own existence as a lesbian trying to survive outside the law and then outside acceptable cultural representation. All of this was familiar to me when it became time to stand up for Palestine. These earlier experiences of understanding and confronting state violence made it familiar and natural to look critically at national constructions and state-regulated loyalties, including my own. I learn from the oppressed, not the powerful, about how to define reality.

Second, my family was pathologically sexist and homophobic to a degree that was so poisonous, thorough, and punitive that I was forced to cohere a critical comprehension of the false loyalty systems families construct. After all, the family is often the first place a person experiences the pain of homophobia and sexism or, inversely, how to benefit from these oppression systems. I explored these questions at length in my book *Ties That Bind: Familial Homophobia and Its Consequences*. As a girl who was both smart and gay, I was betrayed by my family so that they could uphold male and heterosexual supremacy systems. The family is where I first experienced and observed men being artificially inflated beyond their actual accomplishments and merits, a plague that has shadowed my life, contexts, and career. When I needed my family's support in order to face the sexism and anti-lesbian bias in the world, at school, in the workplace, and absolutely in the culture industries of publishing and theater, they couldn't help because they were invested in maintaining those delusions. Ironically, in both publishing and the theater, gay and Jewish men were often the gatekeepers who stopped me, humiliated me, ghosted me, degraded me, and were unable to tolerate smart women with innovative ideas about their power, which is a centerpiece of our experiences. After all, what ultimately makes sophisticated, complex creative work about lesbian life unacceptable is that we see men differently than they see themselves. And the men who run the world and set standards often find this perspective intolerable. Some of my major collaborators have been Black men. Straight Black men like theater director Marion McClinton (the play *Carson McCullers*) and composer Anthony Davis (the musical *Shimmer*), and queer Black men like director Stephen Winter and performer Jack Waters (the film *Jason and Shirley*). Repeatedly these men have recognized the pathologizing systems that I have endured and had comparable and parallel and even more harrowing stories that enabled them to understand what I was experiencing and to validate it. And I have been supported by white gay men like filmmaker Jim Hubbard, lyricist Michael Korie, and scholar Matt Brim, who have all managed to recognize, critique, and transcend the denigration of women by their peers.

Through these resonant familial and professional constructions of elevating white men beyond their ability and degrading women who hold innovative ideas about power, I became immune to arguments about "loyalty" claiming that I should praise something no matter how untrue, brutal, and racist. The idea that I should identify with Jewish supremacy ideology became repulsive. I came to understand through separation from my family and obstruction by men in power that the goal of justice is to erase demography as a basis for identification and rights. It became clear to me that I don't support any power hierarchy in which people have special rights because they are male, straight, or Jewish and denied rights because they are not. There is ultimately no justification for any differential in rights.

The reason the book on familial homophobia and my previously mentioned book on Israel and Palestine were published the same year, 2012, is that *Ties That Bind* was repressed by the publishing industry and took almost ten years to find a venue. I recall one of many rejection letters, this time from Scribner, telling me that the problem with the book was that half of its potential readers already knew about familial homophobia from their lived experience and presumably, according to this esteemed editor, wouldn't want to read about their own lives. And she was sure that the other half—the ones creating familial homophobia—would never care. Twelve years later, the book is still selling, and I am still receiving letters from grateful readers and their families. Still resonating, it was translated into French as recently as 2024. I guess I was prematurely anti-fascist. I still regularly receive reductive rejections for books and plays of new ideas, some of which eventually are allowed to be seen and then sometimes make a significant impact. Ideas change but the shortsightedness and conformity of the gatekeepers remain an occupational hazard. In my lifetime as a playwright and a novelist, the exclusions of authentic and sophisticated representations of adult lesbian life that address male power truthfully are pervasive and consistent.

So, in addition to my Jewish and family-based alienation from American patriotism, I also inherited a gender- and sexuality-based separation from power structures through familial homophobia and the anti-lesbian bias of the culture industries. These three types of rejection—Americanism, nuclear family, and the status quo supremacy structures of the culture industry—all made it possible for me to understand and quickly recognize that the Palestinian experience has been hidden, distorted, and made secondary to Israeli argument and self-description. Once I actually looked, I saw that the assertion that the Israeli wish to dominate was more important than Palestinian life was constructed in the same manner as all the other structures of domination with which I was intimately familiar.

These were all systems of supremacy ideology, and they were masquerading as reality.

My ability to listen and see critically was expanded and reinforced by my immersion in the mass death experience of the AIDS crisis and my subsequent commitment to AIDS activism and then to historicizing it through the ACT UP Oral History Project, cocreated with filmmaker Jim Hubbard (www.actuporalhistory.org), our coproduced film *United in Anger: A History of ACT UP*, and my 2021 book, *Let the Record Show: A Political History of ACT UP, New York 1987–1993*. Once I took the time to listen and to hear what Palestinians were saying about their own experiences, the previously understood structures of being ignored, oppressed, and allowed to die while being lied about resonated with what I had already learned, lived, and witnessed during the height of the AIDS crisis. It was therefore easier for me than for some others to enter into the process of learning about Palestinian life and point of view. By the time the US Congress voted in 2023 that criticism of Israel was the same as antisemitism, I had already learned the hard way, and I came to understand that just because the apparatus made claims of supremacy and innocence did not make it so.

As an employed American, I pay taxes to a government that gives that money to Israel to in turn purchase advanced weapons from US companies. So, as the US markets benefit from these public funds recycled into private industry, Israel then uses the weapons to slaughter Palestinian people endlessly and obsessively while blaming them for the violence being done to them. This double move—the assault and the blame—is both the lie and the game. I want to ask these killers, "How can you believe yourselves? You must know you are lying." But I also know from my close proximity to many people invested in domination in a variety of forms that some of them do know that they are lying, and some of them do not.

THE CYNICAL MANIPULATION OF
THE CHARGE OF ANTISEMITISM

As one of the hundreds of thousands of Jews in the world, and especially in the US, who oppose this injustice and violence, I am constantly being asked about or even charged with antisemitism. There is an actual mass murder of Palestinians in play, but the public conversation is too easily focused on a potential future application of the same tactics to Jews, an application that is imagined from past truths, not current realities. Yet, this imagining is given more importance and more public display than the ongoing slaughter and starvation of Palestinians taking place right now. The people who send me emails and messages calling me "Kapo" and "Nazi" and "JINO" (Jew in Name Only) and telling me I should be raped and murdered and sent to gas chambers, some of them are involved in a frenzied collective mania of projection that overwhelms the reality that we are murdering Palestinians today. I think it is soberly clear that the literal and actual source of antisemitic threat in our time comes from the Christian right, the rising white supremacist power in America. These movements are represented by "replacement theory," the idea that white Christians are being "replaced" by people of color, Jews, immigrants, and Muslims. And these beliefs are also widespread in Europe, where countries with explicit antisemitic histories have elected fascist and right-wing governments across the continent. These racist governments are often consistent in their anti-Arab panic, as they support Israeli policies and collude with their war on Palestinians. Currently the largest Zionist organizations in the world are Christian evangelicals who are invested in Israel out of apocalyptic religious belief in biblical end-time. Christians United for Israel alone has ten million members, which is 25 percent larger than the entire population of Jews in America.

When it comes to Palestinians and whether they are also anti-semitic, I put myself in their shoes. As I go through the process of trying to hear Palestinians, I imagine myself standing in Gaza in my professional role as a teacher, and I look up and see planes killing my students and destroying my schools. On the sides of those planes is the Star of David, the six-point star that is at the center of the Israeli flag but that historically has mystical meaning, as it represented the Jewish people long before the creation of the state of Israel. When I imagine myself seeing what Palestinians see, I am confronted with Israeli soldiers—women and men with mandatory conscription— murdering civilians, destroying people's homes, bullying them, and on their uniforms I see the same star, the one Jews were made to sew onto their clothes by Nazis, and the one I own on a fine gold chain given to me by my grandmother. Everywhere I look I see the Israeli-constructed association between Jews and oppressive brutal violence.

If I were on the receiving end of the violence, instead of its perpetrator as an American taxpayer, I would see the killers' overt claim to be "the Jews." I would be very angry at them. I would see the Israeli soldiers calling themselves "the Jewish state" and presenting themselves as representatives of world Jewry. I would not understand why they are so brutal with no impunity, and I would hate them. This is why so many of us Jewish people who oppose this violence must insist that there is a difference between the Israeli state claiming to be all the Jews, and those of us in active solidarity working toward a tipping point when the injustice will end and Palestinians will have the self-determination that all people want for themselves. We Jews in opposition must show, through our actions, that the Israeli government and their supporters are not us. That they cannot speak in my name. That the false charge that opposing brutality is antisemitic is a created paradox that is nonsensical and cynically dishonest. As Palestinian leader Omar Barghouti said, "There is nothing Jewish about Israel's ethnic cleansing, land theft, apartheid, or genocide. Therefore, there's nothing anti-Jewish per se in supporting BDS to end these crimes and the structure of oppression that perpetuates them."

I have always understood antisemitism as a given in the world. It has always existed and may always exist, for many reasons. In part, Judaism is not an evangelical religion and therefore we understand ourselves as a permanent minority, unlike Christianity and Islam, which are evangelical and have dreams of converting the world. Because we are diasporic and do not recruit, we are always a small group, usually not of the government of each country in which we are living. Consequently, there is a distrust, an otherness, reinforced by stereotypes and specific religious-based myths about the biblical enmity of Sarah and Hagar and the killing of Christ being used as justification for ongoing scapegoating of Jews. Antisemitism functions as a system of collective punishment in which a conflict—whether an actual crime or a projected anxiety—becomes blamed on the entire people, resulting in violence, mass murder, separation, and denial of rights. It is then propagated by clichés, lies, and false accusations about a collective character.

Certainly, as real as antisemitism is, slaughtering, starving, displacing, and traumatizing millions of Palestinians over generations doesn't help the fight against it. Israel is a militarized nation that has chosen the path of subordinating an entirely other people through violence and a justifying propaganda. Because of the complicity of the US government, media, and culture industries with this combination of tactics, many American Jews and most Israelis have not understood that Palestinians do not want to be controlled, and that if we were in their shoes, we would feel the same. It has been hidden from the US and Israeli public that the status quo of domination and suppression is not only unjust but also unsustainable, that inevitably it will explode over and over again. Yet, some are shocked every time it does explode, driving those who identify with the Israeli state into repetitive murderous rages. They cannot place themselves in other people's perspectives, and they are encouraged in this narcissism by corporate media and official culture. Of course, there have always been Jews, like communists or anarchists, who oppose nationalism, or public intellectuals like Hannah Arendt and Albert Einstein, who wanted a binational state of equals, now known as "one state." Arendt and Einstein signed a letter to *The New York Times* warning that Menachem Begin (a former terrorist and subsequent Israeli prime minister) was a fascist. But Israel went in the opposite direction, away from coexistence toward brutal domination and now attempted extermination, while most Palestinians are still standing.

WHO ARE JEWS, REALLY?

Judaism, at its root, is a dialogic religion. Interpretation and discussion are the ways of prayer. Entire holidays are based in analysis and sharing perspectives. For this reason, until the twentieth-century aberration of nationalism, Jews have not been required to agree, but rather to analyze; that is, to understand. It is estimated that if the Holocaust had not occurred, today there would be thirty-two million Jews in the world. Out of the only fifteen million Jews who currently survive worldwide, there are an extraordinarily large number of subsets: secular, Reform, Reconstructionist, Conservative, Modern Orthodox, Orthodox, and various splinter groups within Hasidim such as Lubavitch, Belzer, Satmar, and so on. "Two Jews, three opinions" is a well-known and common refrain in the diaspora. Zionism is a recent nineteenth-century addition to a

5,784-year history. Austrian journalist Theodor Herzl covered the antisemitic show trial of Frenchman Alfred Dreyfus and concluded that Jews would never be safe in Europe. His book *The Jewish State* was published in 1896 in German, cohering the Zionist movement.

Many Jews opposed Zionism for many reasons. Communists believed in one world and were internationalists. Bundists and a range of socialists did not support centralized nationalism and identified with other peoples. Some very religious Jews believe that the Messiah has to come for the goals of Zionism to occur, since religious Jews are still waiting for the Messiah. Some Jews, like Emma Goldman, were anarchists and anti-state. Diasporic Jews wanted to live in the world of others and not be restricted to one place. Zionism changed the concept of Jews from a people and religion to a nationality, and many opposed this. Personally, I imagine a combination of equalizing global access and resources so that people don't have to leave their homes, and opening borders so that all peoples in need can have a place to go; after all, there are now more refugees— 130 million—on earth than at any time in history. I am not opposed to the idea of a country where Jews in distress can go, but not at the expense of the people already existing in this place. One of Herzl's ideas was for Jews to collectively purchase land in Argentina to build trust with their new neighbors, and I wish we had.

A few weeks into the mass murder in Gaza, Columbia University banned the activist groups Jewish Voice for Peace and Students for Justice in Palestine, claiming they had not applied appropriately for meeting space, but this was part of a larger rhetoric employed under the pretense of protecting "Jewish" students. They expressed no interest in the safety, feelings, or rights of Palestinian, Muslim, and Arab students, staff, and faculty. Columbia banned two student groups, including one that is overtly Jewish and the other that has many Jewish members. Clearly, they were only defending Zionism, not Jews. In spring of 2024, Columbia students reached a turning point. Disgusted by their own complicity as Americans, they were influenced by street demonstrations that had been in place since the carpet-bombing of Palestinian civilians began after the retribution killings of Israelis on October 7. Students from Columbia and Barnard College constructed a "free Gaza" encampment that influenced a national flurry of university campuses doing the same. This resulted, by summer 2024, in over three thousand student and faculty arrests nationwide, police violence on many campuses, and campus police forces assaulting their own students and even professors. Yet *The New York Times* and other corporate media, who still had not reported on the long-term incarceration of Palestinian children in Israeli prisons, or on mass graves located in Gaza, continued the charade of pretending that no Jews were involved in the protests, even though they were and have been visible and numerous from the beginning. Jewish Voice for Peace and IfNotNow have conducted many mass actions against the war on Gaza, in which hundreds were arrested in civil disobedience at the Capitol, in Grand Central Station, on the Manhattan Bridge, at Grand Army Plaza, the Stock Exchange, and at the White House. So, the history of Jews opposing Zionism and the prominent role of Jews in Palestine solidarity are deliberately hidden by elaborate misrepresentations by academic institutions, the government, and corporate media.

These institutions of power have no interest in protecting or representing Jews, only people who defend Israeli violence. They make repetitively false claims of Jewish hegemony that are not only anti-historical, but not Judaic. Jews, like every other society, including Palestinians, are multidimensional. We contain multiple religious factions, a full range of political and economic ideologies, a wide range of human conditions and experiences. Yet, on the model of age-old antisemitism and any authoritarian organization of values, Israel and its supporting US media and institutions insist that the collective be homogenous, which is impossible because people are different. As part of the enforcement of this unreachable goal, Israel insists that opposing killing, starving, maiming, incarcerating, and displacing Palestinians is itself anti-Jewish because they falsely claim to own Jewishness. This is confusing to people who don't want to be antisemitic, because it takes a few steps of conceptualization and requires focus to dissect. Because the public space is reductive, Israel and the US corporate university and media can use this untrue accusation as a potent weapon.

Many Americans mistakenly understand Palestinians as an equal power to Israel. They use nonsensical, meaningless phrases like "two sides" and "both sides" as if they were functional concepts. They mistakenly think Palestine has one government, an army, airports. They don't realize that to go to Palestine you must pass Israeli checkpoints and have their permission to travel on. They don't realize that Palestine has no recognized stable borders and does not have contiguous land. They don't know that Palestinians have no autonomy, many have no passports, that some cannot travel, live where they want, attend school, or even keep their homes from demolishment. Most Americans do not have a realistic sense of how overwhelming the control of Palestinians' every day is. Nor do they grasp how literally violent Israeli domination has been for over seventy-five years. Most important, the American public has been acclimated to the idea that whatever Israel wants is how it should be. It is not considered that Palestinians have needs and wants. Americans don't think about Palestinian security and safety, aspirations and dreams.

For me, one turning point came when I realized that I would not want to live under occupation for even one day. This is what we need to make Americans understand. If they were being occupied and controlled, never had safety, and were constantly exposed to repetitive cycles of mass murder and ongoing real violence over decades, wouldn't they do everything they could to change that? Any honest answer would be yes. And the uprising on American campuses across economic class and geography shows that the resistance to propaganda is growing daily, erupting despite constant misrepresentation, rendering the power of these institutions like Columbia University and *The New York Times* less potent—while creating grassroots education, discussion, and consciousness raising that is increasingly powerful and effective. Perhaps most important, the news of this mass protest reached Palestinians. Images appeared of internal Gazan refugees standing outside tents, holding signs thanking students at Arizona State, Yale, Swarthmore, Columbia, and other named campuses, thereby completing the communication.

BUILDING INFRASTRUCTURE FOR RESISTANCE

The effort to keep us misinformed is huge. *The New York Times*, most of MSNBC, NPR, all of the formally considered liberal outlets make daily false equivalencies and obscure key information that would help people think and understand. Watching Al Jazeera, which is now banned in Israel, for even a few minutes on streaming is to see something closer to reality. It is so different; it can actually be hard to take because it is so much more accurate. When we become used to the lullaby of lies, closer-to-the-truth can feel unbearable. Fortunately, despite all the false reporting, institutional pressure, very public firings of journalists and academics, cancellations at establishment institutions like the 92nd Street Y, deposing of the presidents of Harvard and the University of Pennsylvania by right-wing, not Jewish, Republicans, and punishments, firings, and demotions at corporate entertainment agencies like CAA and UTA, all of this intimidation has not kept people from being horrified by genocide. Constituencies in addition to students have started rebelling. Writers have pulled out of lucrative book awards and a prestigious literary conference sponsored by PEN America, when the group under the leadership of Suzanne Nossel refused to make organizational commitments opposing Israeli aggression. Authors have also signed promises not to publish in *Artforum* and other publications that have fired staff because of their anti-genocide position. In February 2024, a coalition of Black clergy called on President Biden to stop sending military aid to Israel. Various locals of the United Auto Workers union have opposed the war. Finally, after years of growing public opposition and nine solid months of global protest, the International Court of Justice, the principal judicial organ of the United Nations, ruled in July 2024 that Israel's occupation of Palestinian land is illegal, that the settlements must leave, that Israel owes Palestinians reparations, and that the world should act accordingly. The force propelling the court to finally decide came entirely from grassroots momentum.

Where does this unauthorized people power and an accompanying resistant understanding come from if it is forbidden in corporate media and entertainment? It comes from below. There are many organizations that have struggled for years to build the infrastructure of this Palestine solidarity movement. Palestine Legal, Institute for Middle East Understanding, Playgrounds for Palestine, US Campaign for Palestinian Rights, the Palestine Festival of Literature, Adalah, Al-Haq, Within Our Lifetime, *The Electronic Intifada*, Council on American-Islamic Relations, Students for Justice in Palestine, Samidoun: Palestinian Prisoner Solidarity Network, Palestine Writes, Palestinian Youth Movement, and many others have been doing the work. Explicitly Jewish organizations have long been organizing, including *Mondoweiss*, IfNotNow, International Jewish Anti-Zionist Network, and Jewish Voice for Peace, founded in 1996, for which I have served on the advisory board since 2010. JVP, as we call it, is the largest Jewish anti-occupation organization in the world, with a rabbinic section, a division of Jews of color, an active political lobbying wing called JVP Action, and chapters on many campuses—legal and illegal. JVP is fighting for permanent ceasefire and is against occupation. It is expressly anti-Zionist and supports BDS (Boycott, Divestment, Sanctions) with the understanding that "Never Again" is for everyone, taking the slogan of Holocaust remembrance and extending it to the world.

Since I became conscious about Israel in 2009, I have written about and protested aerial bombing of Palestinian civilians by US-funded Israeli military. The meaning of the 2014 murder of over two thousand civilians in Gaza by US-funded Israeli warplanes is explored at length in my book *Conflict Is Not Abuse: Overstating Harm, Community Responsibility, and the Duty of Repair*. So, in addition to recognizing the pain and devastation experienced by Israelis whose friends and family members were murdered on October 7, I condemned and recognized the pain experienced by Palestinians on October 6, 5, 4, 3 . . . and in September, August, and all previous days, months, years, and decades before—the precursors to these events.

On October 16, a week after the carpet-bombing of Gaza began, I published the following commentary in *New York* magazine. It is now an artifact, a frozen moment in time:

> I was born in 1958, and like many of my generation, my parents had experienced a world in which Jews were murdered, brutalized, and abandoned. My father knew his mother and

father to have been helpless peasants living under pogroms and without rights in the Russian Pale of Settlement. On my mother's side, my laundry-worker grandmother was financially unable to save her two brothers and two sisters in Poland from extermination. My parents raised me with the idea that Jews were people who sided with the oppressed and worked their way into helping professions.

They could not adjust the worldview born of this experience to a new reality: that in Israel, we Jews had acquired state power and built a highly funded militarized society, and were now subordinating others. No one wants to think about themselves that way. As a Jew and an American who has gone through the complex, painful, and transforming process of facing the injustice against Palestinians committed in my name and with my tax dollars, I have had to change my self-concept. I have had to deprogram myself from the idea that Jews continued to be victims when, in some cases, we had become perpetrators.

This shift in perception would have been unbearable for my parents. The idea that Jewish soldiers could march into villages and commit atrocities was incomprehensible. Yet, for 75 years, Palestinians have been murdered, incarcerated, and displaced with escalating violence by Israeli soldiers, and more recently by settlers. On October 7, these unending, untenable conditions exploded when Hamas broke through Israel's imposed barriers. They reentered the land they consider home. They attacked formerly Palestinian villages and cities, now under the control of Israel. After decades of being on the receiving end of highly organized violence, they switched roles and became the murderers and kidnappers of more than 1,300 Israeli children and adults.

Among political and institutional leaders, there has been a collective refusal to see this horrible violence as the consequence of consistent, unending brutality—paid for by the United States in billions of dollars in aid to Israel per year. Instead, a familiar fog has overtaken so many. They pretend these decades of injustice never took place. That Gazans were not forced against their will to live under siege. That instead, a group of them suddenly—out of nowhere and with no history or experience—emerged as monsters and murdered people who had never hurt them in the past and held no threat over their future.

Selective recognition is the way we maintain our own sense of goodness. Today, we see this process of denial in every aspect of our lives. In this moment, it has become a tool to justify the sustained murder of thousands in Gaza, where the current death toll sits at over 2,600 people. As Israel began its relentless retaliation last week, an accompanying image of Israeli and American moral cleanliness was put swiftly into action. This is called "manufactured consent"—Noam Chomsky's term for a system-supported propaganda by which authorities and media agree on a simplified reality, and it becomes the assumptive truth. We've seen this erasure of history in the uniform responses by Western world leaders, university administrations, heads of foundations, and even book fairs over the past week. President Biden called Hamas's attack "an act of sheer evil" without acknowledging the decades of colonial repression that make this violence legible. Instead he summoned another history, saying, "This attack has brought to the surface painful memories and the scars left by a millennia of antisemitism and genocide of the Jewish people." He then assured Israel it could count on the

United States' military support, as though having been through genocide entitled them to commit it.

Nikki Haley, a former United Nations ambassador under Trump, might be Biden's political opponent for the presidency, but she reinforced his claim of American-Israeli righteousness when she announced that "Israel needs our help in this battle of good vs. evil." This is the binary that has set the tone: *We* are pure, that is to say that *we* have done everything exactly right and do not have to question ourselves. Last Tuesday, White House press secretary Karine Jean-Pierre took a question from journalist Phil Wegmann. He asked her about the president's attitude toward members of Congress who connect Palestinian violence to the Israeli violence that preceded it and have called for a cease-fire. Jean-Pierre replied, "We believe they are wrong, we believe they're repugnant, and we believe they're disgraceful." Here we have a new equation: To ask for the ceasing of bombing and killing thousands of people is not a reasonable thought to consider. Instead, to stop killing is repulsive. To stop killing is a national disgrace.

Within this framework, any public outcry by Palestinians or allegiance with them becomes criminal. France and Germany banned people from showing compassion, solidarity, or pain for Palestinians in public marches. United Kingdom home secretary Suella Braverman called for monitoring displays of Palestinian flags. "At a time when Hamas terrorists are massacring civilians and taking the most vulnerable (including the elderly, women, and children) hostage, we can all recognize the harrowing effect that displays of their logos and flags can have on communities," she said. Aside from the freedom-of-expression issues, there was a symbolic politics being deployed here. A flag that unites millions of Palestinians who live not only in Gaza, the West Bank, the Golan, in refugee camps, and in Israel, but in a global diaspora from Brooklyn and Detroit to London to the UAE—all of these people become unrepresentable.

This continues in the realm of education and ideas, where there have been visible examples of individual writers and anti-occupation groups arguing for context. On Friday, Semafor reported that MSNBC quietly removed three Muslim anchors from hosting duties, despite some at the network believing they had the most expertise on the conflict. *Harper's Bazaar* editor Samira Nasr was forced to apologize for calling Israel's move to cut power to Gaza "the most inhuman thing" she's ever seen. The Frankfurt Book Fair canceled an award ceremony for Palestinian writer Adania Shibli. Donors have threatened the job of the president of the University of Pennsylvania because a literary festival called Palestine Writes took place there in September. Books, literature, ideas, discussion are all considered appropriate fodder for the manufacture of consent.

Humans want to be innocent. Better than innocent is the innocent victim. The innocent victim is eligible for compassion and does not have to carry the burden of self-criticism. Almost every person with authority or at the helm of an institution has declared that Israelis are innocent victims, and that Palestinians are not. On *60 Minutes* Sunday night, Biden reaffirmed his support for Israel while appearing to paint Palestinians as worthy of our compassion, too. He assured the American people that he was confident Israel would follow the "rules of war" and that "innocents in Gaza" would have "access to medicine and food and water."

But in the real world, Israel has cut off the flow of medicine, food, and water in Gaza. Water has already run out at U.N. shelters in the territory. Biden's comments only reinforce that as far as the war is concerned, there are no innocents in Gaza.

At the root of this erasure is the increasing insistence that understanding history, looking at the order of events and the consequences of previous actions to understand why the contemporary moment exists as it does, somehow endorses the present. Explanations are not excuses—they are the illumination that builds the future. But the problem with understanding how we got to where we are is that we could then be implicated. And innocent victims cannot have any responsibility for creating the moment.

What is so ironic is that since 2005, Palestinians have been offering a nonviolent solution: the Boycott, Divestment, Sanctions movement. Just as many of us grew up not buying grapes so that farmworkers could have a union or refusing to purchase South African products to help end apartheid, Palestinians have been asking the rest of us to put economic and cultural pressure on Israel through nonviolent boycott, to encourage them to move away from violent separation and toward negotiation and coexistence. The message here, too, was strategically twisted. The Israeli government and its supporters have led global campaigns to make supporting this boycott illegal. They have developed confusing worldwide messaging claiming that criticizing Israeli apartheid is the same thing as antisemitism. Every aspect of nonviolent organizing for a more equitable solution has been met with distortion as a tool of repression.

There is always, of course, the choice to end the siege of

Gaza and the occupation of the West Bank and end the second-class reality of Palestinians living in Israel. Make everyone equal citizens with the same rights to vote, passports, roads, universities. The reason this solution of just reconciliation, known as "One State," is not yet on the table is because of this selective reality: this panic that equalizing Palestinians in Israel would be allowing an enemy in, one that is fundamentally opposed to Israeli existence. But what this fear overlooks is that Palestine, like every society in the world, is a multidimensional society. Like Jews and Americans and Israelis, Palestinians contain multiple factions and religious perspectives—Muslim, Christian, Druze—and they hold a wide variety of political visions. The only thing they share is the desire to be free. They would never be able to act like a united bloc and all vote the same way, for example, in the same way that we cannot. Because they are human, as we know ourselves to be. To fear unanimity is to imagine they are different from everyone else on earth.

The most difficult challenge in our lives is to face our contributions to the systems that reproduce inequality and consequential cycles of violence. Every person has to face their own complicities, and we start this by listening to whoever is suffering. Even if it is by our own hand. It is this transcendence that can lead us all to a better place.

Since that day, my life has been organized around solidarity with the people of Gaza. I attended the first rally in New York—one opposed by both New York governor Kathy Hochul and Congresswoman Alexandria Ocasio-Cortez. I went to Times Square to support these civilians, was quoted in *The New York Times*, and appeared on *Ayman Mohyeldin Reports* on MSNBC. As a result of this early public stance, I received a steady stream of threatening and distorted messages via my personal and work email and social media. Some doors have slammed shut in my professional life, as I watch colleagues either overtly support Israeli aggression or fear taking a stance. I have spoken in public around the country at universities, bookstores, and community centers and in Europe about how the Palestine solidarity movement can learn directly from the successful tactics of the early AIDS activist organization ACT UP (AIDS Coalition to Unleash Power). These talks included two public conversations in Berlin with Jewish journalist Ben Mauk hosted by Lettrétage, a left-wing literary space, and Oyoun, a people of color collective that lost its government funding for hosting anti-Zionist Jews. Both events attracted hundreds of people, mostly in their twenties and thirties, desperate for an honest conversation about events in Palestine. At that time, March 2024, discussions of the boycott of Israel were repressed in Germany. At both talks we freely discussed the Boycott, Divestment, Sanctions campaign and the academic and cultural boycott of Israel. At that time, Jews made up 1 percent of Germans, and yet constituted 30 percent of people accused of antisemitism. Two weeks after I left, a Palestine solidarity conference in Berlin was broken up by the police. A Palestinian doctor, Ghassan Abu-Sitta, was turned away at the border; Udi Raz, a member of Jüdische Stimme, the German version of Jewish Voice for Peace, was arrested.

In spring 2024, I had the opportunity to go to France to support the French translation of *Ties That Bind: Familial Homophobia and Its Consequences*. Again, I used every platform and public opportunity to speak about Palestine. Because there are so few Jews in Europe—they were either murdered or immigrated to the United States or Israel—public-facing anti-Zionist Jews face more intimidation and the numbers are proportionally smaller. In recent

years France had a very high rate of Jewish immigration to Israel—
many of whom are Arab Jews with origins in former French colonies,
who had to face the combination of anti-Arab bias and antisemitism that is French. A few weeks before my arrival, Judith Butler,
the internationally respected philosopher and a powerful voice
against the oppression of Palestinians, was canceled for describing
October 7 as "armed resistance" instead of "terrorism." The conference they had organized at the Centre Pompidou continued with
Butler sitting quietly in the audience, choosing personal silence
over stopping the full event from taking place.

As a result, while touring various smaller French cities, I found
myself in the interesting position of being one of a few anti-Zionist
Jews whom some audiences had seen speak in public. The reporter
from Mediapart, the country's major left media outlet, told me she
had never interviewed an anti-Zionist Jew before. Of course, the
French anti-Zionist Jews found me, and I had some moving conversations with a few impressive individuals, including a member of
Tzedek who picked me up at the airport in Marseilles so we could
talk, and a young queer art curator with whom I had a moving,
long exchange. During the various book signings that took place
after each presentation, people would take a moment to have a private conversation. Half were young people suffering from familial
homophobia, and the other half were telling me, "I am a Jew,"
struggling with their complex social position of being a minority
within a minority.

In addition to public speaking in a wide range of venues to discuss Palestine and Israel with very diverse communities and audiences, most of my other solidarity work has been behind the scenes
with a diverse range of organizations in which staff or constituent
members wanted their organization to join the boycott, but there
was opposition. I consulted to help individuals strategizing for

organizations trying to advance their positions with failure and sometimes success. These organizations have included Performance Space New York, the Poetry Project at Saint Mark's Church, Queers for Palestine, Queer Art Mentorship, ICA-LA, Committee to Protect Journalists, and the Housing Works employees' union, and I supported a very prominent artist trying to decide between withdrawing major shows from significant institutions and making public statements that would get them canceled. This kind of work has been in coalition with members of Writers Against the War on Gaza, the Palestine Festival of Literature, and others. I have signed every possible letter. I objected to PEN America's refusal to oppose the war on Gaza, supporting writers who withdrew their books from the prestigious PEN awards and the PEN World Voices Festival. I signed a letter begging Olly Alexander to withdraw from Eurovision once the organization excluded Russia for their invasion of Ukraine but included Israel, ignoring their mass slaughter in Gaza. I support students and colleagues at my campus, Northwestern University, in their campaign for university divestment from Israeli institutions. Specifically, at Northwestern, I supported my Syrian colleague Professor Sami Hermez's right to present his book on Palestinian life to the campus community and testified on behalf of two Black students who were arrested for creating a satirical anti-Zionist parody of the school newspaper. Public speaking and writing, behind-the-scenes negotiations with organizations, and support for individuals and for advocacy organizations like Palestine Legal are all part of the wide range of possibilities available to those of us in solidarity. With Dorgham Abusalim, I presented on Palestine at Honcho Campout, a three-day queer and trans festival in the woods of the Allegheny Mountains for people who love DJs and dance music. I went where invited, if the subject was solidarity with Palestine. Combine this with demonstrations in the streets, encampments at universities, opposition to Zionist events, and ongoing educationals. Everywhere I go, it becomes clear that there is a multidimensional movement with many different entry points and a variety of strategic and active approaches available to a wide range of people. All we have to do is act.

3

Solidarity in Action

STUDENTS IN REVOLT AND BOYCOTT, DIVESTMENT, SANCTIONS (BDS)

We have established that solidarity to change embedded injustice requires coming together across lines of power. Grasping that this is more relational than heroic makes it more possible; as seeing the conditions of other people's lives as relevant to our own creates ongoing insight and revelation, bringing us closer to reality. Solidarity is a transformative vision of the real.

Some of the most collective and visible acts of solidarity to end the war on Gaza, as of this writing in summer 2024, were created by the desperation of students, who could not bear to ignore the real-life suffering of Palestinians. Taking responsibility that world leaders would not take, they moved their priorities from themselves to the world and built campus solidarity encampments at:

American University, Arizona State University, Auraria, Barnard College, Berklee College of Music, Brown University, Bryn Mawr, Cal Poly, Cal State LA, Case Western Reserve, City College of New York, Columbia, Community College of Denver, Cornell, CSU Sacramento, Dartmouth, DePaul, Dickenson, Drexel, Emerson, Emory, Evergreen, Florida International, Florida State, Fordham, Gallaudet University, George Mason, Georgetown, George Washington, Hamline, Harvard, Haverford, Howard, Indiana University–Bloomington, Indiana University–Indianapolis, Johns Hopkins, Louisiana State University, Loyola, Miami University, Michigan State, Middlebury, MIT, the New School, Northeastern, Northern Arizona University, Northwestern, Notre Dame, NYU, Oberlin, Occidental, Ohio State, Parsons, Pitzer, Pomona, Princeton, Purdue, Rhode Island School of Design, Rice, Rutgers, San Francisco State, School of Visual Arts, Smith College, Sonoma State, Stanford, Stonybrook, SUNY Albany, SUNY New Paltz, SUNY Purchase, Swarthmore, Syracuse, Temple, Texas A&M, Tufts, Tulane, UC Berkeley, UC Irvine, UCLA, UC Riverside, UC Santa Barbara, U of Arizona, U of Chicago, U of Colorado, U of Connecticut, U of Delaware, U of Florida, U of Georgia, U of Illinois–Urbana, U of Kansas, U of Maryland, U of Mary Washington, U of Michigan, U of Minnesota, U of Mississippi, U of Montana, U of Nevada, U of New Hampshire, U of New Mexico, U of New Orleans, U of North Carolina–Chapel Hill, U of North Carolina–Charlotte, U of Pennsylvania, U of Pittsburgh, U of Puget Sound, U of Rochester, U of South Florida, U of Washington, U of Wisconsin–Madison, U of Wisconsin–Milwaukee, U of Utah, U of Vermont, USC, UT Arlington, UT Austin, UT

Dallas, Vanderbilt, Virginia Commonwealth, Virginia Tech, Washington University in St. Louis, Wayne State, Wesleyan, Yale, and more, including campuses in Canada, Mexico, Egypt, Lebanon, Turkey, India, Germany, Kuwait, France, Argentina, Jordan, Australia, Britain, and many others.

Thousands of students and some faculty were arrested, including three hundred in one day at Columbia and City College, with the public university students facing harsher charges than those at the Ivy. Columbia students later occupied Hamilton Hall and renamed it Hind's Hall to memorialize six-year-old Hind Rajab, a Palestinian girl who was abandoned in a car with the corpses of her family after Israeli soldiers fired 355 bullets. She had called for help but was left to die because Israelis made rescue impossible. These students later refused to make any deals with district attorney Alvin Bragg's office unless the same was offered to students from CUNY who had also been arrested, a further show of solidarity. Then-president of Columbia Minouche Shafik, before her resignation, led a repressive and punitive trend that was followed by some other college presidents, by calling campus police and local police; some schools experienced significance violence. At UCLA the school stood by and allowed Zionists from outside the campus to beat students for hours. At Emory, Atlanta police beat and arrested students and faculty. At Dartmouth, a sixty-five-year-old professor, Annelise Orleck, was knocked to the ground and arrested for telling the police to stop hurting her students. At the New School, faculty started their own encampment. At Columbia, a number of faculty stopped teaching to protest police presence on campus.

But what all these universities and colleges had in common was their demand: divestment. Schools are being asked to divest holdings in Israeli companies and to close collaborative projects with

Israeli state-sponsored institutions. Divestment is the central concept of the BDS movement, which was created in Palestine in 2005. And taking on the demand of divestment is direct solidarity because students and faculty are doing exactly what Palestinians are asking of us.

This nonviolent strategy of economic and cultural boycott is designed to pressure the Israeli state into changing its oppressive policies toward Palestinians, ending the occupation, and facilitating the return of Palestinian refugees. It is based in the 1980s campus movements to divest from apartheid South Africa and inspired by the American Black Civil Rights Movement. Omar Barghouti, a Palestinian leader of the BDS movement, was a graduate student at Columbia in the eighties and witnessed the success of campus civil disobedience, which resulted in Columbia's divestment in South Africa five months after campus demonstrations. And there he derived his inspiration.

For years BDS has been an obscure strategy, difficult to publicize, and considered ultra-left. But by the spring of 2024, it became common parlance and the most widespread strategy in US youth politics, attractive because it is expressly nonviolent, concrete, and possible to accomplish. As students and faculty cohered their politics, became braver, and created the invaluable counterculture of resistance in which we learn, build relationships, and develop leaders for the future, Israeli bombs kept falling on Gaza and we had to face the fact that—so far—there is no consequence on the ground. Our resistance grows but the killing does not stop. The powers we oppose are large, and refusing to be complacent, educating and transforming ourselves, and making winnable demands in strategic ways is a long path, but our best path. Egotistical expectations of quick victories and immediate impact are not our friends when we face such powerful forces as the United States and its paralyzing hold on the United Nations. Renewed creative approaches, fun in growth and togetherness, and supporting each other in refining our strategies are our strengths.

Building BDS is a spotlight on a growing solidarity with Palestine that, like all important solidarities, is a path filled with error, hubris, longing, and above all, the obligation to strive toward the goal of being self-critical, "big picture," and effective, as the bombs continue to be launched and the ongoing trauma of 2.3 million Gazans only deepens. Ironically, we in America benefit from the unity, creativity, and empowerment of BDS solidarity, but because there are no changes on the ground as of this writing, Palestinians continue to suffer. This is one of the terrible elements of a solidarity that is not yet effective but strives to be, which remains elusive even as we do the work to face, internalize, and take it on. It makes us have to ask ourselves hard questions about what solidarity really means if it is not yet working. Each investigation into the meaning of *solidarity* opens up a new range of questions.

ACT UP activist Avram Finkelstein recalls the many years in which AIDS continued to kill unabated, and how activists kept advancing their work because they had no choice. The epicenter of the AIDS crisis lasted from identification in 1981 to the development of effective medications in 1996, 15 years later and ongoing, resulting in, to date, 50 million deaths globally. The European Holocaust, from separation to internment to extermination, lasted from 1933 to 1945—12 years during which approximately 13 million people, including 6 million Jews, were exterminated; 75 million people were killed in World War Two. The occupation of Palestinian land, forcing exile, incarceration, and murder, has lasted for 75 years, with over 6 million, or half of the global Palestinian population, registered with the UN as refugees. The death rate of Palestinians since October 2023 surpasses that of the first five years of the AIDS crisis.

Although these numbers are important to our sense of scale and history, they don't necessarily help us understand how to proceed. We can start by envisioning acting with three guideposts: intervention, listening, and being effective. Over the years, I have come to recognize at least these three basic responsibilities to be at the root of active solidarity.

The Responsibility to Intervene

When we see another person being brutalized, scapegoated, marginalized, blamed for things they have not caused, falsely accused, punished unjustly, shunned, subjected to oppressive state intervention, displaced, incarcerated, or threatened with murder, and that person is asking us to help, I believe that we each have a responsibility to intervene. Even if we don't know the person, even if we don't like the person, justice is, by definition, not a popularity contest, and solidarity does not require love.

We especially have a responsibility to intervene if we are implicated—if our gender, clique, company, family, community, nation, religion, or race are the aggressors. If our university is making money from its investments. If we know the names of the people who are driving the aggression, are providing false justification for the cruelty, or are trying to impose a code of silence about the cruelty. If we have their email addresses, then we have a special responsibility to intervene. The problem arises exactly at this moment, when those taking unjust action are the people we know, live with, or are related to, or if we are dependent on them for approval or access or recognition. When the people acting unjustly are our bosses, relatives, or "friends."

So, solidarity with someone who is being brutalized by people we know or identify with implies a loss. But the fact remains that the "loss" of approval or employment, of money, or of having parties to go to will never equal the loss of the literally millions of people who were murdered, starved, traumatized, and displaced by Israel in Gaza. The bother of having to practice the politics of repetition required to raise consciousness about Palestine, the annoyance of being yelled at or slandered by supporters of the Israeli state, the fear of threats and accusations, censorship, or loss of income and opportunities, even of the violence of the police or Zionist agitators, will never equal being mass-murdered or being surrounded by the death of our contexts.

Palestinian chef and activist Falastine Dwikat, who lives in Nablus, told me, "Solidarity, for me, has the same high standard as friendship." Real friendship is dialogic, not obedient. Real friendship means asking questions, looking at the order of events, challenging assumptions. We are morally obligated to question our governments, families, communities, and friends who are participating (passively or actively) in the shunning or degradation of others, including the subjugation of Palestine. Unfortunately, people who justify group aggression and shunning equate silent submission with friendship. They want loyalty to do the wrong thing. Being in solidarity with Palestine means upholding an ethic of interactive, communicative engagement. And that can be a dramatic change in the way one lives. Engaging the entire process that creates the courage to intervene involves changing the way we see ourselves, changing what is important to us and what diminishment of status we are willing to endure in order to do what we know is right. Swarthmore professor Sa'ed Atshan once told me, "Solidarity means decolonizing your mind." As he often reminds me, this process leads us to find new community along the way.

The Responsibility to Listen and Also to Hear

Palestinians are shunned. That means they are not allowed into the conversation about their experience, reality, condition, and future. As an American, I have to work hard to hear Palestine. I have to look for alternative media like Al Jazeera, *The Electronic Intifada*, *Mondoweiss*, and *Democracy Now!* and slip in through the ever expanding cracks in corporate media. I have to use social media intelligently—follow X from Gaza, for example. I have to attend public talks and read books that are not published by corporate presses. The most personally impactful books I read by Palestinians published recently were from small presses. Adania Shibli's novel *Minor Detail*, published by Fitzcarraldo; *We Could Have Been Friends, My Father and I: A Palestinian Memoir* by Raja Shehadeh, published by Other Press; *My Brother, My Land: A Story from Palestine* by Sami Hermez from Redwood Press; and the British import *The Tale of a Wall: Reflections on the Meaning of Hope and Freedom* by Nasser Abu Srour. None of these were on the bestseller list or selected by Oprah or on *Today* or in Reese Witherspoon's book club. None of these were on *The New York Times* "100 Best Books of the 21st Century" list. I had to think for myself, outside branding and marketing, to find these outstanding and enlightening works.

But I am also challenged to listen to individual Palestinian people whom I now know and work with. For example, when I first began my involvement, I conceptualized solidarity as "support," which meant creating platforms for Palestinians to speak. After I joined BDS in 2009 (at that time one literally "signed on"), my first action was to organize a seven-city US tour for leaders of the Palestinian queer movement: Haneen Maikey, Ghadir Shafie, and Ghaith Hilal Nassar. After that, at the suggestion of Columbia University professor Rashid Khalidi, I co-organized the first LGBT delegation to Palestine, which was led by Sa'ed Atshan. What I did not realize was that support is part of solidarity, but not all of it. After each task was complete, I kept asking the people I was working with, "What do you want me to do next?" Finally, one leader, Haneen Maikey—at that time the director of alQaws, a Palestinian queer organization—just said to me, "It is not my responsibility to think up your strategy." As I recorded in my book *Israel/Palestine and the Queer International*, in Ramallah I met with Omar Barghouti. At one point I asked him, "What can I do?" and he answered wisely, "You are a creative person, you will think of something."

The boycott of Israel was called by PACBI (Palestinian Campaign for the Academic and Cultural Boycott of Israel) and is administered by the BDS movement and the BNC (BDS National Committee)—all are Palestinian organizations based in Palestine. But it is up to us, the internationals, to carry it out. Boycotting is something only we can do. For years, people around the world who have wanted to support the boycott have asked PACBI to scrutinize many cultural projects, events, and organizations, asking them to determine whether they were "boycottable"—were they taking Israeli state funding or partnering with Israeli government-funded organizations? After years and years of responding to these requests for evaluation, PACBI reached an important conclusion: Many of these events and projects fall into an uncertain gray area that is challenging to appraise, but it is important to emphasize that the boycott must target not only the complicit institutions but also the inherent and organic links between them that "reproduce the machinery of colonial subjugation and apartheid."

In other words, PACBI very humanely acknowledged that the point of the boycott is not just a paint-by-numbers set of rules to obey, but a more complex concept of connections to Israeli institutions that might not be direct. So, for example, if a presenting organization like Performance Space New York wants to produce an artist performing a work that is being developed in part by an Israeli state-funded arts organization—although PSNY itself doesn't receive Israeli money—it should not copresent the work. And, as it promised in its 2024 public statement, it will not. The artist has the choice to develop new work without Israeli state participation, and PSNY refusing to be complicit encourages him in that direction. This application of the cultural boycott refuses to normalize Israeli state funding as an accepted part of art-making. It doesn't exclude individuals; the artist has the option to change the way he develops his projects. But PSNY would make it clear that they would not collaborate, even indirectly, with Israeli funding, because they are supporting the boycott.

What good does this do?

Everything.

In the current condition, when the US government is the primary funder of the mass murders in Gaza and the US corporate media is the primary propaganda machine for those murders, grassroots boycott is the only thing that makes a difference. Insisting on making it difficult for projects that normalize Israeli state money creates pressure from below. Ultimately the strategy is for people power to overwhelm corporate and state power, creating the conversations, campaigns, and debates that lead grassroots organizations to participate in the boycott and thereby change the tenor of public discourse and subsequently public values.

When PEN America refused to oppose the war on Gaza and announced the nominees for their prestigious book prizes, including some awards that are very lucrative, writers dropped out of the running, one by one, in protest. Writers did not want to benefit or even be associated with an organization that did not oppose the war on Gaza. Eventually, so many writers chose to boycott the PEN awards despite their prestige, the awards were canceled. And the message was heard loud and clear: Artists want their cultural organizations to oppose this war, to boycott Israeli state funding, and to support people working for permanent ceasefire and to stop the occupation. The murders of writers, journalists, and poets in Gaza made these demands even more acute.

Solidarity with Palestine does not mean doing what you are told, but rather it requires individuals and communities to be conceptual, conscientious, and interpretive—which can be effective only if there is some deep listening involved. Support, friendship, love, and loyalty are not rooted in obedience. We don't do things because someone we identify with tells us to. Because we Americans are funding their destruction, we owe it to Palestinians to hear their ideas, cries, feelings, and strategies, and to turn them into actions that can end the crimes we are committing. We have to be committed to problem-solving.

Sometimes this backfires or becomes incredibly complex.

The Responsibility to Be Effective

For example, in 2013 I had the privilege of working with the Armenian American novelist Nancy Kricorian to realize the first Palestinian writers panel at the PEN America annual conference. The outgoing executive director was Steven Isenberg. For years PEN had resisted this idea and imposed unacceptable obstacles, like having

THE FANTASY AND NECESSITY OF SOLIDARITY

Israelis or American Jews on the panel. But Nancy's leadership helped me understand that we needed to do the work to create a space at PEN where Palestinian writers could speak to each other, unencumbered, for a New York–based global audience, provided by the annual organizational conference, the World Voices Festival. The other big obstacle was that PEN required that every participating country contribute a large amount of money to the festival, but because Palestine is not a "country" with a functional and centralized government with a cultural affairs budget, we had to raise this money independently. Nancy brought me to ArteEast and to private donors, and we reached the required number. Finally, we jumped through all the hoops and PEN invited three Palestinian writers: Randa Jarrar, Adania Shibli, and Najwan Darwish. This would be the first time a Palestinian-only panel of writers would be an organic part of a high-profile mainstream literary event in New York City. We were ecstatic.

Then we heard from PACBI in Palestine. They found the PEN conference to be "boycottable" because, like many of the countries participating in the festival, Israel had also paid the fee required for their writers to sit on other panels, and therefore PEN listed Israel as a "sponsor" along with every country that had paid the fee. And because BDS calls for not collaborating with Israeli state-sponsored organizations, the sponsorship by Israel violated the boycott.

At first I was upset because I felt that PACBI did not comprehend the significance of the event. Yet, at the same time, these principles were more important than any specific event. Many people argue for the exceptionalism of their own actions. It's arrogant. The Palestinian writers, of course, could decide whatever they wanted to decide, but because Nancy and I were in solidarity, we could not ignore PACBI. So, we were highly motivated to find a solution. Only when Judith Butler negotiated behind the scenes with PEN to organizationally reconceptualize the mandatory national donations to a separate category and away from the label "sponsors" was PACBI able to change their finding to "no position," not endorsement and not opposition. Our organizing got PEN to change the way they conceptualized the event, and this allowed the panel to go on. It was a meaningful change at PEN that shifted consciousness, put Israel in a lesser position, and allowed Palestinian writers to be heard without mitigation or obstruction. It required communication, negotiation, and problem-solving. In other words, it required an authentic relationship, neither obeying nor ignoring but listening and communicating, and negotiating with flexibility.

Unfortunately (and that is a gross understatement), PEN's new executive director, Suzanne Nossel, came to power in 2013. She had previously been deputy assistant secretary of the Bureau of International Organization Affairs at the US Department of State and was listed in their directory as having an association with the right-wing Heritage Foundation. Under her leadership, PEN backtracked from the progress we had made with that campaign, and during the 2023–2024 war on Gaza, the L.A. chapter held an event with a celebrity actress who strongly supports the Israeli war policy. Novelist Randa Jarrar, whose participation we had organized for and won, was now relegated to reciting the names of murdered Palestinian writers while seated in the audience at the pro-Israeli PEN event and was captured on film being literally dragged away in her chair by security guards and taken out of the room. Just as some organizations progress, others can decline. Just before the election of 2024, Nossel finally resigned, and the way forward for PEN has yet to be determined.

In short, real applied solidarity requires negotiation, creativity, and twists and turns. And once progress is achieved, it can be easily turned back. So, while PEN's organizational advances were erased when a new, more radically pro-Israel director came to power, the fact that three Palestinian novelists were heard can never be erased, and it gives us a model of how we want our organizations to be run.

RIDING THE EUROPEAN ABORTION UNDERGROUND RAILROAD (1979)

Many of these elements of working for Palestine also apply to other diverse and varied spheres of solidarity. As an example, I want to share an experience I had as a very young person collaborating with a number of collectives in the late 1970s that were helping Spanish women of various political affiliations get abortions. Like all solidarities, this one had unpredictable twists and unsettling terms. But it heavily influences how I look upon abortion in today's American context.

On May 20, 1979, I was arrested with a large group of protesters on the campus of the University of Chicago for opposing an award given to Robert McNamara, the architect of the Vietnam War, for "international understanding." The first woman president of the university called the Chicago police, and we spent the night in jail. I was put in a cell with women who had been arrested for nude dancing. The next day I dropped out of college and the next phase of my life began. I look at students and young people being arrested today on campuses and in the streets in solidarity with Palestine and I know the knowledge gained by these illuminating institutional betrayals lasts forever. And that many of the leaders and visionaries of future progressive movements are trained in these campus rebellions. I took my student loan check, and instead of paying my tuition I bought a one-way ticket to Luxembourg and started a journey south. My plan was to stop for a few days to visit friends in Albi, France, a town of about forty-six thousand in 1980 in the Tarn department; I had met them some years before during a high school student exchange program. I had no idea that an enormous experience awaited me, one that would change the course of my life. That I would participate in an international network of solidarity with women, one in which those being supported would be the weakest link, the ones least willing to cooperate.

We were sitting in my friend's garden in Albi when the phone rang. The rapid Spanish-speaking voice on the other end was Maria-Rosa, whom they had also met as exchange students to Madrid. She was pregnant and coming to France to get an abortion. In fact, she was coming the next day.

We picked her up at the train station and went directly to the office of Dominique Malvy, the local feminist gynecologist. My friends knew Dr. Malvy not just because it was a small town but also because they were in a collective together, trying to start what was then called a "battered women's shelter" in Albi. Maria-Rosa had scars on her stomach from the boiling water that she had poured on herself trying to make the fetus abort. Fascism had just recently ended in Spain when dictator Francisco Franco finally died four years before, and Prince Juan Carlos was facilitating a transitional constitutional monarchy. The first free election was in 1977, producing a fragile coalition, and no one really knew what was possible in Spain and where it was going. Certainly not for women. Dr. Malvy explained that Maria-Rosa was probably twenty-two weeks pregnant and that it would be impossible for her to conduct the procedure. Abortion had been legal in France for two years, but only up to ten weeks, and Dr. Malvy didn't own the necessary equipment. She recommended a clinic in London. Albigeoises (women of Albi) collected money, and I was selected to accompany Maria-Rosa because I spoke English. She did not speak French or English and I did not speak Spanish, so we got on the train in silence and went to London.

The only person I knew in London was the mother of David Kellogg, whom I had met in Chicago when he tried to recruit me to the Trotskyist organization the Spartacist League. He was ultimately expelled, and we became friends. His mother, Dorothy, was a feminist writer and activist and she took us in. The next morning, Maria-Rosa and I took a taxi to the clinic, in a wooded area on the outskirts of the city. The cab driver was familiar with the place, which surprised me. And he had the startling news that it was owned by some doctors from Spain. But when we arrived, that all made sense because the place was packed. I was expecting some demure living room, but this was a large facility, with probably forty women, and many of them were speaking Spanish. What I came to understand as I traveled back and forth from Dorothy's to the clinic as Maria-Rosa healed from her procedure was that according to guards and patients, there were round-trip charter flights leaving Spain every month, filled with women seeking an end to pregnancy. This was despite laws forbidding Spanish citizens to travel to obtain abortions. The setup was so blatant that tickets could be purchased at El Corte Inglés, the Macy's of Spain. Each person I spoke to had paid a different rate, but all the costs were high, and Spain was an economically poor country at the time, still rural and still reeling from the consequences of fascism. This clinic was basically an abortion mill—though clean and operating by British standards—and the profits were going to men.

Maria-Rosa got her late-term abortion and went back to Madrid. I reported back these details to the women of Albi, and it was determined that two of us should go to Spain and try to make contact with feminists there, to tell them about the nature of this clinic and try to set up an alternative in France. In the feminist DIY mindset of the era, les Albigeoises were willing to receive Spanish women who were pregnant up to ten weeks and accommodate them for abortion there and in the neighboring big city of Toulouse. The South of France had a long history of harboring communist and anarchist refugees from the Spanish Civil War, and this would be the next rendition. This was a time of global feminist collectives, and everyone just assumed that these Spanish counterparts were there to be found.

Genevieve and I were selected to go, as she spoke fluent Spanish, and we were given a box of diaphragms and spermicidal cream to bring as gifts. After decades of a complete ban on contraception, it had just been decriminalized in Spain but was hard to obtain. The diaphragm was the most symbolic and popular mode of contraception supported by feminists because it had no side effects, and unlike condoms, diaphragms were controlled by the woman. Unlike IUDs, they could be inserted and removed at will. We took the train across the border, my first time in Spain. Though transitioning to democracy, it still had a full leg in fascism, and the Guardia Civil, the military police force, were still associated as Franco's henchmen, his enforcers, and torturers of opposition. So, when they appeared at customs with their signature tricornio hats worn flat-side out, Genevieve and I got very nervous. They looked at my US passport and waved me through, not opening my suitcase filled with diaphragms. But when they got to French Genevieve, they opened her valise and discovered tubes of spermicidal cream. *Oh shit.* I stood on the other side of the border, watching as they asked her aggressively, "What is this?" Genevieve took out one tube, unscrewed the top, and put a bit of cream on her finger. Then she massaged it into her scalp. "Cosmetica!" she said, smiling. And they waved her on.

We got a small, cheap, dark hotel room in Barcelona and started scouring leftist meetings that might attract women. Genevieve explained that some of the older people in attendance had been in exile for years and were only now coming home to Spain. I watched an old woman telling her story of flight and return before a room of workers. I did not understand Spanish, but I grasped her bitterness, anger, relief, and hope. And at the end of her talk, everyone stood and cheered and then the whole room sang the communist anthem, "The Internationale." During the social period after the event, Gene and I just started telling people who we were and what we were looking for. One short woman in glasses asked us a few questions and then moved on to some other conversations. But by the end of the night, she returned and handed us a piece of paper with an address on it, and instructions to visit the following evening.

We arrived in a seemingly deserted part of Barcelona. Totally silent. *This must be a joke.* We quietly entered the empty building and went up the dark stairs. At the top floor we knocked on a door and walked into a new world. It was a series of waiting rooms crammed with women. Spain in that period, when there was little immigration and few tourists, held a wide variety of racial and ethnic backgrounds of Spanish people, well represented in those rooms: European, Arab, Romani, African, Nordic, and Indigenous women sat in chairs, some with somber male partners, some with children, most alone. Then we saw the short woman with glasses we had met at the leftist meeting. She warmly squeezed us into a corner, and we talked quickly. What we learned was that this underground feminist abortion service was run by three Argentinean communist women who were in exile from fascist Argentina, still under the rule of dictator Jorge Videla, conducting his "Dirty War" that would result in the murder and disappearance of thirty thousand people. Speaking quickly, we worked out that they would start referring women less than ten weeks pregnant to the South of France to try to get abortions women-to-women, bypassing the profiteers.

So, for the next year or so, women would arrive from Spain by train to Toulouse station. They risked arrest because not only was abortion illegal in Spain, but going out of the country to get an abortion was illegal for Spanish citizens. And, as in Texas and other US states today, abetting an abortion was also illegal. The signal was to carry a copy of the French magazine *Des Femmes*. Their French guides would approach, and they would be brought to the offices of gynecologists throughout the South of France. What was so interesting was the way that growing up in fascism had affected these Spanish women who had to take such a risk to get control of their own reproductive lives. Despite the moments of reality that they shared with each other and with their French hosts, for many this abortion was a dissociated experience. Their husbands and friends at home often had no idea what they were doing. Soon French women started to ask their Spanish sisters to do one action of support when they returned home, usually just to speak to a referred pregnant woman who wanted reassurance before committing to the experience. The vast majority refused to complete their tasks. Once they got their abortions, they just washed their hands of the experience, hanging up on pregnant women who called. And even in some cases women denounced the Argentineans once they returned home to their Catholic and fascist contexts.

As heartbreaking as that was then, I understand it so much more clearly now. We see it in white women who vote with their husbands for Trump, against their own gender interests. We see it in men who have historically refused to join the abortion rights movements over the years. We see it in the weird expectation today from the rest of our country that somehow "women in Texas will revolt" instead of the rest of us taking responsibility for our collective well-being. I returned from these experiences to the US just in time to witness the 1979 Hyde Amendment taking away federal funding for abortion in all but seven US states, later adjusted to seventeen. I then committed to the US reproductive rights movement. I witnessed and covered—for feminist newspapers—the unholy alliance being created between the Republican Party and previously apolitical evangelicals in order to get Reagan elected, and then watched the Tea Party people come to define the party entirely.

But it is this question of denunciation that brought these long-ago experiences full circle for me. The withdrawal of *Roe v. Wade* by a corrupt Supreme Court, followed by new state-based anti-abortion restrictions, not only denies American women their constitutional rights, but, like the Spanish fascist laws, implicates and punishes those who assist them in getting the abortions that they feel they must have. Forced motherhood is not enough for the newly empowered forces of regression. They want to punish women for asking for help, for being connected to others, for disobeying. Hopefully we will all soon be similarly accused.

When I returned to the States, a close friend and I hitchhiked to her hometown in the San Fernando Valley in California. By the time we got there, after a stopover at her ex-boyfriend's house in Chicago, she was pregnant. We stayed in the L.A. apartment of another of her ex-boyfriends as she got a free abortion through emergency MediCal. That night, as she was curled up on his couch, recovering, we turned on the television and saw that the Hyde Amendment had passed the Supreme Court, depriving American women in forty-three states of funding for abortion. A week later, we arrived back in New York and went directly to a demonstration against Hyde. The next day was a public meeting in the West Fourth Street church, at that time a gathering place for progressive movements, now the site of high-end condos. I heard a talk by Rhonda Copelon, the attorney who had just argued against Hyde before the Supreme Court, and that night I joined the reproductive rights organization CARASA (Committee for Abortion Rights and Against Sterilization Abuse) and later a national coalition, the Reproductive Rights National Network (R2N2).

These events in 1979 were the product of a grassroots feminist movement that considered itself international and in no way depended or relied on governments, foundations, or dominant structures to achieve their goals. We used collectivity, a sense of adventure and daring, community fundraising, and donated labor as a way of life. We did bold things and succeeded, in the sense that we got abortions for women who needed them without allowing men in power to profit. This did not produce systemic change on its own, but soon France and Spain would have fuller and funded abortion rights, and these kinds of underground actions were part of building the cultural consciousness. The fact that we could not reverse the consequences of fascist thinking in each person by our own examples doesn't undermine what success means. Some women working together ensured that some other women didn't have to have children they didn't want or couldn't care for, and that was a success. It wasn't perfect or complete. But in each of these lives, in that moment, in some way, it was.

NEW APPROACHES ARE NEEDED IN THE FIGHT FOR ABORTION RIGHTS (2024)

As with all exercise of human rights, access is cyclical and constantly reformatting. And so, half a century later, we in the US find ourselves in a protofascist condition regarding childbearing. Forty-five years of thinking about and working for abortion rights has created my perspective about where we are right now.

The personal is historic.

A few weeks before the Supreme Court overturned *Roe v. Wade* in June 2022, now sixty-four years old, I was in San Antonio doing a fundraiser and organizing workshop for Planned Parenthood South Texas. The staff was mostly Latinx young women who were astoundingly brave, strong, and hardworking. And they did their jobs surrounded by lunatics. That week we all knew that *Roe* was in trouble, but we didn't fully realize how bad it was going to be.

The startling reality came crashing down on America a few days later, and my impulse was to sit down and rethink how we approach solidarity with women needing abortions.

It is obvious that despite right-wing "save the children" rhetoric, the rich who prioritize seizing the wealth of the nation, the religious patriarchs trying to seize our minds, and their proxy elected officials do not care about children. Forcing childbirth guarantees lower levels of education, less economic advancement, less autonomy, and less power for the seventy-five million American women currently of childbearing age and their dependents. But we who believe in women's autonomy are responding with rhetoric and resistance tactics about abortion that are outdated. Desperation creates an opportunity for bold new approaches to resistance, and allowing for creative exchange of ideas, even outrageous ones, can only help us in the face of emergency.

Abortion is a collective experience. In the past, women who had abortions were hung out to dry through the tactic of public confession, in which each person bravely, tearfully, or defiantly stood alone and told her truth. While this was initially effective, pre-*Roe*, in making women's experiences visible, decades of repetition have dulled this approach. We have missed the opportunity to convey that along with the one in four American women who have had abortions, the people in their lives and extended communities have also benefited. Abortion is actually a collective experience of autonomy that is good for both individuals and for society. The man involved benefits, the parents of the woman exercising her natural right benefit, her friends benefit, and so do her other children. The collective "we" needs to be brought back into the picture. "We had an abortion" is the appropriate response accompanying an image of the multigenerational, multigender group surrounding each abortion. Especially men. Men who impregnated women who got abortions actually *also had* abortions and need to say so. Places where men gather, from sports teams to gay apps to boardrooms, need to become arenas of support for abortion rights for people who have relied on that right. If men had gotten on board for abortion the first time around, women would not be here now.

Celebrity can be our friend. Because today everyone lives in an information silo, it is very hard to get a message out in the way a movement could when there were only three TV networks. But there are still some people who have the ear of the public. Sports professionals proved this when they took a stand against racist police violence. Although some of us may have a distaste for the shallow constructions of fame, the fact is that actors, pop stars, and other public figures who transcend marketing boxes have money, infrastructure, and the public's ear. Right after the Supreme Court took away the application of a right to abortion, Lizzo did an event with the head of Planned Parenthood at South by Southwest; there needs to be a lot more of that—especially if these individuals are Christian. Celebrities have to pause and shift gears because this is an emergency. As strange as it sounds, the banal falsities of fame must be transformed into statements of personal reality.

The private sector has a role to play. My politics have always envisioned the ultimate diminishment of the power of the private sector, yet the truth is that today they have all the money. The US government is practically the dusty rear subbasement of global capital. The Supreme Court is rogue, and the Democratic Party is the beneficiary of killing machines. So, the private sector must rise to the occasion. MacKenzie Scott and other well-meaning super-donors are currently limited by contributing only to preexisting organizations. But, similar to local initiatives like Texas's Lilith Fund, we need new systems with national reach, in which any woman who wants an abortion can call a number and get travel to a haven state, accommodation, and a procedure all for free. The liberal oligarchs have the power and indeed the responsibility to mitigate the contemporary crisis. I know this money was gained by exploiting labor, avoiding taxes, and eliminating competition, but they own the wealth now and pregnant women need to access it.

Entertainment is part of the problem. The corporate culture, arts, and entertainment sectors must be made accountable. I have been a novelist and playwright for almost forty years, and I also work in television and film. I can tell you from personal experience that there is very little representation of women in American media, arts, and entertainment that is realistic, authentic, and accurate. Flaubert said, "Madame Bovary, c'est moi," and he was right. Men have forever had almost exclusive control of how women are represented, and today many women creators and gatekeepers consciously or unconsciously replicate those distortions in order to stay in the game. The obstacle is that in America we confuse familiarity with quality, and so when writers try to bring in truly complex work from women's points of view, the newness of the material creates anxiety in producers, publishers, and other gatekeepers that they themselves may not even understand. Whereas repetition of tried-and-true distortions feels comfortable and "right," American cultural production has been a big contributor to this current crisis because the truth about women's lives is simply unrepresentable without enormous financial and social risk. And the loss of abortion rights is one of its most severe consequences.

Restrictions on speech raise the stakes. Laws prohibiting speech that helps pregnant women obtain clinical abortions or access to medical abortions in states that still offer access are on the rise. These punitive measures are rapidly evolving in the context of "Don't Say Gay" laws, restrictions on criticizing Israel, book bans in libraries and classrooms, and repression of Black history, the role of American racism, the truth of queer life, and trans existence. Increasingly the state is being used to stop truth-telling. These terrifying acts of overt repression have broad, chilling effects. In fearful anticipation of being silenced, denied publication, or fired from jobs, some people will repress their own ideas. It is much harder to force the authorities to stop us from speaking and may feel safer to preemptively stop ourselves. But appeasement is not safe, because authoritarianism is a ravenous monster that is never satisfied. As my Hunter College professor Audre Lorde warned us, "Your silence will not protect you." It is our own American history of civil disobedience, from workers fighting for unions to Black people seeking rights and power, women insisting on self-determination, and people with AIDS confronting the state until death. If fighting for abortion rights or other basic rights means breaking the law, so be it. And acceptance of this is as essential to our generations as it was to all our predecessors who defied unjust law. As many resisters said before us, it is a time for "no business as usual." And in moments of crisis, that is how positive change gets made.

WILMETTE BROWN:
HOUSEWIVES AND PROSTITUTES UNITE

Like this small group of creative young women in France and Spain providing access to abortions in 1979, throughout my life I have encountered individuals with innovative, risky, out-of-the-box ideas that can transform lives, or at least help out. A year later, when I was twenty-two and back in New York City, I met one such person, Wilmette Brown, and she made a big impression.

In 1980, Sophia Mirviss (later a prominent physician in San Francisco) and I were writers for *WomaNews*, a grassroots, collective-run, feminist newspaper serving the women's community of New York City. Founded in 1979, *WomaNews* emerged in the context of a vibrant, diverse, and dynamic lesbian community that was almost entirely invisible to the dominant culture. Our stories were not reported in the non-lesbian press, our organizations were not funded, our leaders' names were unknown to others. But there was so much activity that a life could be filled to the brim with performances, readings, parties, dances, relationships, affairs, demonstrations, and endless conversations, revelations, hangouts, and fun. There were so many kinds of gatherings for many different kinds of women that we went out every night, constantly meeting new women, regularly hearing new ideas everywhere, reading women's newspapers or books, or having revelations together in person as a way of life. The field of change was so large and vibrant, it was impossible to cover the waterfront. For example, lesbians of color in New York City had multiple groups creating public events: Salsa Soul Sisters, the Committee for the Visibility of the Other Black Woman, Kitchen Table Press, Las Buenas Amigas, Asian Lesbians of the East Coast, Dykes Against Racism Everywhere, Edwina Lee Tyler and a Piece of the World, Retumba con Pie. And there were bars that catered to lesbians of color: Chaps & Rusty's, La Papaya, Philippine Garden, and more. The movement was so alive it was constantly shifting, new women trying out new endeavors, new ways of gathering and of understanding ourselves. All were entirely invisible to the marketplace and to corporate media.

In May 1980, Sophie and I came across a new person on the

New York scene, Wilmette Brown, a Black gay woman who was a spokesperson for something we had never heard of before called the English Prostitutes Collective. We met her as reporters responding to an announcement sent to the *WomaNews* office for a Queens College press conference. We subwayed to Queens College, not knowing what to expect. Rarely did Black women appear on television, and when they did, they were not butch. So, it was exciting when Wilmette took the mic in front of television news cameras. And it was startling when she made the bold announcement that "prostitutes would be raising their prices for the Democratic Convention in New York." We were intrigued by the tactic and by the speaker and quickly requested a follow-up interview. Once we all three sat down together to talk, we found that she was offering many simultaneous states of solidarity and asking for solidarity. But there was a lot to unpack. At the start of the interview, she introduced herself to us as a member of Black Women for Wages for Housework, another organization we had never heard of. What happened to the English Prostitutes Collective? And this woman was from New Jersey, not England. What were all these identities and communities this one person claimed? We were a bit confused.

As the conversation and subsequent reading and research revealed, Wages for Housework was a British movement started by Selma James, an American Jewish woman who had been married to the Trinidadian Marxist leader C. L. R. James. Selma and Mariarosa Dalla Costa had coauthored *The Power of Women and the Subversion of the Community* eight years before, in 1972, which began the Wages for Housework movement. They called for women to be compensated for their unpaid domestic labor. By 1980, a number of front groups or spin-offs had been created focusing on subsets of women who were all underpaid. So, there were groups for Black women, for prostitutes, for lesbians, all of whom were underpaid for their labor in different, specific ways. It was a one-concept materialist movement that had developed satellites of solidarity. And Wilmette was launching a new visibility campaign for them in New York.

The creation of new organizations was part of the vibrant time in which we were living and writing, and the fact that Wages for Housework represented a new analytical system for understanding women's lives and winning our rights was de rigueur for the era. So, Wilmette had our attention. We were interested in the strategic choice of announcing a pay raise for prostitutes working the Democratic convention when they were not organized enough to collectivize pricing. And certainly, this tiny new group, the English Prostitutes Collective, even if they worked with the slightly larger COYOTE (Call Off Your Old Tired Ethics) and PONY (Prostitutes of New York), still had no real impact on sex work in New York. The number of sex workers who were organized into mutual aid groups was minuscule. Wasn't it just a bluff?

Wilmette explained her strategic approach to us. "There is a lot of sex appeal on the issue of prostitution," she said. Her strategy was to communicate with sex workers through manipulating the mainstream media's prurient interest. This was before the siloing of information created by the internet, still the era of three main television networks: CBS, NBC, and ABC. Everyone watched television, and something on the six o'clock news would reach the collective mass. "We can reach the broadest number of women through NBC and CBS. . . . We know that the media is the state. We know that the media is the Man with a capital M. . . . But you can't turn your back on that, you have to use it."

As reporters for an essentially underground newspaper in a country where every large city had at least one feminist paper and one gay paper, thinking about how to manipulate the locked-down corporate media was intriguing. As lesbians we had zero representation on television, and whatever attention gay men received was negative. Then Wilmette connected her media strategy to the economic agenda of her movement. "Everything is going up and women have the right to charge more too. It's making the point that women are not prepared to work for free. We're fed up with being undervalued." In a sense this press conference she'd successfully organized was a piece of performance art, designed to give sex workers (then still called "prostitutes") watching a TV somewhere the opportunity to earn more money for their work. This use of the fake press conference was a clever act of solidarity that would reach more sex workers and their customers than thousands of hours of street corner conversations and handing out leaflets.

She laid out her thought process:

The way you deal with different levels of power is through organizing no matter what angle you are coming in on. The fundamental question is getting money for women's work. Right now, prostitute women are put in the position of getting money from individual men, just as women are put in the position of getting the money through the typing pool or foundations. The money we are talking about getting is the money that business and industry and government have ripped off from women.

The longer we talked, the more we learned about Wilmette's strong history in many of the primary organizations that were cornerstones of then-recent 1960s and '70s political change in America. Born and raised in Newark, New Jersey, she had been on a personal evolution from civil rights worker to Black revolutionary, from working as a teacher in Africa to living as a lesbian-feminist activist, a trajectory that mirrored the evolution of the women's movement to that date. After fifteen years of political experience, she was now focusing her energy on enlarging and developing an economic analysis and program previously lacking. It had been a long road of political grappling with different kinds of coalitions and solidarities as she evolved toward finding what she felt was the most effective way for women to get power.

In 1959, just before Wilmette got out of high school, she joined the NAACP (National Association for the Advancement of Colored People) Youth Council in her hometown of Newark. In the early sixties she moved on to CORE (Congress of Racial Equality) because she liked direct action. Then she moved on to Berkeley because in '64 "that was the place to go to continue organizing." But she found that as a Black woman, she was only welcomed on a very token level and in a token way. "*Oh yes, we have a Black* kind of thing," but there was no way for her to be integrated into the white left. So, she went back into Black groups and was vice president of the first "Afro-American" students' organization at Berkeley. She moved away from campus stuff to join the Black Panther Party, though she was not out as a lesbian in the Panthers.

> I was living a double life of doing my political work, and when I could, steal the time go out to lesbian bars in San Francisco. I say, "steal the time" because the Panthers were a para-military organization, so we all had ranks, and if someone told you to be in a certain place at a certain time you had to be there.

She left the Panthers in 1969 and worked for Black students at San Francisco State University, getting fired as an instructor from their first Black studies program. She learned that in Zambia, Africa—which had won independence in 1964—they had a system in which they hired a lot of ex-patriot teachers, so she taught high school there for three years while working in the broader liberation struggle. She'd hoped that the African movements would be a better place for her as a woman. But "fundamentally it wasn't."

All during this time I was going through a period of *on one hand* I had left the Panthers because I wasn't prepared to give up being a lesbian. *But on the other hand* it was very difficult to maintain because I was cut off from some of the power of the Black movement. Not being part of "Black men and women together, Black revolution together." It was a crock, but you didn't want to be divided off from other Black women. If you're a lesbian and Black, more so then than now, you're super-freak. I kept thinking *well gee, maybe I just ought to give up. Is lesbianism just some trip I'm on or perversion or white influence?* I thought it was white corruption. At the same time, I found the same crap over the division of labor that I found in the states. Who did the typing, as opposed to the content of the communiqués coming out of the bush. When I came back in the spring of '74 I began to check out anything that was going on about women.

Wilmette finally got involved in a Black women's consciousness-raising (CR) group in New York City and began teaching at Queens College. There she met Margaret Prescod-Roberts, who had been inspired by Selma James and Mariarosa Dalla Costa's book and was a member of two related organizations: New York Prostitutes Collective and Black Women for Wages for Housework.

I was fed up with CR, I already felt pretty conscious. It was a form of organization, but it wasn't one that dealt with how to organize. How do you confront the government? How do you confront men? It was the first piece of literature in the women's movement that I had seen that made a connection between Welfare and the rest of what was going on. It brought things home for me because I knew that my fight as a lesbian was a fight against doing the work that women were supposed to do. There is no separation between my fight as a lesbian or the fight of a prostitute woman or the fight of a woman who is on welfare or the question of sexuality as opposed to bread-and-butter issues.

The question she was grappling with was how to get those who have more power than you on your side. "It's the same question when lesbian and non-lesbian women deal with each other. . . . Non-lesbian women can have access to men's money. . . . All women are forced to sell ourselves one way or another. . . . It's a hell of a thing to be a lesbian. It's a battle with all kinds of pressures that translate somehow into cash."

In many ways this was my first conversation about the complexities of solidarity in a historical and racially explicit material context. Wilmette's life had produced the revelation that she didn't have to give up her personhood as a Black lesbian in order to be in a Black movement or in an interracial left. She could offer and receive solidarity simultaneously. And by being strategic she could use the system to help other women get the money that they needed and deserved. It was a personally groundbreaking, paradigm-shifting moment for me. And it informed my own evolution and self-understanding as someone who could both receive and give. Even publishing the interview in *WomaNews* was an act of solidarity toward this impressive, hopeful organizer, as much as it was an extension of her tactic in solidarity with women who had to have sex for money with Democratic Party delegates in order to survive. Did any woman working the delegates actually say, "Prices are up, didn't you see it on television?" In other words, was Wilmette's solidarity successful, even for one person? That, I will never know.

The lesson I learned here, at the start of my adult life, was that creativity was at the source of solidarity. Regardless of the obstacle or the frame, using the imagination to figure out how to take the risk was the only way forward. Wilmette had chutzpah, but she also had a strategy, a high-risk one. But in the end, she did succeed for sure in one arena: She found a way to bypass the exclusion of the Black lesbian voice in corporate media by successfully manipulating the prejudices of the men who controlled it to trick them in the direction of helping women. This was an inspiration and a model, and something I was to find in the practice of many iconoclastic individuals who used innovative methods to reach across lines of access and subjugation.

4

Solidarity and the Problem of Criteria

Our colonizers are superior to us in only one way.

—BETTY SHAMIEH,
Palestinian American novelist and playwright

A S I DEVELOP MY THINKING about solidarity, each focus produces new arenas of understanding: solidarity as a practice, as a creative endeavor, as performance art, as new forms of relationships, as a series of strategies and responsibilities. With each new insight falling into place, I start to understand its social function and its obstacles with more clarity and depth. It becomes clearer and clearer to me that the force keeping us apart from each other is, in a sense, rooted in an idea of supremacy built upon the fiction of *standards*. Qualification seems to be a kind of propaganda, firmly in place to justify the unfair exclusions that require solidarity to dissolve.

In the protofascist period in which we are living, one of the strategies of imposing inequality is creating more and more stringent requirements for people to access basic human rights. *Who qualifies?* is the methodology of exclusion. Who qualifies for health care? The answer should be *everybody*. But instead, health care is restricted to those who can get good insurance, have the time and ability to advocate for themselves, and are able to maneuver the system. Who meets the criteria for rent-controlled housing? The answer should be *everybody*, because when people don't have homes, no other problems can be solved. Yet we see more and more homeless people internationally, and having an appropriate and safe home becomes a rarefied privilege. Who qualifies for a good education? It would be socially beneficial to the whole world if every person had access to a good education, but we restrict this to people with money, time, childcare, and knowledge of how the class-stratified educational system works. Who gets racially profiled and who meets the standard for never having that experience? Whose ideas qualify as genius, and whose are considered annoying? Whose imprisonment merits the front page of *The New York Times*: Israeli hostages or Palestinian child detainees? Whose point of view is considered neutral and therefore valuable? All the hierarchies of power and social control are marketed to the public through an elusive claim of merit. One race and one gender seem to merit the crown of objectivity—while holding the power to admit others who please them—and the rest don't meet the criteria and are relegated to "special interest," having to constantly jump through hoops to prove eligibility for basic rights.

Being in need of solidarity to reach equity means proving that a person or group meets the standard required for justice. The holders of power claim that their standards are defined by something ethereal or aesthetic, by a higher sensibility, a question of taste, or an assertion of convention as a declaration of spiritual superiority. In a sense, the use of criteria, or a claim of superior values, is the primary creator of categories of exclusion, which is the basis for oppression. When it comes to solidarity—the uniting of diverse forces to dissolve injustice and its impact on specific groups of people—

the claims of criteria are the most pervasive justifications and therefore the most difficult and necessary to identify.

One tiny but emblematic example out of many is the international song competition Eurovision, an event that unites claims of "artistic vision" with their underlying foundations in political supremacy. In this annual televised contest, singers representing "European" countries perform kitsch pop songs. In 2024 Eurovision excluded Russia from participation because of their invasion of Ukraine. In turn, thousands of people signed petitions requesting that Eurovision apply the same criteria and exclude Israel (which, by the way, is not European) for their invasion of Gaza. When the corporation would not equalize their criteria, a campaign was launched in which over four hundred queer artists asked the British representative, openly gay performer Olly Alexander, to withdraw in solidarity. Now, if I received a letter from over four hundred queer artists—including some very talented and accomplished people— asking me to consider something as serious as the normalization of genocide, I would think about it. But Olly Alexander responded that he would continue with Eurovision. He signed a statement with eight other competitors explaining their commitment to participation.

We firmly believe in the unifying power of music, enabling people to transcend difference and foster meaningful conversations and connections. We feel that it is our duty to create and uphold this space, with a strong hope that it will inspire greater compassion and empathy.

By his criteria, being on television was of higher importance than standing against the murder of civilians. He came in eighteenth. Israel came in fifth, but 25 percent fewer UK viewers tuned in. Their criteria was stopping genocide. I want to share here the response of the organization PACBI (Palestinian Campaign for the Academic and Cultural Boycott of Israel) to Olly's expression of standards.

> By participating in Eurovision alongside apartheid Israel while it carries out its live-streamed genocide against 2.3 million Palestinians in Gaza, armed and enabled by many European governments, the contestants would be complicit in artwashing these crimes.
>
> Feigning symbolic gestures of support while dismissing the call of the oppressed reflects a patronising and colonial attitude on the part of the contestants that is familiar to Palestinians, and many oppressed communities globally.
>
> Israel is defying the World Court and the UN Security Council. This means everyone has a responsibility to end complicity in supporting or covering up its crimes.
>
> We call on all Eurovision contestants to withdraw from the contest, as a meaningful gesture of solidarity and to fulfil this moral responsibility to do no harm.

Eurovision took place the week that Israel seized control of the Rafah crossing, bombing trapped, starving civilians to death while Israelis made videos of themselves destroying food trucks. The insipid Muzak-like productions of Eurovision did not achieve Olly's claim that they would "inspire greater compassion" except by the large numbers of people who refused to watch it in protest—and those who booed the Israeli performers while yelling "Palestine" in the live audience, which was censored out of the Israeli official video, replacing the real soundtrack with fake applause and cheers. The conditions imposed on Palestine did not meet Olly's criteria.

What is the construction of this mindset of supremacy, coded as *criteria*, that keeps power in some hands and deprivation the status quo for large numbers of people? I want to look at a number of examples of how claims of criteria or standards are excuses for maintaining supremacy systems. I'd like to start with the case of an incarcerated poet, Dareen Tatour, and how non-incarcerated people defined their criteria in determining whether to call for her release. Then I want to apply this idea in a much larger way to the question of class divisions in American higher education—how we justify to ourselves the separate systems of elite selection and open admissions. And then extend this to look at the experiences of some women artists, like Alice Neel, whose life experiences were determined by the consequences of claims of aesthetic criteria that were actually used to silence, impoverish, and marginalize. And how this shifted only when a political movement of women artists, pushing against institutions, forced criteria, finally—in this one example—to change.

THE CASE OF DAREEN TATOUR: IMPRISONING A POET

The targeted killing of writers, poets, and journalists in Gaza in 2023 and 2024 is the bloody consequence of a long history of imprisoning and silencing creative writers. As just one example, in 2018, the Israeli government sentenced a poet to five months in prison. For a poem. That year Dareen Tatour, a young Palestinian woman, posted these words in Arabic on her Facebook page:

Resist, My People, Resist Them

In my Quds I dressed my wounds
Recounted my sorrows to God

And put my soul in my palm
For an Arab Palestine
I will not agree to a peace solution
As long as the poison is spreading
And killing flowers from my country

I will never lower my flags
Until I take them out of my homeland
I will defeat them when the time comes
Resist them, my people, resist
Resist the settler's greed
Shred the shameful constitution
Which carried the depressing humiliation
And prevented us from reclaiming our rights

Resist them, my people, resist
And follow the convoy of martyrs
They burned the innocent children
And at Hadil* they sniped in public
Murdered her in broad daylight
They plucked Muhammad's† eyes
Crucified him and drew pain on his body
They poured hatred on Ali‡
Set fire
And burned hopes in a cradle

---

* The martyr Hadil from Khalil was murdered by Israeli soldiers at one of the military checkpoints because she didn't agree to remove her hijab while crossing.
† The martyr Muhammad Abu Khdeir from Quds was tortured and burned to death by three extremist settlers.
‡ The martyr baby Ali Dawabshe from Duma was murdered along with his mother, father, and brother when their house was set on fire by a group of settlers.

Resist the Mista'arev's* evilness
And do not listen to the collaborators

Who tied us to the illusion of peace
Do not fear the fire tongues of the Merkava tank[†]
Because the belief in your heart is stronger
As long as you resist in a homeland
Which experienced invasions and did not get tired
For Ali[‡] is calling from his grave
Resist, my rebellious people
Write me as parts of the incense branch
And you became the response to my remains

—ENGLISH TRANSLATION BY DAREEN TATOUR

As any reader can see, this is not an act of violence or of domination, nor is it an action to conquer another people. This poem is, instead, a call to use whatever the reader feels will succeed, to end ongoing violence, the killing of children, the occupation of land, the imposition of degradation and humiliation. Dareen is calling for a reversal of oppression.

For the Palestinian people, the internet is the only consistent site of cohered community; of the 14.3 million Palestinians in the world, all live under occupation, separation, siege, exile—or as second-class citizens in Israel, where they are subjected to more than fifty discriminatory laws. To maintain this oppression, the Israeli government is increasingly policing virtual space. Annual reports from

---

* Israeli soldier disguised as an Arab in order to carry out a military operation or to gather intelligence.
† Israeli tank.
‡ The martyr baby Ali Dawabshe as previously mentioned.

Hamleh, the Arab Center for Social Media Advancement, shows 150 Israeli arrests of Palestinians in 2016 based on Facebook posts, through the charge of "incitement through social media." The year before Dareen's arrest, three hundred Palestinians were arrested by Israelis in 2017 for posting online.

Historically, poets go to prison when unjust systems reach a level of control so brutal that no opposition can be tolerated. Russian Anna Akhmatova was declared a nonperson by Stalin. South African poet Dennis Brutus was imprisoned on Robben Island with Nelson Mandela. Of the thousands of poets and writers arrested or exterminated by the German Nazi government, the best known perhaps is Martin Niemöller, a Christian, who wrote the "First they came for . . ." piece that has inspired a wide range of resistance movements for over a hundred years.

While free speech has always been a principle and a marker of democracy, the Israeli crackdown on poetry came at a very specific moment. In 2005, Palestinian civil society inaugurated a strategy of nonviolent resistance by asking people worldwide to show their support through joining BDS, which had grown increasingly popular around the world. The years surrounding Dareen's arrest had shown remarkable victories for BDS, as recognized artists like pop performer Lorde and formerly incarcerated Russian performance art group Pussy Riot canceled concerts in Israel. In Britain, the High Court ruled that the Conservative government acted unlawfully in trying to prevent local councils from divesting from firms involved in Israel's military occupation. So many international filmmakers pulled out of the state-funded TLVFest, an LGBTQ film festival in Tel Aviv, that *The Jerusalem Post* claimed, "It has never faced a campaign this successful against it."

Following appeals from 250 writers, the literary powerhouse

PEN America, before the leadership of Suzanne Nossel, quietly acknowledged that they no longer accepted funds from the Israelis for its World Voices Festival. Norway's trade unions, the city councils of Dublin and Barcelona, the Presbyterian Church USA, the United Church of Christ, the United Methodist Church (UMC), several Quaker bodies, and significant voices within the British Labour Party had all endorsed some element of BDS.

Dareen's poem appeared after the 2014 Israeli war on Gaza, in which 2,300 people, mostly civilians and many children, were killed by Israeli aerial warfare and ground invasion. Schools, mosques, and hospitals were destroyed. Her conviction took place as Gaza's nonviolent Great March of Return reached its sixth week. Al Jazeera estimates that more than 266 Palestinians have been killed and 30,398 wounded as part of that enormous mass protest in March 2018, including journalists wearing "Press" vests and two medics, as a precursor to the current wholesale murder of journalists in Gaza. It was a dress rehearsal for 2023.

Palestinian strategies of nonviolence had proved increasingly successful in garnering international support and attracting Israeli rage. Thus, poetry, the epitome of nonviolent resistance, becomes symbolic of this new surge of organizing to overturn oppression, and in this way exposes the heart of the Palestinian experience. Yet, Israeli intransigence and impunity, moving further to the right, exploiting and overpowering Palestinian nonviolence with more murder, arrests, and domination, left Palestinians in a place of frustration and desperation. While incarcerated in Damoun Prison, Dareen wrote new lines:

> The soul asks who am I?
> I am the confession of the conscience
> A person who reveals the question.

One of my responsibilities at this time was to find prominent American writers who would be willing to sign a letter protesting Dareen's imprisonment. This is always a complex task, because the system of asking for solidarity from people whose signatures may be influential for your cause is a process of asking up, which—regardless of the necessity and value of the ask—is often regarded by those with more power as a favor instead of an opportunity or moral privilege. And asking for favors for other than oneself from those with more currency in one's own field can have negative consequences later. They can resent the request, and they can become punitive. Also, the higher up the ladder they are, the more approval from the machine they hold, and therefore the more they feel they have to risk. One very well-known writer whom I approached did email me back, but with the request "Send me the poem." This was a startling example of the introduction of criteria. The famous writer had standards for poems posted on Facebook that resulted in poets being incarcerated. The poem had to meet their criteria to win a signature.

Of course, I did as this writer asked. And of course, I understand the hesitancy. This person didn't want to go on record supporting a poem that might have some content that could be found objectionable. So, I complied, and they did sign. But I have thought about that exchange for years. After all, do you have to agree with what a subjugated person says about their own experience, especially one that you have never known or lived, to say they have the right to create a poem? Can you imagine any poem posted on Facebook that would merit someone being arrested and incarcerated? I cannot.

When it comes to supporting poets being arrested and incarcerated for posting poems on Facebook toward the end of their subjugation, I must admit that I, Sarah Schulman, have no criteria.

OPEN ADMISSIONS AND THE PROBLEM OF CRITERIA

One of the clarifying examples I have encountered of criteria used to exclude and to inflate became apparent in a long-term extended and significant opportunity to offer solidarity: my role as a teacher.

For twenty-three years, until 2022, I was a professor at the College of Staten Island (CSI), which is one of twenty-five campuses that make up the City University of New York, a public system of five hundred thousand people that provides education on an open admissions system. That means any person who had a high school diploma or GED equivalence could enter my classroom simply because they wanted to. My job was to teach everyone who was there.

Of course, these students faced a lot of obstacles in their daily lives. They had to have enough time to come to class, including time off from work, which was often a problem. Time to study was rare. They had to have childcare, and sometimes they brought their kids to school with them. The College of Staten Island provided a childcare service for day students, but it was expensive, and there was nothing for evening and weekend students. Most had to pay for a part of the approximately seven thousand dollars per year in tuition. Eighty-nine percent of students were on some kind of financial aid, but DACA (Deferred Action for Childhood Arrivals) and undocumented students could not qualify for financial aid. So, if I had students who were clearly poor and they had no financial aid, that was a good indicator that they had an immigration status problem. They had to pay subway and bus fare to get to and from campus, and sometimes students would message me that they did not have enough money to travel to class that day. Many did not have enough food, and the school maintained a pantry.

Open admissions also meant that many students entered their college years needing remedial courses. Many got frustrated at that level and dropped out. Our school is heavy with overworked and underpaid adjunct professors. My department, English, had thirty full-time professors and one hundred adjuncts. Many adjuncts were teaching fourteen-week courses for six thousand dollars per class and might be teaching four classes like this at three or four different CUNY campuses, running from borough to borough. So, students' first experience of college, at the crucial introductory level, could be met by committed but exhausted poverty-stricken adjunct professors who could barely pull together the clothes appropriate to teach. Also, lack of funding meant that we often did not offer the classes that students needed to fulfill their requirements because the required minimum of twenty to thirty students in a foundational course was not met and the classes were canceled. As a result, students were thwarted in their efforts to graduate. All studies show a direct relationship between funding per capita and successful outcome per student. In the end, CSI had a graduation rate of 34 percent after eight years. In other words, we defeated almost 70 percent of our students. Our school was just too poor to do what was necessary for all of our poor students to fulfill the dreams that they expressed by enrolling in higher education.

Yet, our annual graduation ceremonies were poster events for the American dream. Our typical dean's list or honor graduate would be a woman of color, often an immigrant, in her late twenties or thirties, with multiple children, living in a multigenerational household, who finished her bachelor's degree over five to ten years while maintaining her employment, heading for a master's program. But behind each of these marvels were our average students, who struggled through, barely made it, and basically disappeared into the world.

For many years I taught fiction writing on Friday nights. My night school students often worked full-time jobs, in recent years at

Staten Island's mammoth Amazon warehouse. There were young parents, who were immigrants or lived with immigrant parents and grandparents, and many had trouble with English. They came to class exhausted from a week's labor. One night in class, we were working on the depiction of *thinking* in creative writing. I asked the class to think, and to write down the process. The goal was to reveal that people think in fragments, not sustained sentences, and therefore when writing a character thinking, the construction should be different from the narrative voice. But, as usual, I learned more than I taught. When they shared their writings, the most common element in their collective consciousness was what they were going to eat when they got home that night at ten thirty and could finally have their dinner. They were hungry.

When COVID forced me into the students' homes via Zoom, it became apparent that a number lived in one room with their partners and children, and that room was in a house occupied by their parents, siblings, and grandparents. Very few had their own room, or any private space to do class. The students had to take their classes with their partners and children in the same space—sometimes with their child sitting on their lap, or with the TV on in the same room, or with their parents sitting on the same sofa. One kid's mother and sister had to leave the studio apartment the three of them shared, every Friday night from six thirty to ten, so that he could Zoom our class. Often the family had one computer, insufficient Wi-Fi, no Wi-Fi, or no computer. Some students had to take class on their phones. The same conditions applied to some of our underpaid faculty. When I observed an adjunct during COVID, the poverty of open admissions was made even more apparent. Only three of twenty-five students showed up for his class and none of them would turn on their cameras. He and his wife and infant lived in a studio. The child was screaming. The professor was clearly having a breakdown, and he was not earning enough money to live.

There is a connection between the financial deprivation attached to public education and the fact that it is open to everyone. Even though it is better for society for more people to be educated, we lost track of that understanding a long time ago. Instead, we have embraced a punitive exclusionary system in which respecting people's gifts, recognizing their dreams, and extending their abilities is considered a reward, and it is only offered based on social currency and derivations of race, class, gender, and immigration status. Special opportunities are tied to all kinds of criteria, especially which candidates fit the admission committees' images of the students they want to teach. Palatability is an enormous element to these decisions. Identification between gatekeeper and candidate is another. But the most significant factor in which of our students could get access to better educational circumstances was information. They needed to know that those opportunities existed. And then they needed to understand how to access them. These were huge obstacles.

But what I want to focus on here is what this means for the teacher who tries to be in solidarity with her students.

For most of my teaching life, my job has been to work with anyone who made it into the room. Whenever I came to class on the first day the only thing I knew I would find for sure was difference. I often averaged fifteen or sixteen different ethnicities, with Puerto Rican–Italian as the most common mix on Staten Island, and ages ranging from seventeen to seventy. It wasn't only the demographic difference, but more important was the range of internal difference. I had students who were brilliant, who were slow, who were bored, who were exhausted, who were developmentally disabled, who were deaf, who cared, who were indifferent, who were high, who were in bare-knuckle recovery, who were revolutionary, who were reactionary, who were illiterate to the extent that they could not read out loud, who were sophisticated autodidacts, who were rude, scary, racist, violent, who bragged about being connected to the Mafia, who were homeless, hungry, hardworking, who had never read an entire book, who had written six novels, who were super excited about school, talented beyond measure. I had cops, corrections officers at Rikers, soldiers, formerly incarcerated, veterans, women who were pregnant and did not want to be but for whom abortion was not an option and who dropped out or graduated against all odds, strippers, queers, trans people, waitresses, lots of construction workers, security guards, bank tellers, preschool teachers, charter school teachers, religious school teachers, lots of home health aides, maids, cleaners both industrial and private—every dimension of New Yorker was present in my class.

In order to find the place of potential solidarity with each student, I needed to work to individuate them as quickly as possible. I had to assess where each person was starting from, so I could teach them individually and build each one's progress based on their starting point. I usually began the first day by being transparent that this was my approach. I would write the word *individuation* on the board (I had to bring my own chalk and eraser) and explain that this meant it was *my job* to find out who they were and where they were at so that I could help them learn on their own terms. Then we would go around the room and I would ask them the following questions: How old are you? Where were you born? What languages do you speak? What does your name mean? And we would spend the first hour writing each person's name on the board and trying to figure out what their name means. The results established the extremes of our collective starting position. One student would say, "I am from Ghana, I speak four languages," and they would know exactly what their name meant. The next student would say, "I'm from Staten Island, I speak English, I don't know what my name means."

Quickly the divide between immigrants and Staten Island–based Americans started to become articulated. The first- and second-generation immigrant students are the hungriest for upward mobility. They are outsiders, and so they know there is an inside. And for many, their parents will do anything for their children to surpass them. The multigeneration working-class white kids are coming from an entirely different experience. Italian American is a protected category in CUNY, and Italian Americans are the white New Yorkers with the lowest rate of upward mobility in the city. This explains the Puerto Rican–Italian majority identity. Italian Americans tend to stay in key neighborhoods, maintaining working-class city jobs that they get grandfathered into, like cop, construction worker, firefighter, sanitation worker, while other groups pass through on their way to the suburbs. When I was a kid, the classic New York mix was Irish Italian, but the Irish assimilated a long time ago. Now it is Puerto Ricans who are on the rise, and so they are sharing social and living space with Italians as they pass through on the way up the ladder. While immigrant students may have big dreams, often Italian kids don't even know what professions are out there. I had one student, Sharon, who was literally a genius. Turned out her grade point average was 3.98. So, I asked after her career goals.

"Preschool teacher," she said.

"Really? Because you can get a free ride to law school."

She thought for a moment. "Ahh, no thanks."

"Wait a minute. Don't blow it off so fast. Bring in your parents; we can all talk about it."

But more conversation would reveal that her parents wouldn't want her to, and she didn't want to leave home and her boyfriend. Besides, no one she knew had done something like that.

And that was the problem. Open admissions is often a struggle between the teacher and the family, who wants the female student to have a predictable future. Of course, that was a specific case, and everyone is different, but the working-class American white kids in my classes were more likely to have parents who just did not want their children to surpass them. My colleague Daisy Hernández shared with me that based on kids she grew up with in New Jersey, she understands that some working-class parents may live in fear of losing their kids. "They know intuitively that class mobility may be a loss from which their children never return."

There was an expectation among a sector of my CSI students that they would live at home until they got married and then they would live across the street. At the same time, one of my primary goals was to get the smartest, most talented kids—their children— to escape from "the island," to get away from Republicans, familial control, and parochialism and expose them to how things work, how the apparatus is constructed, and how concepts are created and imposed. My dream for them was to make them literate regarding the mechanisms behind the short range of ideas available in official American discourse.

Once, early on, I taught playwrighting, and out of twenty-eight students, only three had ever seen a play and one was *The Phantom of the Opera*. So, I first had individual meetings with each student, and we talked about what a play is. That a play is what people *do* and *say*. It was a private conversation; I just felt that if I did it in class, collectively, a significant number would miss the point. Then we sat down as a class and read and talked about *A Streetcar Named Desire* for a month. This turned out to be a good choice. Most people in the class had examples from real life that they could relate to of a drunken bully and of a freeloading relative. Even though those are not exactly the character profiles, they work for letting the story unfold. Finally, each student wrote their own scene, rewrote it, worked on it with another student, cast it, and presented it in class. This was the moment of truth, when I was grateful that they had never actually seen a produced play on the other side of the ferry ride in "the city." Because my students, who were all races, made themselves the protagonists. A fifty-year-old Caribbean woman who worked as a home health-care aide wrote a play about her family in which her job was never mentioned. A Polish woman who cleaned houses wrote a play about an immigrant whose boyfriend is back home and doesn't understand what America is really like. If these two women actually attended the American theater, they would have come away with the news that they could not be protagonists and could only appear as home health-care aides and accented blond maids.

In twenty-three years in open admissions, I sent ten kids to creative writing MFA programs. Overwhelmingly they did very poorly. Getting them in turned out to be easier than having them thrive. There were so many obstacles. The most visible was that the professors did not mentor them, and they could not make friends. They were highly stigmatized socially for being working-class from Staten Island. Some of them finished, some did not, and some just disappeared. A few relied on me and their other Staten Island professors to mentor them through the programs because their professors from Bennington could not give them helpful notes. One very talented Panamanian kid got into the highly ranked MFA program at Brooklyn College. He was the only Black student, there were two kids from Harvard, and when he showed me the notes he got from his famous professor, I was appalled. She did not get inside his work. She was shallow and exoticizing and clearly did not believe he could have a career. I checked back with some of these students during COVID and invited them to speak to my current under-graduates. One of the most successful, who had gotten into the New School, was still working on her first book ten years later. She described her MFA experience as very difficult. Students made fun of Staten Island and had no curiosity about it. And she had trouble building networks and relationships because she could not afford to go out for drinks. Now she still lives on Staten Island, has four children, and is writing in her car. In open admissions, these tal-ented students thrived and were appreciated and welcomed on their terms. Once they survived a selection process, they were de-feated. Part of the goal of selection is triage, to force people out, often for reasons that are unrelated to their potential contribution.

In 2022, at age sixty-four, I started a new job at Northwestern University's creative writing program. Many of my friends were re-tiring, my CUNY job was known to me, and Northwestern was offering me a substantial raise and a brand-new life experience. Plus, my partner, Leslie M. Harris, lives in Chicago. *Change is good*. And I feel very lucky to have been offered a chance to actually make some money and have a brand-new final act as I approach the end of my teaching career. As the kind of New Yorker who can never leave New York, I still live here, but I move back and forth to and from Chicago. There is a lot that is very attractive about Northwestern. My colleagues include some of the most exciting creative writers in the country: Natasha Trethewey, Chris Abani, Charif Shanahan, Juan Martinez, Daisy Hernández. The writing faculty is mostly people of color, and half queer. But most of all, every student ad-mitted to the master's program is given a free ride plus an annual stipend of forty-five thousand dollars and health insurance. This means that we can take anyone we want, without asking them to take out loans or go into debt. And Northwestern is so rich—its endowment is $13.7 billion, more than most countries—that they have all kinds of support systems for students. The College of Staten Island, with an endowment of $19 million, can't afford copy paper. Northwestern has a program that buys students winter coats.

Suddenly, in the middle of one night, I woke up, terrified, realizing that for the first time in my life, I was going to have to grapple with something I had never thought about before: *criteria*.

To me, teaching had always meant walking into a room and teaching whoever was inside it. And I loved this. I have had great students, I have changed lives, I have meant something to my students' futures, and I have been exposed to and learned from a wide range of people from a variety of circumstances with all kinds of perspectives, goals, and dreams.

Criteria meant abandoning this. It required re-creating the very selection systems that had defeated my most talented students, the ones who had managed to get admitted to MFA programs.

What were my criteria and how did it impact being in solidarity with my students? Certainly, I don't believe in the idea of "the best writer." When *The New York Times* surveyed over five hundred writers in order to compose a list of the "best" one hundred books published so far in the twenty-first century, my list of ten was one of the samples they published. Only one of the books I selected, *Citizen: An American Lyric* by Claudia Rankine, appeared in their master list. So the writers I am in solidarity with, whom I appreciate and learn from, are not the ones relegated to the status quo of "best." In this case, *criteria* seemed to be a euphemism for bias, rooted in the past, and often homogenous—not necessarily by demographic, but certainly by form and point of view. We reward the kind of "difference" that stays within boundaries while reinforcing our norms, and gatekeepers find this comfortable and in fact entertaining. But works that question our sense of ourselves as objective, neutral, or value-free are the works that gatekeepers reject. Because supremacy thinking is rooted in the deep-seated belief that the supreme is inherently objective. And turning that over is intolerable to people in power, who emotionally need to justify their status and access.

When I think of open admissions, I think of my friend, the great theater artist Jeff Weiss, who recently passed. Jeff was a huge force in my development and appears in two of my books. I wrote him into a scene in my 1986 novel, *Girls, Visions and Everything*, and ten years later I dedicated *Stagestruck: Theater, AIDS, and the Marketing of Gay America* to him and his partner, carlos ricardo martinez.

There is so much to say, but I think the most relevant experience was a very specific one. This took place in the 1980s. My former girlfriend G was a working-class woman who had a naturally beautiful voice and sweet, charming demeanor. She had auditioned for a part at a theater company that was mostly composed of children of celebrities and the wealthy. The playwright was someone close to us, and he had asked her to audition. But between the invitation and the decision, he was transformed by his desire to fit in with the famous and rich people, and so even though she was the better choice, he chose the far less talented daughter of a famous actor.

Devastated by surprise, we were sitting on a stoop on East Tenth Street trying to process the creation of this humiliation by its imposers. Jeff and carlos walked by at that moment and stopped to talk. We told them exactly what had happened.

Jeff had ethics and he had values about making art. This applied to treating people with respect and honesty. And one of his and carlos's core values was to never pander to the powerful. First, he told us to never talk to this man again. Then he told us something phenomenally surprising. He was about to do a collaboration with these very same people. They had chased him and cajoled him for years to work with them, and he had finally promised, only on the condition that half the cast would be his loyal, reliable old friends—his freakish, unconnected, special, iconoclastic artists with whom he had built his vision.

So, without ever having seen G perform or ever having heard her sing, he went on his instinct and invited her to be in this upcoming show.

And for the next two years, she performed with these wealthy, connected, and dynastic people every weekend for four- to six-hour shows, each week with a new script. And, in fact, she had a beautiful voice, and week after week she enriched and filled the hearts of the audience and her coactors—both celebretantes and East Village nobody/everybodies—as she sang "Please, Let Love Pass Me By." And of course the people with pedigree and entrée were no better and were often worse than the inappropriate, freer, wilder, and less streamlined East Villagers. And that was one of the greatest lessons I have ever learned: Say yes. Trust people. Let go. Welcome others. And include. Community is for everyone, and by operating like a community, you get the same rate of excellence and duds. But there is a lot more range.

Another example of the rewards of open admissions is my longtime collaborator Jim Hubbard, with whom I co-founded the MIX NYC Queer Experimental Film Festival, which lasted for thirty-three years and has recently been revived by a new generation. Jim said yes to every kid, queerdo, and nerd who wanted to be part of MIX. There was no entrance requirement, no criteria. And you may be interested to know that from this open-door policy emerged people like Shari Frilot (now chief curator at Sundance), notable filmmaker Thomas Allen Harris, Cannes director Karim Aïnouz, and Rajendra Roy, film curator at MoMA. None of them had to apply, provide references, or be interviewed. And no one was refused, because Jim saw MIX as a community, not a company. This open admissions produced excellence, leadership, and the future.

So, here I am at a crossroads, finally becoming a gatekeeper myself. I am thinking about what the criteria for this opportunity at Northwestern should be. The success of talented students should not be based on whether they can afford to go out for drinks, or whether faculty, with our own anxieties about status and approval, can relate to them. In other words, we have to remove the comparatives that dominate the field. I am realizing that these three students whom we will be admitting every two years in my area, nonfiction, don't have to be young, don't have to have gotten their BA recently, don't have to be in the know, and should not be people who today would get approval from *The New Yorker*, Penguin Random House, or Iowa. They should be the kind of writers who raise the ick factor, the discomfort level, the lack of repetition required for approval. Writers whose points of view are not acceptable, and who therefore don't reinforce all preexisting hierarchies. And who are not formulaic.

In education, in publishing, in theater, the slight variation on the standard repetition is the money shot. After all, entertainment tells us what we already know, whereas art expands how we think. Open admissions, with all its difference, means less money, because more people's needs are met, and criteria means fewer people to share the money. Open admissions is a model for solidarity, for an open city and a much more accessible and equitable larger society.

Certainly, my job conditions at Northwestern are beyond excellent. My colleagues are top-of-the-line, everything is highly functional, and there is enough money and infrastructure for both students and faculty to excel. And I don't have to bring my own chalk to work. But open admissions is actually culturally healthier, because it reflects difference, while so far our existing concepts of criteria reproduce the status quo and maintain exclusions of people who are widely denied solidarity.

Trump-appointed US courts are now intent on creating even more obstacles for poor people, people of color, and the overlap of those two categories to enter elite institutions. Even though, for example, Black women are only 4.4 percent of American PhDs, the Trump Supreme Court decided to make it even harder for Black people to access quality higher education, while protecting white legacy admissions. But when exclusions are removed individuals can achieve, create new arenas and perspectives on scholarship, and expand what education offers the society.

However, the past that produced the inequality does not retrospectively get reevaluated. To reevaluate the past would mean to admit that a mistake was made. That not only were the gatekeepers wrong when they excluded earlier renditions of the individuals they now trumpet, but it would also acknowledge that mediocre white male artists were elevated, overpraised, overvalued, and endowed with powers they did not actually possess. Saying that women were cheated in the past means that men were cheating. And that admission is unbearable. Now that we accept more queer content, are we going back to the lesbian and gay writers who created the current moment and rereading those books we overlooked and relegated to the margins? Is *The New Yorker* reconsidering all those lesbian stories it rejected in the eighties, nineties, aughts, and last week? No, because while we may be more inclusive now, we still have *criteria* that cannot look back.

My ultimate goal is that America would have one higher educational system, which would be free—and available to everyone. I think it would be good for the collective if more people were exposed to one another. As it stands, open admissions doesn't even know what the cafeterias of criteria look like. What a ruling-class salad bar looks like. The differences are unimaginable. My dream is that the people who guard the borders of our insanely stale, constrained, uptight, and boring cultural production would be re-created to be highly accountable and flexible individuals whose job is to welcome the world and refuse repetition, not only of content, but of perspective beyond demographic.

Open admissions as a value offers us a great deal beyond the educational model. As a way of life, it invites a widening of community, while criteria reinforces the privacy of power. Open admissions is the public, and criteria creates the corporation. The more we have open admissions, the weaker the centrality of the corporation, for, as we all know, the hoarding of resources destroys the community.

ALICE NEEL: AHEAD OF THE DIMINISHING WORLD

No silencing or exclusion exists in a vacuum. Zillah Eisenstein used the phrase *capitalist patriarchy* in her 1978 anthology, *Capitalist Patriarchy and the Case for Socialist Feminism*. Similarly, books from the 1970s and '80s like *This Bridge Called My Back: Writings by Radical Women of Color* popularized "women of color feminism," which later became known as "intersectionality," a recognition that different groups of people and spheres of social dynamics of power are relational. The observation of resonant patterns on the continua of exclusion, erasure, imposition of poverty, and infliction of violence—all the components of imposed defeat and repression—reveals larger structures of control, of which each illustration in this book is an example.

Alice Neel is now considered one of America's greatest painters. Unlike most female geniuses, she finally became successful, but it was in legacy. Why she was so marginalized, despite her ability, like so many of the people and examples we have visited here, is helpful in illuminating the function of exclusion and marginality itself—and how the excuse of inferiority is a deception facilitating power. Her life and career are worth revisiting because as she practiced solidarity, she also asked for solidarity. She was controlled by criteria. And she had a radical vision, both political and aesthetic. She also is treated as an individual, but as I will show, she is actually part of a century-long tradition of the avant-garde, and of New York experience, that spans the twentieth century and intersects with my own story. It was the rising feminist art movement that propelled her out of the prison of obscurity late in her life. So, that she is known and valued today as an individual is the consequence of collective solidarity by other women.

The white straight woman sits between both positions as she is precariously mistrusted by both the safe and the endangered. No one admires her. Her complaint is considered inelegant. If she is not a mother, we don't understand why she demands attention. If she is, then she is always wrong until she is idealized. And yet a mother's errors have the greatest consequences. We project frustration and blame on the white straight woman. She is the hinge on which a door swings open, though when it slams shut she is the one left on the outside looking for her key. Her currency depletes rapidly and occasionally becomes branded: emblem of brilliance ignored. She is depicted as annoying, a role.

Alice Neel divides the canvas in a painterly manner we find energizing and exciting. But this is not about her painting style, but rather the question of solidarity between the artist, born with the twentieth century, and her normally marginalized subjects. When living with a rich Cuban husband in Havana in the 1920s, Alice had her first exposure to the contrasts of extreme wealth and extreme poverty; she attributed her communism to this shock of blatant injustice. Her first experience as an artist in the world was in Cuba; unlike many of her peers, she didn't visit Europe until her sixties. In New York, post-divorce, her subsequent single-motherness and poverty brought her into community with the poor. She moved into a poor building, and the neighbors she painted were poor people. It all scans. It was her reality and her world. And yet it is somehow considered surprising or exceptional by those who foolishly assume that because of her race she should not be poor. But because being a woman alone with children made her poor, should she therefore have been thwarted in her desire to make art? Presumably every poor woman—if she had the obsessive compulsion to make art no matter what—would paint the other poor people with whom she lived. Or write about them or photograph them or compose music that took their music into account.

The scarcity of such examples is less a measure of Neel's equality vision than of how few women manage to sustain art-making in the face of deprivation. So, this ability alone makes her remarkable. Yet later she painted famous, influential, and wealthy artists and political leaders, some of whom were gay or bisexual. How did she get these people to take her seriously if she was as marginalized as her Puerto Rican neighbors? She shared space and needs with her Latino neighbors and her Puerto Rican boyfriend's family, whom she painted, but she had other advantages that they never had, which became, naturally, part of her vision of the world. There is an equality in her portraits, repeatedly discovered—they feel alive in the moment. Her ability to be interested in people of color was rare; most white people did not and don't care. And as Neel rose in access, that interest did not dissipate. Despite her passionate politics and integrated rejection of the corruption of wealth, there was simultaneously a sense of distanced interest that seemed to drive her visual ideas. She chose some subjects that were socially marginal, and she was against people being punished for difference. Yet her subject selection was not only a social corrective but also a disobedient interest in people who were not supposed to matter. I wonder if it was the interest that predominated, not the impulse to equality.

Oppression means not being seen accurately at your level of merit, actively rendered not worth being remembered or grappled with, not being allowed to speak from inside the apparatus. Was Neel's deprivation equal to the deprivation of her subjects? In the case of some of her Latino and Black subjects, they ultimately became seen because she was recognized. And this applies also to some of her obscure feminist art critic, artist, and curator subjects, whose greatest notoriety is that they sat for portraits by Alice. On the other hand, her gay male subjects held a currency that helped propel her to acknowledgment. She thought she'd become a portraitist from studying her mother's face, "which had dominion over me," to detect any sign of a possible outburst of "dissatisfied morbidity." She watched and saw people as a defense against their unpredictability. This was later cast as a social value. "I always loved the working class and the most wretched," she said. "But then I also loved the most effete and the most elegant." Most of the queer people Neel painted were not powerless. I would daresay that all the gay and queer men she painted were more functional and savvier within capitalism than she was and knew better how to position themselves in order to have some autonomy. Frank O'Hara, Henry Geldzahler, Andy Warhol, John Perreault, John Gruen, even the closeted mayor Ed Koch had power over her, the power to help her be seen. To declare her important. As notoriously lonely as she and many of them were, they had other men's power to aspire to, which is itself a recognition of collectivity. When you are a lonely white heterosexual woman, what does a homosexual couple mean to you?

They have belonging and they have love, even if they don't appear as protagonists in movies or have familial approval or legal rights.

One of the exceptions to the power-gay theme is the paired portrait of Jackie Curtis and Ritta Redd. Penny Arcade, the performance artist whose lack of institutional recognition parallels Neel's first sixty-four years, wrote a stunning tribute to Redd in her play *Invitation to the Beginning of the End of the World* (1990). A middle-aged middle-American woman is standing bewildered on an East Village street corner at the height of the AIDS epidemic. Seeing she is clearly out of place, a kind young gay man stops to ask if she needs directions; she wonders if he knew her son, Ritta Redd, who has just died of AIDS. The man has never heard of him, and the bereaved mother is even more confused. "He did shows," she says over and over again. "He did shows." Finally, out of kindness, the passerby pretends he remembers the deceased artist, just to give the woman a confirmation of her son's life purpose. A search on Redd turns up almost nothing besides the Neel portrait; Redd and Curtis are erroneously described as a "couple." As Penny told me:

> Ritta Redd was Jackie's handmaiden and lieutenant for a while, 1969 till 1974. Jackie moved on to other identities and other people. That Jackie and Ritta were lovers is a complete myth created by people who need a reason of why Alice Neel painted them together other than the simple reality that they were joined at the hip.

The more I find out about Alice Neel, the more personal connections I detect through the multigenerational history of the New York avant-garde. The two gay men she painted who were closest to my life were both by association. Geoffrey Hendricks, the Fluxus artist, sat for a portrait with his partner Brian Buczak, who would die of AIDS in 1987 (*Geoffrey Hendricks and Brian*, 1978). Geoff and I became friends later when he partnered, until his own death, with my pal Sur Rodney (Sur), gallerist, archivist, and East Village neighbor. To celebrate the sixtieth birthday of our common thread, Brad Taylor, a group of ten of us East Village artists, all longtime friends, celebrated by sharing a house for a week on the Mediterranean coast near Naples. Geoff brought me to Jill Johnston's eightieth birthday party, where he did his signature headstand performance. She published her book *Lesbian Nation: The Feminist Solution* (1973) with iconoclastic punctuation and a corporate press, which would be impossible today. And her most important and invisible book, *Jasper Johns: Privileged Information* (1996), explored the twin powers of the closet and male bonding to build power for gay men in the art world.

But, for me, the most influential of Neel's subjects was Roger Jacoby (*Rose Fried's Nephew*, 1963). Although we never met, Roger was the lover of my lifelong collaborator, Jim Hubbard, before Jim and I met. Roger was a pioneer of the hand-processing technique for Super 8 film that Jim has used all his life. And it was Roger's death from AIDS that was partially the impulse for us to co-found MIX in 1986.

In a way, asking to paint someone is very flattering, and these men, with their own ambitions and loyalties, all said yes. There is an affect Neel displayed that can be observed in some white heterosexual women before feminism—a kind of childishness, a diminution to make herself less threatening to men or to elicit mercy from her father. In some cases it became a performance of dottiness. In some cases it was a protective cover for fierce intelligence and ability. In others it was an internalization of inferiority signified by helpless confusion. In art school Neel started taking money from boyfriends in order to make art; it became a lifelong practice. In archival footage, she often exhibits this kooky front, even when speaking profound ideas or fierce opinions. It softens her and makes her easier to take or more annoying, depending on your preferences for white heterosexual female behavior. Her white ability to appear helpless while also sexually powerful so she could paint, constructed her exterior without interfering with her actual work. Even powerful gay men were attracted to this; recognizing her talent, I think, would not have been enough or, in some cases, even possible without the charm.

Neel had only six solo shows from age twenty-seven to sixty-four, and then sixty solo shows from that point until her death. Many of us women artists and writers can identify with this disappearance in plain sight. While men with power may have admired her spunk, it took them four decades to recognize her talent. If we applied what we now know retrospectively, we would find decades if not centuries of overpraised mediocre men with bad values being told that they are marvelous. Yet this excavation is never done; even with the new inclusivity, the rotten canon is expanded but not sorted, and so we never discover that we live with bad standards and false claims. This deception created one of Neel's narcissistic wounds. Even near the end of her life, even on *The Tonight Show Starring Johnny Carson*, she was reciting her laurels of recognition, not seeing that the attention itself was its proof. Because being seen at the last minute solves some problems but not others.

She was on the Works Progress Administration in the 1930s, and then on welfare—a program with unjust constraints. After all, people should be able to spend whatever money they can gather the way they wish to. Alice spent hers on a second home in New Jersey. She was the kind of hustler that people who are not allowed to exist as themselves learn how to be, or perhaps a kind of survivor living under a system of bad values that makes bohemians into hustlers. The hustle was a rebellion against the control and confusion of deprivation that was ever trying to stop her from making art. Interestingly, it was a woman, Muriel Gardiner, a psychotherapist, who actually handed her money: starting at sixty-four, Neel received a six-thousand-dollar annual stipend for life. This understanding of the falsity of praise when owned by men never goes away; therefore, the damage of the earlier stupid discarding can never heal.

When Neel talks to Barbaralee Diamonstein in 1978 we find out that she is glad her sons were not homosexual because she wouldn't want them to be part of a "little group," which feels imprecise because she did want them to be artists. She contrasts the "sophisticated painting" of the Gruen family with "simple" Puerto Ricans. So, she was far ahead of her time, yet she held prejudices because she was a human—the kinds of prejudices that have long defined white people and straight people who are far ahead of the diminishing world and reject its exclusionary practices. Today, though, those same contradictions are increasingly found unforgivable, because in the long run they do not create structural change.

The queer subjects Neel chose were very far away from my own experience and my own world, because they had something that she wanted, while my queer world downtown in the 1970s and '80s comprised an entirely different kind of person. As Vivian Gornick reminded me in a smart but negative review of my novel *Rat Bohemia* (1995), bohemians leave, but the lesbians, gays, and people with AIDS at the center of my world were thrown out. And that is a significant difference. Looking back, I actually have to start in the 1950s, because I was born on Tenth Street in 1958 and so was exposed in some unconscious natural way to queer life from the beginning. The first words I learned how to read were *Hotel Albert*, the large green letters that hung off the side of the building across the street. Later I learned that the people hanging out on the corner below, getting welfare checks from the open wooden mailboxes behind the hotel's desk, were the trans/drag reason that the Cockettes chose to stay there when they made their New York debut at the former Yiddish theater on Second Avenue. I remember hearing about a gay man jumping from the now-abandoned police station on Eleventh Street and getting impaled on the spiked iron fence below. Our next-door neighbor was a never-married, strangely Protestant woman named Grace who had moved to the village in the 1920s and had an apartment filled with furniture from the 1930s, who lived mysteriously *alone.* What was she doing there, I vaguely wondered. Though I didn't know it, homosexuals were everywhere. On Sunday mornings my father would go buy rolls at a bakery called Sutter's and I would stand out front waiting (helicopter parenting did not exist), staring at the Women's House of Detention across the street. Women yelled out the window and other women and men stood on the sidewalk yelling back. Only later, when I read Joan Nestle, did I learn that women were arrested in bar raids on Saturday nights, and on Sunday mornings—as the Schulmans got their rolls—their lovers and pimps and friends would yell up to them from the sidewalk.

It was around that same time, in 1962 at age three, that I first crossed paths with a queer subject of a Neel painting: John Gruen, the father of my nursery school classmate, Julia Gruen. John was an art critic, married to the New York School painter Jane Wilson, Julia's mother. Neel had been reviewed by him favorably in the *World Herald Tribune* in 1966; four years later, in 1970, she painted *The Family (John Gruen, Jane Wilson, and Julia).* I remember playing with Julia, who would grow up to be the founding director of the very queer Keith Haring Foundation, under the table at her parents' apartment on Tenth Street between Avenues A and B while her mother may have been painting on coats. John was a Jewish Holocaust survivor and bisexual, and after his death he was included in the "In Memoriam" section of the LGBT Lambda Literary Awards annual gala slide show.

When I was rejected by my own parents for being gay in 1975, my life became chaotic, and yet, as a consequence of their stupidity and cruelty, I was rescued from being embedded in a ridiculous family and a dead world. The night of the great 1977 blackout, my high school girlfriend came to meet me at Circle Repertory Company, where I worked, and we finally had the nerve to go into the Duchess, the lesbian bar next door, with its blacked-out windows and Danny, the bouncer from the Israeli mafia. We weren't carded because of the exception of the blackout; the usually dark place was lit by candles on tables—and, surprise, the waitress was a girl from our high school! Even though the lesbian world was still part of the criminal class, the presence of our classmate serving the bottles of beer made that whole world more welcoming and sensical, and soon the underground society of lesbian culture, romance, predation, aesthetics, partying, disobedience, and codes would become the center of my life.

When I dropped out of college in 1979 and returned to New York, I rented a room on Seventh Street and Avenue C from a white woman named Tennessee. Every morning, walking to the subway to go to my job as a substitute bartender for the Brew and Burger chain, I would pass a beat-up pizza place on Seventh and A where a strange woman, of the category I then thought of as "bag lady," sat talking to the pizza man. And when I returned at night she would still be there. Then Tennessee told me it was Valerie Solanas, the playwright who shot Andy Warhol for mocking and disrespecting her. Alice Neel famously painted Warhol with a bare chest, revealing the scar left by Solanas's bullet. Soon I had a job working for an all-women trucking company that drove old post office delivery vans painted pink to bring gay male pornography to corner newsstands. The business owners had previously run a feminist newspaper called *Majority Report*, and stacks of back issues sat in the rear of the garage. I found one that covered the Warhol shooting, the remanding of Solanas to the same Women's House of Detention, and her representation by attorney Florynce Kennedy. But most interesting to me were the letters back and forth on the editorial page of *Majority Report* debating whether Solanas was setting an example for the collective and whether the moment had finally come for women to "take up armed struggle" against male derision.

The East Village was not a destination neighborhood until the galleries started the gentrification process in the early 1980s. People did not come there unless they lived there, and in many ways that was what attracted queers to the area. Basically, you could go outside dressed any way you wished without appearing odd (weirdly, that is still true). Unlike the gay male West Village, the East Village was cheap, and gay women were poor. Most "clones" wanted the West Village or, later, Chelsea, but lesbians and hippie, faggy, transie gay men came to the East Village because it was affordable and we could disappear. The primary exception to the closed-world feel were the cars with New Jersey license plates looking for heroin. Rent was so low that people really didn't need to work. I could work ten to fifteen hours a week and live. I started at Leroy's, the first coffee shop in Tribeca, where the food was so bad the waitresses brought our own lunch from home. And this became the material for my third novel, *After Delores* (1988). I waited on icons like Meredith Monk, Yvonne Rainer, John Kelly. A bunch of gay-girl artists in the East Village started a food club. Everyone put in $2.50 a week and I would cook. Banana omelets, rice omelets, bananas and rice, kasha varnishkes. Breakfast at Veselka was ninety-nine cents with coffee, and even cheaper in dirtier places. We bought and sold our clothes in an open-air market on Astor Place in front of Cooper Union. I also worked doing "put-in," which was a standard lesbian job. Trucks filled with equipment for putting on shows would arrive at the venue and we would carry everything into the theater. I did all kinds of stage crew jobs, did telemarketing for Learjets for two days, and once dressed up like an eggplant to advertise a farmers market. Our lesbian lives were very connected to being artists. Many of us would not have stuck with being artists if we were straight. There was no reason to. But once you were out there on the lesbian limb, the world looked like a pretty phony and hypocritical place, so it was hard to aspire to fit into it. There was so much that needed to be said.

Alice Neel did paint some women whom I identified with or met—she did commissioned portraits of Adrienne Rich and Kate Millett for *Parnassus: Poetry in Review* and *Time* magazine, respectively, and painted Annie Sprinkle. I, like many East Village artists, made cameos in experimental film, and a generation before, male directors had wisely cast Neel in avant-garde film and video in surprising vignettes. Alfred Leslie and Robert Frank cast her as the bishop's mother in *Pull My Daisy* (1959), and Michel Auder had her bantering with Cookie Mueller in Gary Indiana's *A Coupla White Faggots Sitting Around Talking* (1981). Looking at Neel's work, I often think of Nan Goldin, who also recorded women's realities, her own chaotic decisions, bruised faces; both artists reflected and then articulated their own historic moment, representing people who are well-known, those who are forgotten, the dead in their open caskets. Goldin and Neel were both able to see other people as individuals no matter who they were, and no matter how chaotic their own lives became. That ability to make other people real in the storm of self-destruction is almost impossible, and yet they both achieved this immense solidarity. Each constantly exteriorized, physically, her interest. I see this in my own work as well. My forty years of novels about the complexities and nuances of lesbian life are as difficult to publish and to have taken seriously today as they were when I started, in 1984. But when I write nonfiction that centers on gay men, suddenly I am considered a good writer or smart, and the work is treated as important. But when I return to formally varied and innovative lesbian work, the approval dissipates almost immediately. So, I really understand this back-and-forth, high-and-low dilemma and attraction, though books function socially and financially on a much more modest scale than fine-art objects.

Everyone can now see that Neel's content of sexuality, reality, body, the truths of motherhood, relationships, and the physical self were feminist, in that they spoke truthfully—against the grain—about her life as a woman. But she seems to have never been interested in the collectivity aspect of the feminist art movement. Later in Neel's life, as the emergence of a feminist art consciousness helped open social space for her, her sister artists and critics saw the vital meaning of her content and her existence but complained that she did not share the spotlight or let other people speak on panels and at community events. Yet she painted their portraits, and for some women, this ended up being primarily how they are remembered, as her subjects.

As a communist, she spent her life at demonstrations, later publicly picketing the very institutions she and other protesting artists wanted mercy from, because she could not ignore their power—the Whitney Museum of American Art for creating exclusively white male exhibitions and the Metropolitan Museum of Art for the infamous *Harlem on My Mind* (1969) show. As she said, the Depression made artists confront poverty; many became communists or joined social movements and stood with others, even if it wouldn't advance them professionally. It is hard to imagine artists as a collective behaving that way now. Wealthy and successful Black artists are often thinking about and referencing community in their work, and some—like Julie Mehretu, Kehinde Wiley, and Jacqueline Woodson—have used their money to create artists' residencies and advocacy organizations, like Claudia Rankine's Racial Imaginary Institute. But there is nothing close to a grassroots artists' movement with a global freedom vision, as Alice Neel experienced. Perhaps it is the protofascist cloud over everyone's sensibilities, the fact that professionalization and MFA programs create a selection network that is homogenizing, that visual artists are propelled by a private triangle of curators, collectors, and dealers, and the general public lags far out of sight. Contemporary artists are expected to cooperate with institutions, especially when they hold bad values, and even questioning power is a frightening prospect. I think of the artists, both struggling and wealthy, who in 2023 fearfully removed their names from a letter they had already signed in *Artforum* protesting the killings in Gaza. They were afraid of losing sales. The lack of truly active artistic political resistance and analysis leaves today's artists more vulnerable to the falsities and punishments of market aesthetics. Neel's integration of politics and principle may have underlined her structural exclusion as a woman artist with an individual eye, but it also created the heart of her vision. For Neel, art was a search—for visual ideas, for belonging, for income, and for recognition—but it also was a search for understanding among difference and, visually and materially, for a more just world.

5

From Fantasy to Necessity: The Case for Strategic Radicalism

I T IS SPRING 2024, AND I have been working in tandem with Amelia Bande, Kyle Dacuyan, and Shiv Kotecha to help Performance Space New York (PSNY) call for a ceasefire and make a commitment to not partner with any institution that receives Israeli state funding. It has been a long and complex process because of the presence of conflicted Germans and Israelis on the organization's board. But we've all been talking and moving forward. One day, on Instagram, I see that a person I have never heard of is publicly challenging me regarding Performance Space New York.

"I want you to go full PACBI," she writes. I ask myself, *What is "full PACBI"?* I know that PACBI stands for Palestinian Campaign for the Academic and Cultural Boycott of Israel, an organization in Palestine that I have been supporting for fifteen years. But how do you "go full" on an organization?

"We are all working on this right now and are in the middle of the process," I answer, still in public.

It is normal for me to be strongly addressed on social media by names I have never heard before, most of whom are bots or multiple identities or account names for people who work for Hasbara ("the Explanation"), the Israeli government propaganda system that, among its many tentacles, has a program that recruits people to follow social media accounts and spam them. Whenever someone I don't know and have never seen before pops up to contest something about Israel, I usually think it is Hasbara.

"Don't wait!" she answers. "Go full PACBI now! This is very important to me. I am telling my friends who work there to boycott."

OK, I am thinking. *Who the hell is this? Anyone who knows enough avant-garde artists connected to this forty-year-old East Village arts center (formerly known as PS 122) to ask them to withdraw their work would be someone whose name I would recognize.* So, I take the conversation to private.

What I finally learn after a few rounds of back-and-forth is that this is one of the many thousands of people who have joined the Palestine solidarity movement in the past few months, who don't really know what they are talking about and don't understand how we make progress—but are understandably desperate for change. "Go PACBI," or "Full PACBI" is a telltale sign of this confusion. PACBI is a group of people in Palestine. BDS is the name of their strategy. What the person meant is that she wanted PSNY to join the cultural boycott of Israel, or "Go BDS" or "Full BDS," meaning boycott *and* divestment *and* sanctions. This woman was starting off strongly in the fantasy stage. She wanted it all right now, without any idea of how to get there, who the players were, or what values the movement she was joining had developed.

Of course, I understand the urgency. When someone's eyes are first opened to the reality of Palestinian oppression, it is literally mind-boggling. Over and over, I have seen friends who just tolerated me for years suddenly wake up and become obsessed, repeating the same behaviors that I exhibited fifteen years ago. They are reading everything; Palestine is dominating their thoughts and conversations—the reality is so shocking once a person notices. And of course, they then are in deep fantasy, wanting to change everything immediately, not grokking how powerful the forces that oppose us are—in fact, so powerful and so in possession of the tools of camouflage that for most of our lives, my friends and I never even noticed what these power structures were doing to Palestinians, even though it was all in plain sight. Especially with so many thousands of students participating in divestment campaigns on campuses and pouring into this movement, it is very easy to want change immediately and get angry or accusatory—to condemn each other, to create hierarchies of radicalness or other forms of blame—when change doesn't go your way. We feel so terrible when we realize, and we want to feel better. But creating change when you are opposing the US government, corporate media, your own university's administrations, the New York City Police Department, and the never-ending death machine that is the Israeli government, with the support of most of its citizens and the US entertainment and culture industries that propagandize for it all or deliberately ignore these power structures, is probably the most difficult obstacle many of these important and needed new activists have ever faced.

Fortunately, on May 15, 2024, the BDS movement, of which PACBI is a member organization, issued a thoughtful, helpful article to aid US campus encampments dealing with growing pains and miscomprehensions about how to move forward, in a way that is clear and enlightening. I am reproducing that document here, not only to disseminate it for further study, but because it is an excellent model for how solidarity movements can operate effectively and inclusively against great odds.

Campus Uprisings for Palestine: Strategic Radicalism, Ethical Principles, and Incremental Wins by the BDS Movement—Excerpts (May 15, 2024)

Strategic radicalism calls on the movement to employ multiple tactics that take local contexts into account to mutually build on and amplify each other. A strategic and incremental win for one campus is a win for all.

Given the diversity of tactics used by students and administrators, and many questions they are receiving, the BDS movement wanted to outline, from Palestine, how "to move forward collectively." This is based on their "tried-and-tested principles":

- Gradualness (incremental process of building power to affect policy change)
- Sustainability (defending and building on previous achievements by steadily widening support for them)
- Context Sensitivity (being sensitive to the particularities of every context without losing track of the overall movement objectives)

Divestment and academic boycott are and must remain the goals of campus movements. However, **these goals will not be met in a few weeks** in almost all universities, given the dominating power structures and nature of investments in the Israeli state. We must achieve reasonable gains that can be continually built on and reestablish our new positions. **The**

only path to justice is an incremental, strategic approach with patience and ethical commitment.

Each university has its own context with varying resources, faculty, histories of activism, board of trustees composition and relations, administrations, Zionist entrenchment, and student compositions (especially with regard to class, race, and prevalence of international students in danger of deportation). Importantly, in the US context, some states have anti-BDS laws. While these unconstitutional laws are being fought in the courts, the reality is that it may be difficult for some institutions in the US to explicitly announce divestment from or boycott of Israel, and therefore, there is a need for solidarity groups to find creative solutions there. **What is possible on one campus may not be possible on another.** As such, we should recognize that **power comes from a diversity of tactics** that keep the overall goal in mind.

Campus groups have to make tough decisions on what is achievable now versus later, and whether currently negotiated agreements allow us to build on them later. Regardless of the path, in all our movement actions and statements, we must always center Palestinians, Palestinian rights, and the absolute urgency of ending the genocide in Gaza. This is a priority even as we push for divestment and academic boycotts. They are not mutually exclusive.

All deals with university administrations that center Palestinian rights and commit, in a reasonable time frame, to financial disclosure and/or a divestment process and/or academic boycotts are important gains that should be defended by all in our movement. They are significant contributions to long-term movement building and grassroots power accumulation. . . . And while there certainly can be bad deals, it is important to recognize that most, if not all, of the deals reached with administrations so far were impossible to imagine even a few months ago. This, in itself, is a radical change and another indicator that we are approaching "Palestine's South Africa moment."

When reaching agreements, solidarity negotiators on campuses must be vigilant in recognizing that many university administrations, often equipped with experienced legal teams, will try to use a deal as a stalling mechanism to undermine student mobilizations. **Thus, any deal that is conditioned on forbidding all future solidarity actions or that takes as given that administrations have limited authority over how their endowment is invested should be an immediate red flag.** The campus movement should be planning, ready, and committed to push for further gains, use the agreements as building blocks for further mobilization, and return to protests should administrators renege on commitments. This ensures that incremental gains can be protected and built upon.

Coordination and communication across our movement and across campuses is important, and it is even more necessary when deciding to escalate or reach agreements. This is both to **understand each other's context to prevent public attacks and factionalizing,** and to amplify messaging that can energize our movement. We are all working for Palestinian liberation, including the right of refugees to return. This is a time to unite around the Palestinian people's express demands and the points of unity that the overwhelming Palestinian grassroots networks, coalitions, and organizations call on solidarity movements to adopt.

ACT UP AND THE EVOLUTION OF QUEER
SUPPORT FOR PALESTINE

Reading the BDS document, and their very human and realistic call for the allowance of difference and against factionalizing, made me think of ACT UP—the AIDS Coalition to Unleash Power. This AIDS activist organization helped transform the AIDS crisis and the place of queers and people with AIDS within the larger society. Writing my six-hundred-page synthesis, *Let the Record Show: A Political History of ACT UP New York, 1987–1993*, allowed me to cohere an understanding of what strategic and social elements helped make ACT UP one of the most effective social movements in recent memory.

Of course, the big difference here is that the BDS movement is conscious in calling for radical democracy, recognizing different contexts, and giving one another a break. Although ACT UP developed many of these same elements, it was an organic evolution in which the terms were unspoken and, in many cases, not explicit. It was only through the experience of interviewing 187 surviving members of ACT UP over eighteen years, through the ACT UP Oral History Project, that cofounder Jim Hubbard and I were able to realize that ACT UP was structured in a way that allowed individuals to do what they needed to do, even if others disagreed— from its founding in 1987 through its split in 1992. No one had decided, nor was it discussed, that ACT UP would proceed this way—it just seems that when you have to win, when you are desperate for change and must be effective, radical democracy is the only path that works.

There has to be a bottom line; otherwise an organization has no foundation. The BDS movement's bottom line is that "in all our movement actions and statements, we must always center Palestinians,

Palestinian rights, and the absolute urgency of ending the genocide in Gaza." For ACT UP, the bottom line was made clear in a one-sentence statement of unity: "Direct Action to end the AIDS crisis." But in the case of both movements, which were and are in practice nonviolent, if your goal is the stated bottom line, you can do what is appropriate for your context.

And what the Palestinians call "factionalizing"—claiming that your strategy toward the common goal is better than someone else's—is the downfall of movements that depend, like ACT UP, on many different approaches, tactics, and actions all aimed at the same goal. It is the breadth of tactic and response that, in ACT UP's case, created the paradigm shift.

But reading this statement calling for flexibility and context from the BDS movement reminded me of the basic takeaways Jim Hubbard and I cohered from our decades of study of ACT UP.

1. ACT UP was not a consensus-based movement. Their statement of unity, "Direct Action to end the AIDS crisis," emphasized *direct action* in contrast to social service provision. Basically, if someone had an idea that would move us closer to ending the AIDS crisis, they could do it.

    When others disagreed, they would debate and argue. ACT UP was a very confrontational place as a result of the high pressure of the suffering among us, combined with pre-gentrification New York culture. Lots of yelling. But if in the end *you* had an idea that was *direct action to end the AIDS crisis* and *I* didn't want to do it, I wouldn't try to stop you from doing it. I just wouldn't do it. I would go find my five people to do my idea. And in this way, there was a broad range of many different kinds of actions with different methods and aesthetics, aimed at different social milieus, that would take place at the same time.

My own study of history shows me that movements that try to force everyone into one analysis or one strategy always fail, and I can't find any historical exceptions. Trying to make people all agree on approaching the problem the same way is not effective, and this is because people are *different* and therefore can only be where they are at. It took me decades of therapy to accept this. But the fundamental truth is that people will always be different and therefore real leadership is rooted in facilitating people being effective from where they are at.

2. Second, ACT UP went action first, not theory first. The reason was not ideological. ACT UP was driven by people with AIDS whose clocks were ticking. They had immediate needs that had to be won as soon as possible, and so the method had to be effective. As a result, there were concrete goals; our job was to figure out how to make them winnable by coming up with solutions that were doable.

Part of this process was people in ACT UP becoming the experts on the issues. They avoided the infantilization process that comes with asking the powers that be to solve problems. They will never solve our problems, primarily because they don't want to and don't know how to, since their power is derived from the status quo. So, to create change, we have to be highly informed and design the reasonable, winnable, and doable solutions ourselves. This means taking action in the realm of the real.

As Maxine Wolfe, one of the leaders of ACT UP, often pointed out, if we go action first, our theory will emerge because we have to make decisions about how to enact the action. And this is how our values are cohered. If instead we went theory first, we would be instantly polarized by theoretical differences, with nothing concrete at stake.

3. The final point I emphasize in public talks aimed at building Palestine solidarity is the role of women and people of color in ACT UP, which was primarily a white gay male organization. Some of the older gay men in ACT UP had been in the previous movement, gay liberation, but most of the younger men had never been politically active before. This was the era of fascist dictatorships in Chile and Argentina, producing a group of highly politicized Latin American exiles, including veterans of the Mexico City student movements. And lesbians in ACT UP were veterans of the previous decade's feminist movements in reproductive rights, feminist women's health care, and the women's peace movement. So, because of previous political experience, women and people of color in ACT UP had influence beyond our numbers.

One of the effects of this experience was that women and people of color rarely stopped the action to correct speech or to demand consciousness raising on race or sex. Instead, they kept their eyes on the prize and figured out how to marshal the ample resources of the larger white male membership to advocate for Latinos and women with HIV constituencies.

For example, ACT UP had an art auction that raised $650,000. So, when the Latino caucus realized that people with AIDS in Puerto Rico didn't have any political support, instead of having to fundraise, they could go to the fundraising committee of ACT UP and get the money necessary to start ACT UP Puerto Rico. When women with HIV needed funds to travel to demonstrate or testify, and people were not feeling well and needed hotels, women in ACT UP didn't have to find the money for their low-income communities. They could go to fundraising and get this money.

In this way, by focusing on fulfilling the needs of their constituencies instead of controlling or correcting other people, women and people of color were able to win substantial victories, including a four-year campaign that won access to experimental drug trials for women with HIV, and access to benefits. These made ACT UP perhaps the only white male movement in history that won transforming victories for women, poor people, and people of color.

From the beginning of the wave of new actions by an expanding Palestine solidarity coalition, which started in October 2023 in response to Israeli carpet-bombing and systematic killings, activists consciously looked to the ACT UP playbook. This was partially because ACT UP had been so successful, but also because of a profound shift in the location of the radical queer movement.

The reason an autonomous "gay and lesbian" movement emerged in 1969 was not because queer people wanted to be alone. It was because the existing range of progressive movements decided that we did not meet their criteria for solidarity. The Communist Party notoriously excluded homosexuals. As everyone now knows because of the feature film about his life, the Black Civil Rights Movement sidelined Quaker Bayard Rustin—one of their most effective organizers—because of his homosexuality. The women's movement had a series of lesbian purges, many of which have not yet been historicized. It was because we queers were excluded that our own movement(s) emerged and transformed.

When ACT UP was formed in 1987, eighteen years after Stonewall, they still faced a lack of solidarity from most of the country for people with AIDS. However, ACT UP's successful use of video, graphic design, and manipulation of the media, as well as a long series of significant intersectional victories including winning needle exchange in New York, winning benefits for women with AIDS, starting Housing Works for homeless people with AIDS, and more, were the catalyst for starting to change how the rest of the country, and especially younger people, felt about queer and trans people.

WHY THE PALESTINE SOLIDARITY
MOVEMENT IS SO PRO-QUEER

Today, the Palestine solidarity movement is very queer, for a number of historical reasons. First of all, in the post–ACT UP era, the social and political emergence of trans and nonbinary expression and organizing has produced a present-day reality in which every progressive movement in America has openly queer and trans people integrated into their leadership. The radical queer movement now lives inside the left.

As this integration became the norm here, queer Palestinians emerged in the West Bank and in Israel with early organizations like Aswat, alQaws, and Palestinian Queers for BDS. Their visibility also attracted global queers to Palestine solidarity. The founders of Jewish Voice for Peace included many gay and queer women and still does, with trans people in significant regional and national positions. And Palestinian Americans welcomed queer people into the US movement at the same time the queer Arab movement started to fully emerge in the US with groups like Tarab NYC, and in Lebanon with organizations including Helem and Meem. In 2013 the Lebanese Psychiatric Society announced that homosexuality is not a mental disorder and does not need to be treated. Arab and Muslim queer groups increasingly emerged in the 1990s and 2000s in the diaspora. Black for Palestine released a statement in 2015 with a thousand individuals and thirty-nine organizations including groups like Coalition of African Lesbians, and queer filmmakers, writers, scholars, and community leaders like Aishah

Shahidah Simmons, Alexis Pauline Gumbs, Angela Davis, Christina Sharpe, Darius Bost, Lynette Jackson, Gina Dent, Malkia A. Cyril, Rinaldo Walcott, Shaka McGlotten, Tavia Nyong'o, and many others. When I entered into the preexisting and ever-expanding matrix of Palestinian solidarity in 2009, it felt like a very queer and queer-friendly place. And they have never let us down.

On April 12, 2011, Omar Barghouti and I went on the progressive independent GRITtv, and he told host Laura Flanders that his vision for the future of Palestine included sexual and gender rights. In Palestine, Aswat moved in and out of coalition with Kayan, the Palestinian feminist coalition. Groups like Queers Against Israeli Apartheid (QuAIA) and Queers Undermining Israeli Terrorism (QUIT!) were founded in a number of cities from Toronto to New York to the Bay Area. When Haneen Maikey, then the director of alQaws, gave the keynote address at the Homonationalism and Pinkwashing Conference at the CUNY Graduate Center in April 2013, she challenged the sold-out audience to extend their support from queer Palestine to the rest of Palestinian society. "There is no pink door in the apartheid wall," she said. Given that many significant voices in the queer solidarity movement at that time heard that talk or saw the video, the message got out loud and clear.

So, decades of work within Palestinian society, the American left, and the Jewish left combined with the inclusion of queer and trans solidarity in a wider range of progressive movements created a base from which queer and LGBT people can openly oppose the horror of Israeli war crimes on their own terms.

Several key actions were taken directly from ACT UP. The occupation of Grand Central Station on October 27, 2023, and accompanying two hundred arrests organized by Jewish anti-war activists were an exact replay of ACT UP's January 1991 "Day of

Desperation" action, occupying Grand Central Station to protest the first Gulf War, with the slogans "Money for AIDS, Not for War" and "Fight AIDS, Not Arabs." ACT UP in San Francisco stopped traffic on the Golden Gate Bridge to call attention to the state of emergency, a tactic enhanced by Black Lives Matter decades later and now used often on highways, on bridges, and at airports by activists against the killing in Gaza. Another direct influence was ACT UP's affinity group creation of a fake *New York Times*, called *The New York Crimes*, based on the paper's abandonment of people with AIDS. Writers Against the War on Gaza re-created the same project for their first action protesting the distorted pro-Israel coverage at the *Times*, and then altered the name one step further: *The New York War Crimes*. Even ACT UP NY resuscitated "Money for Healthcare, Not Warfare" in 2023 to protest the billions of US dollars Biden sent to Israel to kill Palestinians. And they replaced the pink triangle at the center of ACT UP's most iconic T-shirt, "Silence=Death" with a pink, green, and black watermelon—the symbol of the Palestinian people that has been used in places where the Palestinian flag was banned. In October 2024, Jewish Voice for Peace re-created ACT UP's fall 1989 action, closing down the New York Stock Exchange. So, the resonance between the two movements has been intentional and public from the start.

As the Israeli propaganda machine constantly escalates its efforts to discredit Jews who oppose the occupation and genocide, they also move steadily to discredit queers who support Palestinian autonomy and work for permanent ceasefire. The rhetoric against us has been systematic and contrived. In fact, this campaign was developed by prominent advertising agencies and put into place over decades. And in turn we have developed our own name for this propaganda: pinkwashing.

PINKWASHING

Right now, in the United States, hard-won legal gains by queer people are being revoked and attacked and are under threat, depending on what state you live in. In Florida and Texas, for example, there are new laws and restrictions removing LGBTQ content from public school libraries and classrooms, and keeping rights from trans people—especially medical rights and rights of social integration—and there are states challenging queer adoption and fostering. The Trump Supreme Court ruled that businesses can discriminate against gay customers who want to buy a wedding cake. Some places have lesbian mayors, governors, and senators, but—in the representational gap—none of them can see sophisticated, complex, and sexually active adult lesbians as protagonists on a Broadway stage.

In the eyes of the Christian nationalists and their manipulative Republican allies, rights for gay or lesbian or bisexual or transgender people is a symbol of a corrupt and dangerous world. Yet just a few years, months, weeks ago, the conflicted United States was a different kind of symbol for queer people—a combination of queer promise and queer imposition. When, what NYU professor Lisa Duggan called "homonormativity" was on the rise, the way Americans did gay rights was imposed, along with other US products, as a global standard. Countries that did not tolerate demonstrations were encouraged to hold pride parades, where the marchers—like Russians, for example—got beaten up and arrested. Women whose cultural context means they wouldn't talk to their parents about sexual experiences with men were suddenly supposed to "come out" and tell them they were having sex with women. Gay imperatives went hand in hand with US cultural imperialism. Meanwhile, in the West, the more rights white gay men got, the more conservative they became. Jasbir Puar named this "homonationalism," as white gays in European countries with full legal standing increasingly joined right-wing political parties and took stances against immigrants, especially Muslims, using an assumed homophobia as the criteria for exclusion. Are we free or oppressed, second-class citizens or the new average American? It really depends on where one lives in the US and what one's family is like. The wide range of difference in how queer and trans people are treated is not stable or coherent and just doesn't make sense.

In 2011, after a ridiculous amount of hoop jumping and the submission of hundreds of pages of background for a short opinion piece, I finally succeeded in publishing an article in *The New York Times* on "pinkwashing"—the cynical use of limited gay rights as an attempt by Israel to claim themselves progressive, thereby whitewashing or "pinkwashing" the occupation. I first heard this word in a talk by Ali Abunimah, the editor of *The Electronic Intifada*. But its appearance in the *Times* gave it mainstream exposure, and thirteen years later, in 2024, I heard many conversations in France and Brussels about "le pinkwashing," used naturally as though it were a French word. The concept penetrated and resonated with queers who did not want to be used to justify occupation and now genocide.

On June 21, 2024, Benjamin Netanyahu, in anticipation of his highly contested planned speech before the US Congress, told *Punchbowl News*, "If you are gay in Gaza, you'll be shot in the back of the head. Women for Gaza. What are women in Gaza—they're chattel and other such absurdities," as he continued to murder gays and women and everyone else in Gaza with bombs and starvation. This is the nexus of pinkwashing—pretending that Palestinians or Muslims or Arabs generally deserve to die and be occupied because they are falsely represented as all straight and viciously antigay. Even though this mischaracterization is untrue, the logic of the argument is even falser: Do we think that religious Jews in Israel who object to homosexuality should be aerial-bombed and starved to death? Do we want to carpet-bomb Florida because the Republican leadership is banning books and forcing queer and Black history out of public schools? That anyone would think this is a legitimate argument shows the twisted logic coming out of Netanyahu's war crimes. He has no reason to mass-murder all these people, but he is reaching into ignorance and misperception of women and queers to try to justify his actions. Where did pinkwashing come from? Let's review its history.

A Brief History of Pinkwashing

According to the *Jewish Daily Forward*, in 2005 the Israeli foreign ministry, the Prime Minister's Office, and the finance ministry concluded three years of consultation with American marketing executives and launched Brand Israel, a campaign to rebrand the country's image to appear "relevant and modern" instead of militaristic and religious. "Americans don't see Israel as being like the US," explained David Sable, CEO and vice president of Wunderman, a division of Young and Rubicam that conducted extensive and costly branding research for Israel at no charge. His conclusion was that while Israel, as a brand, is strong in America, it is "better known than liked, and constrained by lack of relevance." Sable elaborated that Americans "find Israel to be totally irrelevant to their lives . . . particularly 18–34 year old males, the most significant target." Brand Israel intended to change this by selecting aspects of Israeli society to highlight, bringing Americans directly to them. They started off with a free trip for architectural writers, and then another for food and wine writers. The goal of these "and numerous other efforts" was to convey an image of Israel "as a productive, vibrant and cutting-edge culture."

In July 2005, the Brand Israel Group (BIG) presented their findings to the Israeli foreign ministry. In 2006, they conducted a study of Israelis' own perceptions. In 2007, the foreign ministry organized a Brand Israel conference in Tel Aviv, which marked the official adoption of the campaign. Foreign minister Tzipi Livni appointed Ido Aharoni to head Israel's first brand-management office and awarded him a $4 million budget, in addition to the already established $3 million in annual spending on Hasbara and $11 million for the Israeli tourism ministry in North America. In this way, Israel began its wooing of young males by first niche marketing to heterosexual men. David Saranga, of the consulate general of Israel, initiated a project with *Maxim* magazine, a photo shoot titled "The Women of the Israel Defense Forces," which shows, in swimsuits, model-like Israeli women who served in the army. Saranga said, "Approaching *Maxim* allowed us to gear our message to the younger generation, especially males, and towards a demographic that did not see Israel as relevant or identify particularly with Israel."

A follow-up study revealed that *Maxim*'s readers' perceptions of Israel had improved as a result of the piece. Saranga was pleased but knew he had a lot of work ahead of him. "Rebranding a country can take 20 years or more. It involves more than just generating more positive stories about Israel. The process has to be internalized and integrated, too. Israelis must share in and believe what we promote."

In 2007, *The Electronic Intifada* reported that Saatchi and Saatchi was also working for Israel, free of charge. David Saranga told *PRWeek* that the two groups Israel was targeting were "liberals" and people age sixteen to thirty. Gideon Meir of Israel's foreign ministry told *Haaretz* that he would "rather have a Style section item on Israel than a front page story."

In 2008, Aharoni's office hired TNS, a market research firm, to test new brand concepts for Israel in thirteen different countries.

They also funded a pilot program called "Israel: Innovation for Life" in Toronto. Aharoni predicted "the execution of a program that will support the brand identity. This might include initiating press missions to Israel, or missions of community influence; it could include organizing film festivals, or food and wine festivals featuring Israel-made products."

In 2008, PACBI published a sample contract that Israeli artists signed with their government when the artist was "invited" to an international event, the kind of invitation that every Israeli artist craves and must have in order to establish a broad reputation. The contract text reveals, interestingly, that this is not an invitation at all, but rather that it is the Israeli government that is inviting itself to international events. The artist is paid with a plane ticket, shipping fees, hotel, and expenses by their own government. The contract does not assume any funding from the "host" country. In return, the template states:

> The service provider is aware that the purpose of ordering services from him is to promote the policy interests of the state of Israel via culture and art including contributing to creating a positive image for Israel.

Yet...

> The service provider will not present himself as an agent, emissary and/or representative of the Ministry.

The challenge facing Brand Israel was huge. In the 2009 East-West Global Nation Brand Perception Index, Israel was 192 out of 200, behind North Korea, Cuba, and Yemen and just before Sudan. That year the International Gay and Lesbian Travel Association

(IGLTA) announced an October conference in Tel Aviv with the goal of promoting Israel as a "world gay destination." Helem, a Lebanese LGBTQ organization, responded with a call for a boycott.

> For some time now, Israeli officials and organizations such as the Aguda, who are cooperating closely with IGLTA, have been promoting LGBT tourism to Israel through false representations of visiting Tel Aviv as not taking sides, or as being on the "LGBT" side as if LGBT lives were the only ones that mattered.
>
> It is implied that it's okay to visit Israel as long as you "believe in peace" as if what is taking place in Palestine/Israel is merely a conflict between equals, rather than an oppressive power relationship. Consistent with globalization's tendency to distance the "final product" from the moral implications of the manufacturing process, LGBT tourists are encouraged to forget about politics and just have fun in a so-called gay-friendly city.
>
> Even more importantly, Tel Aviv's flashy coffee shops and shopping malls, in contrast with the nearby deprived Palestinian villages and towns, serve as evidence that the Israeli society, just as the Israeli state itself, has built walls, blockades and systems of racist segregations to hide from the Palestinians it oppresses. The intersection of physical and societal separations and barriers have justly earned the term apartheid, referring to an historically parallel racist regime in South Africa against the indigenous Black population of that country. Leisure tourism to apartheid Israel supports this regime. It is not neutral and it certainly is not a step toward real peace, which can only be based on justice.

The four-hour symposium took place despite opposition. In its newsletter the travel association acknowledged and dismissed the protest. "It has been fascinating to us that Tel Aviv has an Arab community living in peace here with the Jewish community," said IGLTA president and CEO John Tanzella, who spoke about the 1,400-member association. "We are meeting gay business professionals from all religions and backgrounds within the Middle East."

Protests at the event focused on Israeli occupation of Gaza. "They were using our gathering as a means to make their concerns public with all the radio and TV that came to meet us," Tanzella said. "We certainly welcome freedom of speech, but it should be noted that our focus is to support LGBT businesses around the world, wherever they might be located."

That same year, the Zionist organization StandWithUs's fellowship program told *The Jerusalem Post* that they were undertaking a campaign to "improve Israel's image through the gay community in Israel." The foreign ministry told Ynet that they would be sponsoring a gay Olympics delegation "to help show to the world Israel's liberal and diverse face."

The January 2010 conference of the Interdisciplinary Center Herzliya, the Lauder School of Government Diplomacy and Strategy, and the Institute for Policy and Strategy brought together representatives of the foreign affairs ministry, University of Haifa, the Prime Minister's Office, Reut Institute, and private communications companies to discuss "Winning the Battle of the Narrative," reaffirming the need for rebranding.

The conference had some very interesting findings:

— That many criticisms of Israel will stop when policy toward Palestinians is changed.

— Israel correlates with the phrase "daring and independent" but not "fun and creative."

— Fifty percent of people in Western countries are disengaged and do not have an opinion on Israel, and can therefore be won over by marketing.

— "Narratives of victimhood and survival adapted by Israel over the years are no longer relevant for its diplomatic efforts and dialogue with the West. Nowadays Israel's opponents capitalize on using the same narratives to achieve and mobilize support."

— "People respond well when addressed in a familiar language that uses well-known terms and are susceptible to simple, repetitive, consistent messages."

— "In order to succeed online, one has to detach one's self from strictly official messages and to develop an online personality."

By 2010, the Israeli *Globes* reported that the Ministry of Foreign Affairs had allocated 100 million shekels (over $26 million) to branding.

> The Globe found that the activity will focus on the internet, especially on social networks. This is following research performed by the Ministry of Foreign Affairs in which it found that surfers will show sympathy and identify with content that interests them, regardless of the identity of the political affiliation of the publisher.

Also in 2010, Scott Piro, a gay Jewish public relations and social media professional, announced in a press release on his letterhead that Israel's Ministry of Tourism, the Tel Aviv tourism board, and Israel's largest LGBT organization, the Aguda, were joining together to launch Tel Aviv Gay Vibe, an online tourism campaign to promote Tel Aviv as a travel destination for European LGBTs.

"Campaign Branding Tel Aviv Gay Destination Underway," July 21, 2010, Ynetnews.com

BY DANNY SADEH

With an investment of NIS 340 million (about $88.1 million), an international marketing campaign is being launched to brand Tel Aviv as an international gay vacation destination. The campaign will be run in England and Germany, two locations with considerable gay and lesbian communities.

The campaign will include ads on gay community websites and magazines and will display everything the city has to offer by way of gay tourism. Designated Facebook and Twitter pages will be created to support the effort and promote Tel Aviv as a new gay capital. A new website has also been built: Gay Tel Aviv. It starts off with a sentence encapsulating the very essence of the campaign: "Rising from the global shores of the Mediterranean, stands one of the most intriguing and exciting new gay capitals of the world."

The decision to brand Tel Aviv as an international gay destination was supported by an international study conducted by Out Now, a leading company for consulting, branding, and marketing to the gay community. Etti Gargir, director of the VisitTLV organization, said that the tourism ministry and Tel Aviv municipality invested NIS 170 million each in the project. "The increased discount flight capacity from England and Germany increases the capability of Tel Aviv to compete with other cities in Europe," said Gargir. "This is in addition to the Out Now study that found Tel Aviv to be an attractive city to those who like culture, restaurants, nightlife and shopping. The study also showed that the city is good for any budget. In other words, there is a range of entertainment and accommodation options at prices that anyone can afford."

About a month before, Tel Aviv municipality submitted an official application to host the international gay pride parade in 2012. The tourism ministry reported that it supports targeted marketing campaigns likely to increase tourism to Israel. The article was appended with the following comments from readers (verbatim):

1. Surely nothing to be proud of. Shameful
2. Haredim!!!!
3. Gay avek also cute slogan (Yiddish for go away)
4. Thanks for warning now I know not
5. Yes by all means bring hordes of aids
6. Inviting destruction full speed

By 2010, pinkwashing was already in general use by queer anti-occupation activists. The phrase was coined in 1985 by Breast Cancer Action to identify companies that claimed to support women with breast cancer while actually profiting from their illness. In April 2010, QUIT! in the Bay Area used the word *pinkwashing* as a twist on *greenwashing*, in which companies claim to be eco-friendly in order to make a profit. Dunya Alwan attributes the term to Ali Abunimah, saying at a meeting in 2010, "We won't put up with Israel whitewashing, greenwashing or pinkwashing."

In April 2010, Brand Israel launched Israeli Pride Month in

San Francisco. This was not a grassroots expression by Israeli queers living in San Francisco but an event instigated, funded, and administered by the Israeli government.

By March 2011, Ynet reported that for the first time, the Israeli stand at the International Tourism Fair in Berlin encouraged gay tourists to visit Tel Aviv. According to Tel Aviv council member Yaniv Weizman, "The gay tourist likes urban vacations, he forms attachments with the community in the cities he visits, enjoys partying and usually returns to places he has had a good time in. This is established tourism which draws in young tourism and sets trends which other sectors of the population adopt."

The Tel Aviv tourist association filed a formal request with the International Gay and Lesbian Travel Association to host World Pride in 2012. In July 2011, the Anti-Defamation League hosted StandWithUs's Yossi Herzog, who spoke on gay rights in Israel and gay presence in the Israeli Defense Forces. In August, *The Jerusalem Post* reported:

> The Foreign Ministry is promoting Gay Israel as part of its campaigns to break apart negative stereotypes many liberal Americans and Europeans have of Israel. The initiative flies in the face of the swelling protests set against Jerusalem's Gay Pride parade set for November 10. But even as its organizers are receiving anonymous threats of holy war against them, gay activist Michael Hamel is traveling in Europe and North America working on publicizing Gay Israel. A portion of his work, he told *The Jerusalem Post* by phone as he sat drinking coffee in a California airport, has the support of the Foreign Ministry. "We are working very closely with them," said Hamel, who heads the AGUDAH, Israel's LGBT organization.

(Speaking on condition of anonymity, a foreign ministry official told *The Jerusalem Post* that efforts to let European and American liberals know about the gay community in Israel were an important part of its work to highlight this country's support of human rights and to underscore its diversity in a population that tends to judge Israel harshly, solely on its treatment of Palestinians. Still, it is such a touchy topic, he did not want his name used.) But David Saranga, employed by the New York consulate, was clear about wanting to promote gay Israel "as part of showing liberal America that Israel is more than the place where Jesus once walked. Gay culture is an entryway to liberal culture," he said, because in New York it is that culture that is creating "a buzz." Israel needs to show this community that it is relevant to them by promoting gay tourism, artists, and films. Showing young, liberal Americans that Israel also has a gay culture goes a long way toward informing them that Israel is a place that respects human rights as well, said Saranga.

By 2023, after devastating Gaza with aerial bombing, murdering over eleven thousand people, and cutting off water, food, and medicine, Israeli land troops invaded with tanks. One soldier had a photo taken of him standing in the rubble of a place he had participated in annihilating, holding up an Israeli flag, with the Star of David that once represented an ancient diasporic people, and surrounding that star was . . . a rainbow border.

1. *Is Israel pro-gay?* LGBTQ people are included in obligatory military service in Israel. To the American eye, this could look progressive. The state supports events like the Tel Aviv International LGBT Film Festival. There are enclaves of Tel Aviv where being out in your complete and daily life is possible, and some people are able to do this. However, overall, Israel is a

profoundly homophobic society. The dominance of religious fundamentalists, the sexism, the proximity to family, and family oppression make life very difficult for most people on the LGBT spectrum in Israel. According to Aeyal Gross, professor of law at Tel Aviv University, "Gay rights have essentially become a public-relations tool," while "conservative and especially religious politicians remain fiercely homophobic."

2. *How homophobic is Palestine?* The Occupied Palestinian Territory is a homophobic, sexist arena. The goal of pinkwashing is to justify Israel's policies of occupation and separation by promoting the image of a lone oasis of progress surrounded by violent, homophobic Arabs—thereby denying the existence of queer Palestinian movements and of secular, feminist, intellectual, and queer Palestinians. By ignoring the multidimensionality of Palestinian society, the Israeli government is trying to claim racial supremacy that in their minds justifies the occupation. Yet, nothing justifies the occupation. "While Palestinians in Israel, Jerusalem, and the Occupied Territories of the West Bank and Gaza constitute one community," said Haneen Maikey, "our different legal statuses and the different realities of each of these locations—including, for example, restrictions on the freedom of movement of Palestinians from the West Bank and Gaza—severely constrain our ability to meet as a community."

Why Queers Are Susceptible to Pinkwashing

What makes LGBTQ people and their allies so susceptible to homonationalism and pinkwashing is the emotional legacy of homophobia. The vast majority of queers have had oppression experiences, often in the searing realm of family, reflected by the confusing status of fluctuating legal rights and reinforced by distorted representations of both LGBTQ life and freedoms in arts and entertainment. The relative civil equality of white gays in the Netherlands and Germany has only been achieved within a generation, and still does not erase the pain of familial and cultural exclusion. As a consequence, many people have come to mistakenly assess how advanced a country is by how it responds to homosexuality. Yet, in a selective democracy like Israel, the inclusion of LGBTQ Jews in the military and the relative openness of Tel Aviv are not accurate measures of broad human rights. By deliberately pinkwashing, the Israeli government ends up exploiting both the Israeli and Palestinian LGBTQ communities to cynically claim broad personal freedom that the ongoing occupation and slaughter insistently belies.

JEAN GENET IN PALESTINE

Just as pinkwashing has a history, so does queer support for Palestine. In fact, we can trace the relationship between openly gay solidarity workers and Palestine as far back as the 1960s. French novelist and playwright Jean Genet's bold solidarity with Palestine was the complex product of a lifetime of contradictory experiences. And his example, when visited in detail, shows us how solidarity is possible without ideological purity, without 100 percent didacticism of motive, and yet despite contradictions, it can still be important, evolve, and have an impact.

Throughout his early life, Genet was subjected to overly punitive incarceration by the French state for petty crimes and poverty. He was marginalized and stigmatized as a homosexual. Yet, as a white European, his reciprocated sexual attraction to Arab men coincided with the experience of supremacy of French colonial military service. Genet received solidarity from France's most famous writers, at the same time that French Jews and communists were being deported from occupied Paris and exterminated. He was on every side of both oppression and domination, and from this complexity, his solidarity impulses sprang.

Genet wrote his five novels in five years, from 1942 to 1947. After seven years of sadness and silence, he wrote three iconic plays—*The Blacks*, *The Balcony*, and *The Screens*—in two years. The subsequent 1960s were filled with death as his lover, Abdallah (a high-wire performer), died by suicide, his agent and English translator, Bernard Fruchtman, died by suicide, and Genet himself attempted suicide. Then he entered into the other utopian endeavor: activism. From 1970 until his death in 1986, Genet was aligned with oppressed people and supported them in energetic ways, on their terms and his own. American writer Edmund White, in his book *Genet: A Biography*, called him "the apostle of the wretched of the earth."

White's use of the word *apostle* is, of course, an open invitation to question it. Apostles believe that the mortals they adore are not mortal. And in that way, they err. Jean-Paul Sartre, who, White points out, was an atheist, called his 625-page homage *Saint Genet*, so there was an ironic anti-religiosity to the book. But Genet was a man for whom adoration was deification; he often described his lovers as gods, for his love had superhuman qualities of possibility, rebirth—and annihilation. Genet's devotion to outsiders was not necessarily rooted in political analysis, as he fiercely loved his Nazi soldier lover-apparition turned underdog, who was left behind in liberated Paris, in the novel *Pompes Funebres*. Although Genet had been poor, outcast, and incarcerated, he looked longingly toward the ex-Nazi debased by his country's ruthless ambition, providing an erotic outcome of compassion and attraction to a man newly downtrodden by his former fascist power.

Born in 1910, Genet had already been arrested eight times by the age of seventeen for running away, for taking trains for free, for embezzling money to go to a carnival, and for stealing pens and notebooks. He was sentenced to two and a half years at an agricultural detention facility for juveniles. White tells us that in order to get out of Mettray prison (a place that looms large in his work), Genet joined the army and was promoted to corporal. He then volunteered specifically for duty in the eastern part of the Mediterranean known as the Levant. In other words, at the age of nineteen, he chose to be in an Arab place—in this case Syria. So, the Arab world offered him an escape from the pain of an incarcerating and despising France. The Arab world is to the young and French Jean Genet what France becomes to the young and American Edmund White: a place of permission. And permission is a kind of romance. It's a rhapsody of relief, indulgence, and lightheaded elevation. Of course, Genet's arrival as a French soldier gave him a different source of his permission than Edmund White, who loves not only men but also graceful, stylish, beautiful things, sophisticated ways, and elevated traditions. Genet also found in the Levant male beauty, ancient cultures, and intoxicating aesthetics, but his permission to do so came with the power of the French state. He had a uniform, a gun, a rank, and a historically imposed social role. The marginalized, punished, and alienated Genet came to his place of peace as a colonial. White had only the willingness to be reconstructed as a Francophile.

In his biography, Edmund White describes Genet's commitments to Palestine and to the Black Panthers as support for the "homeless," as Palestinians are living in exile and diasporic displacement, and carry and elicit elaborate dreams of repatriation, resolution, and repair. Even Palestinian intellectual and Columbia professor Edward Said understood Genet's pro-Palestinian position as the identification of one oppressed person with another. "Genet made the step, crossed the legal borders, that very few white men or women even attempted," Said has written. "He traversed the space from the metropolitan center to the colony; his unquestioned solidarity was with the very same oppressed identified and so passionately analyzed by [Frantz] Fanon," he continued, referring to the Afro-Caribbean psychiatrist, philosopher, and revolutionary concerned with the psychopathology of colonization. And while it is easy and truthful to say that Genet also was homeless, in the most intimate sense of the word, unlike Palestinians, he did have a nation state, a passport, and la langue natale, which allowed him to be a writer with readers who also have nation states, passports, and a celebrated, accessible literature in their own language.

White writes of Genet's perspective of himself as an exception in the eyes of the various Arab communities he was sent to occupy. Of course, we don't know what the Syrians actually thought of him, but we do learn that he felt they saw his difference in a positive light. Like Genet, I also see myself as a "friend of Palestine," and yet I do understand that that has nothing to do with whether individual Palestinians like me. Political relationships of solidarity are rife with the problem of supremacy, no matter how alienated or excluded the dominant party feels from their own societies. And it is easy to project one's own enthusiasm of connection onto the less powerful partner. White wisely acknowledges this by pointing out that one of Genet's favorite fantasy tropes is that of the benevolent or enamored cop, or complicit soldier, transgressing the rules of punishment because he is so moved by a vulnerable—and fictionalized—Genet. Once in the colonial army, the roles are arousing and disturbing in their reverse, as he fled and reentered the military's insiderness and France's marginalization with a repetitive compulsion.

At the age of twenty-one, Genet reenlisted, this time volunteering to go to Morocco. In 1934, at twenty-three and out of the army for only six months, he signed up for a third tour of duty, this time volunteering for Algeria. In 1936, he did not show up for roll call and deserted. He falsified his passport with the name Gejietti and was arrested in Albania. Then he was arrested in Yugoslavia. Then Vienna. Then Czechoslovakia, where he asked for political asylum. Despite a level of asylum status, he fled again and was arrested in Poland before crossing over into Nazi Germany. (Nazis were never a problem for Genet.) He got to Paris and was yet again arrested, this time in a department store for stealing twelve handkerchiefs. Over the next two years, he was arrested and incarcerated for desertion, expelled from the army, arrested for more free train riding, for stealing bottles of aperitifs, for carrying a gun, for stealing a shirt, for vagrancy, and for stealing a piece of silk. At the age of thirty, he spent ten months in prison for stealing a suitcase and wallet from a store, then another four months for stealing history and philosophy books. He worked as a bookseller on the Seine, where he met readers, writers, and intellectuals. Then he was arrested near Notre Dame and sentenced to three months for stealing a volume of Proust. In prison, at the age of thirty-one, he started writing his first novel, *Notre Dame des Fleurs*. Two former customers, one of whom was a right-wing editor, introduced him to writer-filmmaker Jean Cocteau, who helped him immeasurably. Arrested again for stealing a rare edition of Verlaine, he was then eligible for life imprisonment, but Cocteau argued in court that Genet was "the greatest writer of the modern era"; he was sentenced instead to three months, during which he wrote *Miracle de la Rose*. Three weeks after being freed, he stole more books and was jailed for four more months.

It's a manic cycle, and most obviously filled with pervasive disregard for the obvious consequences of actions that might have alternatives. In this place and this time, Genet was a man who could not solve problems, unless his goal was to remain in prison. Certainly, the meeting with Cocteau was lucky, but even luckier was the fact that Cocteau helped him at all—and to the extent that he did. I have to disclaim here that Edmund White himself helped me by reviewing my lesbian erotic, formally complex 1994 novel, *Rat Bohemia*, in *The New York Times* and thereby elevated me with his accomplishments in the tradition of Cocteau's helping Genet. But I assure you that most people with real power in literature do not help people who cannot help them back. That Cocteau, himself the homosexual author of *Les Enfants Terribles* (about a love affair between a brother and sister), understood Genet's talents and bothered to make the effort is just a rare fluke of literary history. Lucky, lucky Saint Genet.

It was now 1943 and France was in the midst of its Nazi occupation. French people—especially the Jews among them—were being deported to concentration camps in Poland and exterminated. Genet found himself held in Caserne des Tourelles, a deportation site. He was visited by Marc Barbezat, the powerful publisher of the magazine *L'Arbalète*, who, with other powerful people, got Genet released. I have no idea what effort this publisher or Cocteau or any of Genet's other powerful supporters committed to interfering with the deportation of Jews. Cocteau famously attended a party in the Nazi-occupied home of the exiled French Jewish Rothschild family. And Cocteau's 1946, film *La Belle et La Bête*, depicted a hook-nosed Jewish usurer, a timely flirt with the soon-to-be-departing German power elite. Simultaneously, other artists, like Max Jacob and Robert Desnos, were deported and exterminated for being anti-Nazi or Jewish. Genet's protectors were not deported and continued to publish during the occupation. So, despite his homosexuality, his desertion, and his endless incarcerations for crimes petty and pathetic, this homeless man's life was saved in a period when thousands of citizens of far greater social standing were sent off to be murdered because they were Jews, communists, and anti-Nazi resisters. He qualified for a solidarity that was denied these doomed others. Was that the model for his own future actions toward Palestinians?

Sartre claimed Genet was an antisemite but understood it—in opposition to Edward Said's interpretation—as a revulsion to other oppressed people. White quotes Sartre: "Since Genet wants his lovers to be executioners, he should never be sodomized by a victim. What repels Genet about Israelites is that he finds himself in their situations." But actually, no, he was excused from their situation. So, given that he had more power than Jews, just as he had more power than Arabs, there is a contradiction in the theory that the reason Genet was pro-Palestinian was because he identified with the oppressed. We all sit in these different hierarchies that are constantly changing and defy reductive categories. Even Palestinians live within hierarchies of status and power, defied only by Israeli bombs.

In 1944, still under Nazi occupation, Genet's first novel, *Notre Dame des Fleurs*, appeared in excerpt in *L'Arbalète*. He met Sartre, also still in France, at Café de Flore, which was still open despite the Nazi seizure of resources and severe rationing. And Genet's lover, Jean Decarnin, died on the communist barricades fighting to liberate Paris. Strange juxtaposition of events: One dies, the other drinks coffee. From then on, most of Genet's important love relationships were to be with Arab men. The Nazis were defeated in 1945 and three years later Sartre and Cocteau petitioned for amnesty for Genet. In 1951, the prestige publisher Gallimard issued the complete works of Genet. All his books were banned in America until Grove Press broke the restriction in 1963. This was another good reason for Edmund White, future author of sexually explicit gay literature, to have been enamored with France. It offered him a legacy of freedom in contrast to ever-Victorian America.

But there is such a strange imbalance of values in all of this. A France brutally colonizing the Arab and African world—and deeply complicit in the deportation of Jews—listens to its own intellectuals and frees, publishes, and awards its own homosexual experimental writer ex-convict. Then again, perhaps the things that made white homosexual men intolerable to American culture—principally the refusal to build families and reproduce—didn't really matter that much to the French. Overt empires reproduce in their own brutal ways, and histories such as Adam Hochschild's *King Leopold's Ghost*, which is about the colonization of the Congo by Belgium, depict colonial culture as a homoerotic, homosocial, and, in many cases, a homosexual refuge. It is similar perhaps to our own genocidal westward expansion and homoerotically male separatist cowboy culture.

In 1970, Genet was arrested with Marguerite Duras at a demonstration protesting the death of four African immigrant workers. As a Frenchman, he had often traveled in Africa, especially in French colonized countries. Yet he had little contact with African Americans besides James Baldwin, who was in sexual and racial exile in France. But once he surfaced as an activist, Genet was contacted by Black Panther Connie Matthews, one of the women in international leadership, and Michael Persitz (the lover of Genet's lover Lucien Senemand's stepson—what we now call "chosen family") to speak out against the jailing and government murders of much of the movement's leadership. How the Panthers made the decision to ask Genet for help is unclear. A lot has been written about the macho nature of the Panther party, and much of that has also been softened, retrospectively. Huey P. Newton, the party's minister of defense, famously said, "Maybe a homosexual could be the most revolutionary," which is certainly very far from the white left, who were busy yelling, "Take her off the stage and fuck her," when Marilyn Webb of women's liberation tried to talk feminism at an anti-war rally that same year. Certainly, the handsome Panther, Huey P. Newton, and the stylish rank and file were a lot sexier than white leftists whose torn, baggy jeans and flannel shirts desexualized working-class clothing, which would soon be tightened and re-masculinized by gay clone culture.

Wanting to help the Panthers, Genet was denied a visa by the US because of his homosexuality, and so he crossed the border illegally from Canada. For two months, he traveled the country as a fugitive from US officials, giving many public talks at universities and to the press on behalf of the Panthers. His diverse American adventures included a cocktail party at Stanford University's French department, where he compared the Panthers to the Marquis de Sade because of their shared authenticity. He had a crush on Panther leader David Hilliard. Jane Fonda proposed doing a film with Genet. And one night he danced for some Panthers in a pink negligee. He may have been a Marxist, but he was still camp. The Panthers gave him a black leather jacket, later de rigueur for clones, leather queens, and AIDS activists. He met twenty-six-year-old UCLA philosophy professor Angela Davis, who was a fluent French speaker from a family of learned French speakers. On May 1, he spoke to twenty-five thousand people in New Haven, Connecticut, and his speech was published by the Black Panther Party. He then hastily departed America when contacted by the office of immigration. Back in Europe, he published a defense of Angela Davis, who was now on FBI wanted posters, named "public enemy number one." When she was arrested, he agreed for the first time to go on television, where he delivered a talk, "Angela Davis Is at Your Mercy." In

Prisoner of Love, Genet showed his artist's sense of aesthetics by remarking, "The Panthers' symbolism was too easily deciphered to last. It was accepted quickly, but rejected because it was too easily understood."

As the Panthers were overthrown and fractured, Genet became friends back in France with Mahmoud Hamchari, the Paris representative of the Palestine Liberation Organization. His wife told Edmund White that Genet would come to their house unannounced and have long talks with Hamchari about the division and corruption within the Panthers. So, as one political partner crumbled, another was born. After disastrous events in Jordan, known in Palestinian history as Black September, Genet accepted an invitation to visit Palestinian refugee camps for one week. He stayed for six months and returned four times over the next two years. In November 1970, he met Yasser Arafat for less than thirty minutes. But Arafat did give Genet a pass permitting free travel in any PLO territory and asked him to write a book about Palestinians, which Genet completed fifteen years later. White writes that Genet "preferred to think the Arab world should be Palestinized rather than that the Palestinian revolution should be Arabized." For many Westerners in solidarity with Palestine to come, there was also an exceptionalism to the love. "To Genet," writes White, "the only positive vision of the future should be socialist, not theological: his analysis of the failure of Zionism was that it had begun as a socialist experiment but had degenerated quickly into a theological state."

Just as in Syria, there is not much information about how the Palestinians experienced Genet, most of the details coming from Genet's version of the relationship. As in Syria, he described himself as well-liked. Genet says that he shocked Palestinians by telling them he was homosexual and an atheist, "an avowal that made them burst out laughing," he claimed. But who knows what really happened? I am fascinated by Genet's "invitations." As an openly lesbian woman who is a "friend of Palestine," I wonder if Genet was the first out Western queer in political solidarity with Palestinians, as opposed to homoerotic French colonial soldiers whose only investments were a sexual interest in Arab men.

The visit took place after the 1967 Six-Day War, and much of the world was troubled by the Israeli occupation of more territory and the creation of yet more refugees on top of the people still in exile from their expulsion by the Nakba, the founding of the Israeli state in 1948. Although Palestine is and was a "place," the specific geographical boundaries of this "home" were different in people's minds than in legal realities. In fact, "Palestine" was now the West Bank, Gaza, Palestinian citizens of Israel, refugee camps in Jordan and Lebanon and Syria, as well as a global diaspora of refugees from Kuwait to London to Brooklyn and Detroit. Palestine was also the memories, the still-standing houses now lived in by Israelis, and the land, sea, and hills that many Palestinians would never see again. Genet's visits stimulated a series of articles and petitions and participations with Michel Foucault on anti-prison work and with Gilles Deleuze in support of Arab workers in France.

At the age of sixty-four, Genet met his last lover, Mohammed El Katrani, in Tangiers. They lived together in a small apartment in Saint-Denis, a suburb of Paris. At seventy-two, suffering from throat cancer, Genet moved to Morocco. From this base, he traveled to Lebanon with Leila Shahid, a young Palestinian activist. In September 1982, Genet was in Beirut when Israelis invaded. This assault enabled Christian militias to massacre Palestinians in the Sabra and Shatila refugee camps, where Palestinians are still living today, as Jim Hubbard and I witnessed when we visited Sabra with Lebanese queer activist Lynn Darwich in 2013. Genet was one of the first outsiders to enter Shatila, on September 19, 1982; he found the place strewn with corpses. He wrote "Four Hours at Shatila," which was published in the *Journal of Palestine Studies*. I don't know if he chose this venue to support the journal, or if the piece had been rejected by more widely read and mainstream publications. Returning to Morocco, he started to write *Prisoner of Love*, based on fifteen years of notes about the Black Panther and Palestinian experiences. On April 15, 1986, he died of cancer at the age of seventy-six. He was buried in Larache, Morocco. *Prisoner of Love* was published one month later.

If Genet ever had a "home," it was in the Arab world, a world he first entered as a colonial soldier. It was as a colonial soldier that he had his first experience of authority, group belonging, sway. It was in the Arab world that he found lovers, often younger, poorer, with less social currency. It was Palestine that "invited" him, while America refused his request for a visa. American homosexuals now have what University of British Columbia professor Jasbir Puar named "homonationalism": Those gays who are white and male, who marry and reproduce, who are documented, who are not incarcerated, who have homes, and who support the military and US imperial wars are now invited to identify with and build the American, Canadian, British, German, French, Dutch, and Israeli state apparatus of punishment and enforcement. Despite being a homosexual convict, Genet experienced this same elevation by being a French soldier. But the status of Palestinians has not changed since Genet walked into Shatila and witnessed murdered civilians lying on its grounds in 1982. Palestinians are still mass-murdered; they are still denied a "home."

There are still questions for us to grapple with regarding Jean Genet. Was his support for Palestine—which was unusual, energetic, sincere, effortful, and significant—rooted in the identification of one homeless person with another, one marginalized, unjustly punished person with another? Was it simultaneously a relationship of a French person to an Arab one, a Frenchman whose only place of supremacy in his own cultural framework was in relationship to the Arabs he could love and to whom he could make a difference? Or was he primarily erotically attracted to the Palestinians and the Black Panthers, who needed "Jean Genet"? Solidarity is still welcomed, impactful, and necessary, even when its powers are dirty and dependent on historical supremacy, and even when they are rooted in erotic desire and fantasy, both colonial and individual. Even with all this contradiction and simultaneous meaning, conflicted solidarity is welcomed and needed and makes some difference, sometimes regardless of its source.

6

Threats of Punishment
and of Complicity

In late February 2016, the City University of New York (CUNY) announced it was launching a task force on antisemitism. This move followed lobbying by the Zionist Organization of America (ZOA), a right-wing group that supports West Bank settlements. They sent a letter to the CUNY chancellor complaining about antisemitism and demanding that CUNY "publicly condemn the SJP [Students for Justice in Palestine] and its hateful, divisive, and antisemitic actions" and "hold this group accountable for violation of CUNY rules and policies." As faculty adviser to the chapter of SJP at the College of Staten Island, I was charged and brought before the CUNY task force on antisemitism.

I must admit that I was frightened of losing my job. Being summoned by my employer and charged with antisemitism was a double threat. This was the beginning of the propaganda campaign to conflate criticism of Israel with antisemitism, and I knew that I was facing a lying structure. I also knew that if this new, false definition of *antisemitism* were to enter the system, public critiques of the Israeli occupation of Palestine would be reconstituted from political discourse to "hate speech." And I knew that if I were convicted of hate speech, it could trip the moral turpitude clause of my tenure. I have to admit now that my first impulse at that time was to be outraged at being accused of antisemitism when I am obviously so Jewish, with two Jewish names (*Sarah* and *Schulman*)—but one of my heroes, Rebecca Vilkomerson, then the director of JVP, firmly reminded me that this had to be addressed politically, not personally.

CUNY did not have a task force on racism or Islamophobia, so I knew this special investigation was designed to intimidate Palestinian students and their allies. I assumed I was caught up in the chaos because I was the faculty adviser, although I was denied any evidence until the actual hearing. SJP at the College of Staten Island had a predominantly Palestinian membership, including significant movement leaders like Nerdeen Kiswani, who would later be the valedictorian of her graduating class at CUNY School of Law and went on to cofound and chair Within Our Lifetime. WOL would become a leading force in street resistance in New York against the Israeli war on Gaza in 2023 and 2024. They led demonstrations daily, through snow and rain, and inspired the student rebellion at Columbia. But this was seven years earlier.

I was accompanied by my attorney, Jed Eisenstein, chairman of the board of Jewish Voice for Peace. I also had support from Palestine Legal and the Center for Constitutional Rights. One member of the CUNY task force prosecuting me, Paul Shechtman, was not present at my hearing, but his reputation cast a shadow over the events. He is an attorney who, in addition to being on this task force, represented the NYPD officer who killed Akai Gurley, and his firm also represented Dominique Strauss-Kahn when he was charged with raping an African woman while a guest in the NYC hotel where she was employed. In his absence I was interviewed by Judge Barbara Jones.

As I arrived at the designated Park Avenue office, I was presented with a fourteen-page list of accusations filed by ZOA. Once a mainstream Jewish organization, it had become a small extremist right-wing group. Even though ZOA has been running a press campaign calling me antisemitic in the *New York Post* and *Daily News*, I was not actually named anywhere in their documents. Instead, they went after the students. Jed and I were handed this stack of charges and then left alone in a room to systematically wade through all the accusations, *all* of which were fabricated and absurd.

For example, SJP was accused of drawing swastikas on the walls of our college. However, the only record of such an incident ever taking place was three years earlier, in 2013, and the chancellor's report agreed that there was no connection to SJP; it was a false accusation. Personally, my experience of Nerdeen and other Palestinian student leaders with whom I worked is that they were and continue to be very, very offended by charges of antisemitism, with which they have been harassed all their lives.

The stack of charges was really just a list of slanders against Muslim students. Over and over were vague charges that "a Muslim student" said something unpleasant to a Jewish student. But neither these Jewish students nor the Muslim students were ever identified. No details of any incident were presented. And there were no dates provided. Furthermore, never was there any evidence that this composite Muslim student had anything to do with SJP. But what did become apparent was that the unnamed but presumed first-hand accusers were students attached to the Hillel center on campus. When I went to college, any Jewish student could go to Hillel. But in recent years it had become overtly Zionist. Not only did they forbid anti-Zionist Jews to speak, but there was a national organization that was paying the costs of putting full-time Hillel coordinators on campuses all over the country. At that time the College of Staten Island was about 30 percent Muslim and 2 percent Jewish, mostly recent Russian immigrants. But Hillel didn't need a significant Jewish population to justify a full-time person. They were even opening and staffing centers on historically Black campuses. So, on our campus, and presumably on many others, the full-time Hillel staff member was the only paid person on the university grounds who was hired and salaried by an outside organization. It seemed like Hillel was the source of these anonymous student testimonies. If they weren't fabricated, where else could they have originated?

When the panel returned to the hearing room, Jed and I pointed out the vagueness of the accusations, and the lack of substantive evidence, revealing that this was not rooted in fact but was instead designed to frighten Palestinian students and their supporters and to freeze debate and discussion on campus. In addition to making these points, I also spoke about the students themselves: how much I respect CUNY students, and how much I had been enriched by working with them. How many of our SJP students' families had been displaced, and their relatives had been held in illegal detention. The students had often been denied entry to Israel and Palestine because of their political activism. I told the task force that I had come to know the students and some of their family members. That they had *never* been antisemitic or homophobic or done anything that justified any kind of negative institutional response. That, quite the opposite, they were enhancing and deepening campus life, and providing necessary information in the form of educationals and public discussions, with guest speakers expanding the lives of the

students, staff, and faculty. Some of these speakers had included
Steven Salaita, Ali Abunimah, and Ghadir Shafie, a representative
of the Palestinian lesbian group Aswat.

One of the accusations was that an unnamed "Jewish student"
hid her Star of David when she saw Muslim students. Besides the
fact that this has nothing to do with SJP, I explained to the task force
that there are some Jews who have dehumanizing views of Arabs,
Muslims, and Palestinians, and project enormous anxiety onto them.
But this has nothing to do with Muslim students themselves—and
certainly is not their fault. Then we discussed the relationship between Zionism and Judaism. I testified that since the onset of Zionism, since Theodor Herzl published his book *The Jewish State* in
1896, there has been disagreement among Jews regarding Zionism.
That for its entire history, for over 5,700 years, Judaism has been a
dialogic religion rooted in commentary and inquiry. And that this
current moment is the only time that Jews have been told to be
homogenous in thought. That in fact, this impulse to force all Jews
into one opinion is ahistorical and not Judaic.

Finally we got to the question of the inquiry itself. I detailed for
the task force how the Zionist Organization of America had been
harassing me on Twitter, posting ten to forty tweets a day to my
publisher, reviewers, friends, and colleagues calling me a terrorist,
how they sabotaged my Wikipedia page, inserting a false claim
that I went to Gaza as a "guest of Hamas" (I have never been to
Gaza and I have no contact with Hamas), and that they had been
using the media to harass me because we hold different values.

I then raised the troubling question of Abe Foxman (long-
standing former head of the right-wing Anti-Defamation League)
being quoted in the *Daily News* saying that he approved of how
CUNY was handling me. "How does Abe Foxman even know how
CUNY is handling me?" I asked. "How does a group of bullies

who are not even reputable get to file a list of absurd accusations and get CUNY to go to the trouble and expense of creating a task force?" And I said that I saw an inappropriate relationship between ZOA and CUNY. Finally I asked, "Why are we even here?"

At the end of the meeting, I was asked what I thought the task force should include in their final report. My suggestion: "That Students for Justice in Palestine should be treated like every other student group." Six months later the committee report exonerated me from the charge of antisemitism but criticized a tweet on my personal account in which I questioned the use of the concept of "Jewish values" given Israeli military assaults on Gaza.

As frightening as this experience was, it felt easy to support my students. However, even though the university failed to label me an antisemite, I know from the examples of Steven Salaita and other Palestinian academics who lost their jobs that mine was saved because I am Jewish and the charge was therefore too absurd to stick. Yet, I was soon to learn that it may be easier to stand up to an absurd bureaucratic machine than to one's own inner circle. This is why, throughout this volume, I maintain that the violent state destruction of Palestinian people in Gaza is related to the systematic under-education of the working classes in New York City, to the imposition of mandatory motherhood through the denial of abortion rights, to the branding and enforcement of culture industry hierarchies. That all these oppressions that control individual and collective lives are imposed through false standards and fake claims of supremacy and superiority. And that we can see these structures of containment in the lives of women artists, just as we see them in congressional subpoenas and justifications for silence or even complicity. A witness has a distance of safety. A participant shares a vulnerability.

AFTERNOON OF A FASCIST

The question of complicity is—of course—an institutional one and a governmental one, but it also is expressed in our most personal relationships. It is an inescapable fact that when we are in a position to offer solidarity, in the most basic possible way, we have a choice. At the same time, the person needing the recognition and intervention has no choice. This means that from the start, solidarity is conditional and fragile as long as it can be withdrawn, unless we become so intertwined and identified with the threatened party that we lose our protective shield and become inescapably subject to offshoots of their punishment. This potential scenario looms larger than is imminent, for it is a long, long journey from tentative to no return. As a result, most solidarity takes place in a state of contradiction. Denying this can be as absurd as trying to erase it. Better to be clear about the inequality. Trying to self-impose deprivation in order to disappear the contradictions is a foolish effort because the end goal is to share advantage and protection, not to increase the numbers of people who live without it.

One of the many ways that these contradictions show themselves is that we may witness, experience, and tolerate expressions of hatred and threat that we oppose because, in the moment, it is the most practical thing to do. Most people hear racist, homophobic, sexist, anti-immigrant, Islamophobic, antisemitic drivel at times but say and do nothing in response. And while this is often a question of safety, it very often also has to do with the exceptional conditions we have created for family and friends. We put allowance and tolerance in place in order to maintain relationships, possibly because we see patience as a potential strategy for change, or simply to make our lives easier. That maintenance may exist because of convenience or sentimentality, function or nostalgia. Or it may be because we hope that with time the conflict will simply fade away. That our friends' and families' attitudes and actions on behalf of inequality or even domination hurt others while we are silent is one of the daily life contradictions of our wishes to be part of change. I know because this is something I've watched myself do: be silent in the face of racism, because it belonged to the son of a close friend.

It was three weeks after the American affliction produced Trump's victory that I flew to France to visit my old friend Anne-Marie. We've been through a lifetime of friendship and were now circling sixty. Anne-Marie is funny, smart, and interested in the world. But when things get tough emotionally, she disappears. She's been through a girlfriend, a few boyfriends, and an alcoholic ex-husband with whom she produced an adult son, Antoine. That night at dinner, everyone seemed in good form. Antoine was funny and warm and charming, and he loved my present of a wool hat with a built-in rechargeable headlight for his motorcycle. The food, sausage and lentils, was served, the wine was poured, and then the conversation turned to Trump.

Now, these people are leftists, atheists, and in this way typically French. Also typically, Anne-Marie's sister, Claudette, has become increasingly racist. Like many white French women, she opposes hijabs and burkas and supports them being outlawed. Appalled, I have had this one out with her over and over again. Yet, her contempt for Muslims increases year by year, and becomes more rabid. Like many white French people, she believes in a state of mind that I think does not really exist. It's what she calls "laïque." Technically this is the French word for *secular*, but when analyzing French society, what she sees as secular, I see as Christian. Sundays, Christmas, common names, costumed nuns and priests, the central nature of Christian art and buildings are all foundations of the national identity. As a person who grew up as a religious minority, I know the United States is a Christian country, even if it says it legally is supposed to have a separation of church and state. But as a Catholic growing up in France, Claudette has no perspective on the Christian nature of her point of view. Like many dominant cultural people, she considers her very subjective perspective to be objective and neutral. She cannot imagine that her desire to forbid women living in France to wear what they want or express their religious beliefs the way they want to is anything but secular.

At this point Antoine pipes up, and he too is impassioned. In fact, I am dismayed to see that he has that same scolding, monologuing tone that his aunt Claudette has acquired. This newly liberated racism is a lecture, a recitation of grief, of anger, of intense emotions all generated from within. And he is even more explicit than his aunt. He has started reciting lines from some tract he read about Islam, pointing his finger at me, and spitting as he drowns out our protests. I know it won't do any good, but my conscience requires me to disagree. It doesn't make him madder, because he is not listening. He is ranting. He can't stop himself. Every false statement possible about Islam is being vomited into our lives, and the rest of the family looks at one another helplessly.

As I watch his emotions contort, I realize that Antoine is in a different phase of this distortion than his aunt. Claudette is a run-of-the-mill French racist, the kind of white person who is overtaking Europe as they have overtaken America. She believes in her own superiority, and she blames less powerful people for her country's flaws. Her worldview is frightening, destructive, divisive, and dangerous and has brought both countries to despair and potential ruin. And yet, I am exposed to her whenever I visit because she is my friend's sister. But Antoine is something else. He is not using racism to avoid himself and blame others, as is that daily practice;

he is living on racism. It is his air. In his daily emotions, conversations, pursued interests, and what he reads, takes comfort in, and declares, racism is running his life.

After everyone left, Anne-Marie and I sat down and had a shaken reality check. She was clearly embarrassed that I had witnessed her son's compulsive hatred. And she was equally very concerned that Antoine could not control his venomous outbursts. As we tried to find a way to understand what was happening to him, in the futile gesture of looking for a solution, we traveled over a range of areas: It is true that many more white people hold those views today than they did in our youth. It is not as freakish to be a hate-filled twenty-nine-year-old white man; in fact, it is somewhat status quo. Instead of being a nutcase in a basement looking at scary websites from obscure places, one can hold this dedication to hatred openly, publicly, finding a lot of support for it in open society. "In fact," Anne-Marie said about herself and me, "we are now the strange ones."

In our generation of post-1960s white progressives, we developed an understanding of ourselves as people with privileges that are unjustified, who—despite our desires to contribute to dismantling racism—have to be constantly vigilant and self-critical and open to other people's criticisms to limit the damage. And we are learning how to carry and integrate this information about ourselves, and to act on it without being paralyzed by it. In Antoine's perspective, this way of thinking about one's white self is impossible. Multidimensionality equals fault. The idea of white people having to think about ourselves subjectively is something that feels to Antoine's cohort like an assault, instead of feeling enriching. It is an ideological battle between the wielding of complexity as a source of depth and complexity as a weapon of diminishment.

The next day Anne-Marie and I were in a pho restaurant near Antoine's apartment. It was a Saturday afternoon, and she knew he would be sitting home alone and so invited him for big bowls of steamy beef and rice noodles. This time there was no warm-up. "I want all the Arabs out of France," he was shouting, in a public place this time, with a Vietnamese proprietor. "It's *my country*! *MY* country!" His mother was in the trap of trying to counter with facts, but he only took it as opposition and got louder and more frightening. We decided to retreat to his nearby apartment if only to spare the Vietnamese restaurant owner from having to spend one more minute listening to this threatening discourse.

We started walking toward his street, and I noticed right away that his neighborhood had become distinctively more Arab. Most of the businesses were now Arab, and the streets were filled with covered women with children, and young men hanging out in groups, smoking, playing music, and talking. In fact, I started to realize that this lonely, isolated, and increasingly distorted young white man was surrounded by Arab people in groups, in families, with friends, while he had retreated into isolation. We entered his lobby and most of the names on the mailboxes were Arab names. He opened the apartment's front door. Anne-Marie and I were stunned. There was dirt and broken shards of unidentifiable objects on every inch of the floor and every surface. The place stank of cigarettes and dope, and there were burn marks on the tables and filthy furniture. There was absolutely no place to bring any friends. It was an apartment designed to ensure that no human connection would take place. While all around him, Arab people were building businesses, families, and community, Antoine was living in self-imposed filth.

We were shocked, and frightened. At home again we had a long talk. Showing us the disaster of his apartment was an action that we had to interpret as a cry for help. He was suffering, and we understood for the first time that his distorted thinking was progressing, had gotten much worse, and would not correct itself. His mother would have to do something before he hurt someone or ended up in jail. She'd have a long road ahead, and we both knew this. But it was a crisis. An emergency.

In the airport waiting for my return flight, I was filled with questions. Is racism a form of mental illness? In Antoine's case, it clearly is, because it is tied to suffering, it is an exteriorization of his internal anxieties, and he is tormented, and instead of saying, "Help me, I don't know how to live," he blames Muslims. But what about his aunt Claudette's increasingly normative racism? Is that just old-fashioned supremacy? There is real pain out there in the world. There is the pain that produces the racist, but more important, there is the pain that the racist produces for others. Claudette's racism is willful, I've finally decided, and Antoine's is compulsive; it may have an obsessive biological component. With the right medication and the right caring treatment, some of those anxieties might be tamped. And in this way, the person out there whom he could hurt or even kill would be protected. But there is no strategy to counter Claudette. She will continue feeling self-satisfied and superior, and unfortunately, for the near future, her nation and mine will be cheering her on.

Cut ahead and the neoliberal Emmanuel Macron, the New Popular Frontist Jean-Luc Mélenchon, and the fascist Marine Le Pen faced an apocalyptic runoff for the French presidency, and the fascists scored a terrifying first-round victory, to be locked into a three-way split. Russia has self-destructed through destruction of others. We are now in a proxy war and Ukrainians are the fodder. It is Antoine who occupies my mind. And then a message from him pops up on Facebook. He is suffering, he tells me. He has had to give up the two most important things in his life: going to work and traveling. Why? Because they both require vaccination, and he won't be controlled. He is a free man. He won't let those immigrants tell him what to put in his body. Like so many American anti-vaxxers, he is deranged. Like the Russians who somehow accept that they are liberating the corpses they create, he is very far from a viable future. Other people are the problem, not his own internal anxieties. Like so many in our world, Antoine will be controlled by his demons, but he won't be controlled by the cure. And I don't know what I am supposed to do.

FROM CAMPUS TO CONGRESS: THE CASE OF NORTHWESTERN UNIVERSITY (2024)

As the carpet-bombing of Gaza began, campuses were slow to respond. Grassroots organizations like Within Our Lifetime, Jewish Voice for Peace, IfNotNow, Palestinian Youth Movement, Writers Against the War on Gaza, and others were conducting street demonstrations daily, through rain and snow. Mass arrests were taking place, usually around planned civil disobedience actions, but the police were getting testier and had started arresting people haphazardly. Preexisting student organizations like Students for Justice in Palestine and Jewish Voice for Peace were increasing their memberships, reactivating or starting new chapters. And a number of schools, including Columbia University and Brandeis, were banning both. By November a new national US organization, Faculty for Justice in Palestine Network (FJP), had formed to enlarge the infrastructure of support so that students taking chances would not be hung out to dry. The number of chapters, 120 by summer 2024, grew rapidly from coast to coast, enhancing the power and solidarity of campus organizing.

During the first few months of mass killings in Gaza, we were able to communicate with Gazans via X (formerly Twitter). Grassroots Palestinian journalists, university professors, and everyday citizens were keeping us informed with images of daily violence and suffering that was impossible to fully comprehend. As the Israelis and President Biden were claiming that the bombing was tactical or contained, and speaking endlessly about the threat of Hamas, X was telling us the opposite. Daily evidence was being presented by individuals and broadcasters on Al Jazeera of wanton, systematic bombing destroying entire families, crushing people to death, and blowing off their body parts, organs erupting from ruptured bodies, endless live footage of endless parents carrying their children's corpses, suddenly orphaned children hovering over their parents' mangled remains. The Israelis were targeting journalists, murdering them and their families. Every university was decimated; their professors, administrators, and students were murdered. Poets and writers were targeted and killed. And thousands and thousands of Palestinians were maimed, losing limbs, eyes, feet—as Jasbir Puar predicted in her 2017 book, *The Right to Maim*.

I remember one photograph of stacks of children's severed legs. And then there were the scenes of Palestinians screaming, "Stop it! Stop doing this to us!" as the floors of the remaining hospitals were filled with bodies and then the hospitals also were destroyed. In turn, American grassroots activists continued endless rapid-response demonstrations, but the US media was tepid. Reporting was weak and distorted. Only platforms like X showed Gazans as human beings made to deliberately and unnecessarily suffer a degree of pain and trauma that would carry through many future generations. *The New York Times* was particularly savage. When Palestinian experiences were touched upon, it would be in the passive phrasing "Palestinians died" instead of "Palestinians were murdered by Israel."

The first sign of administrative response to growing activism that I experienced at work was in the early weeks of 2024, two months after the mass murder in Gaza had begun. I had been invited by the Middle East and North African Studies (MENA) program to conduct a book talk with a Northwestern colleague, Sami Hermez, about his new book, *My Brother, My Land: A Story from Palestine*, which had just been published by Stanford University Press, widely considered the top publisher in MENA studies. I read the book and thoroughly appreciated it. It is an innovative collaboration with Sireen Sawalha about her brother's experiences with Israeli brutality and how this led him to join resistance movements, choose violence as a strategy, face long incarceration in an Israeli prison, and join Palestine Islamic Jihad. The book succeeds in humanizing and representing the experience of young Palestinians facing severe repression and helps us understand how that pain and pressure produce certain kinds of choices. I found the book to be important and making a considerable contribution, and I was looking forward to the event. One of the major consequences of the media blackout on Gazan suffering and Israeli violence was that Americans never heard from Palestinians about their experiences and did not understand where seventy-five years of oppression had brought them. This book was a major contribution toward making that information available.

Even though this event would have been held during lunch in a small room, attended by thirty to fifty people, it had more significance than I anticipated. I was very surprised when I received an email a few days before, letting me know that the event had been canceled. Dr. Hermez was the director of liberal arts at Northwestern's Qatar campus and had already taken the long flight from Qatar. He was waiting in Evanston when word of the cancellation had reached him. So, whatever had occurred had happened suddenly and quickly. I was concerned, of course, that two colleagues at different branches of the same institution had been forbidden to discuss a leading book in the field, scheduled by an academic program.

I witnessed that the censoring of Arab voices was resonant among public and corporate universities—perhaps the only thing they had in common.

After a number of conversations with Dr. Hermez, administrators, and colleagues, what I could piece together was that his talk that had been scheduled for a few days before at Johns Hopkins University in Baltimore had been canceled through the efforts of some censorious Zionist faculty members, who had actually contacted their counterparts at Northwestern's Evanston campus, who then engaged the administration and achieved the cancellation of our conversation. The excuse for this repression of discourse was that after combing Dr. Hermez's personal X account, this group had located one tweet questioning *The New York Times*'s claim of mass rapes by Hamas members during the violence and killings of over 1,200 Israelis committed on October 7. Now, a quick search of media shows articles in *The Nation* magazine and *The Intercept*, and by Northwestern journalism professor Steven Thrasher in *Lit Hub* and many others questioning aspects of *The New York Times*'s claims. The *Times* actually retracted their podcast on the coverage because of errors. One of the coauthors of the article had a questionable background. So, regardless of how anyone interprets the *Times*'s claims, some of which were later walked back, questioning them was a legitimate position within a reasonable range of opinion. Certainly, this was not grounds for canceling an academic conversation. After a cycle of protests by faculty, a new date was scheduled for fall 2024. But certain members of the administration had shown that they were susceptible to coordinated pressure for censorship.

A few weeks later I attended a job talk on campus in trans studies by Oxford historian Dr. Zavier Nunn. It was a fascinating presentation raising the possibility that while both trans and gay Germans experienced the rise of subculture in Weimar, Germany, it was possible that trans people did not experience the same degree of repression, incarceration, and death as gay men and (with different specifics) lesbians during the Nazi period. Dr. Nunn gave a few examples of trans people who had been studied and treated in clinics during the Nazi era, while gay people were being deported. During the discussion I raised the issue of gay and trans collaboration or identification with supremacy and fascism that has occurred at different historical points, and I detailed queer and trans participation in "white supremacy, Christian supremacy, and Jewish supremacy via pinkwashing" as being historically consistent with aspects of Dr. Nunn's presentation. After the talk, a man I did not know, trembling with rage, approached me in the hall. He identified himself as a Northwestern professor and told me, with great anger, that I was "mouthing Nazi ideology" and sounding like the classic tract of antisemitism, *The Protocols of the Elders of Zion,* by using the phrase "Jewish supremacy." I introduced myself and shook his hand, trying to calm him down, but actually I was scared. I calmly replied that this was part of my research and work on pinkwashing. He repeated the accusation that I was conveying Nazi ideology and said that I "should not say those words in public." This kind of behavior is extremely inappropriate for the culture of a place like Northwestern. The predominant tone is "Midwest nice": calm and boundaried. Whereas at CUNY people were capable of yelling as part of New York culture, our collegial gatherings at Northwestern were very *appropriate.* So, this raging, accusatory style after a job talk was entirely out of the norm. I calmly replied that I knew it was very upsetting that Jews were acting in supremacist ways, and that it was very personally distressing but that it was reality. I tried to be as polite as possible, but his behavior was so inappropriate professionally, and his affect, language, and accusations were so aggressive and distorted, I felt shaken. Of course, I

THE FANTASY AND NECESSITY OF SOLIDARITY

wondered if he was one of the faculty who had gotten Dr. Hermez's book talk temporarily canceled, and what his next move would be. Was this a sign of more to come?

That spring of 2024, when I was on leave and not in Chicago, an encampment in solidarity with Gaza was created on the Northwestern campus. Columbia students had been inspired by previous grassroots street demonstrations and had endured simultaneous months of repression by the university's administration. Famously, the president of Columbia, Minouche Shafik, fresh from a shakedown by the congressional committee that had forced out the presidents of the University of Pennsylvania and Harvard, called the NYPD, had students arrested, suspended, and evicted from their campus housing, and turned off the electronic faculty ID cards so that teachers could not get on campus.

Our encampment at Northwestern included students and faculty from SJP, JVP, and F4P and many others and unfolded very differently. On the first day, Northwestern president Michael Schill— or someone in administration—called the Northwestern University Police, a deputized private police force. My impression from watching videos is that the police overreacted and were excessively physical and aggressive with peaceful students. Faculty, including journalism professor Steven Thrasher, my colleague, formed a marshaling line to protect their students from police violence. One supervisor, a Black woman officer, could be seen on tape calming down officers under her supervision who were overreacting and physically attacking faculty. After this event, I joined my faculty colleagues in writing letters and making phone calls to administrators begging them to not bring the police back to campus; it was dangerous. The next day the police were not called. After a few more days of peaceful demonstrations, teach-ins, study groups, engaged discussion, and protest, a chosen group of student negotiators were able to create an agreement with the administration, and the encampment de-escalated in return for the beginning of a conversation toward the number one demand of the encampment: divestment from university money and affiliations in Israel, and some other points including the very crucial promise to house at-risk Palestinian scholars and other adjacent issues. In this way Northwestern joined Brown, Union Theological Seminary, Wesleyan, and a number of schools whose administrations chose negotiation toward divestment over police violence. This group differed dramatically from schools like UCLA, Columbia, Emory, USC, and Dartmouth, whose presidents chose combinations of violence against students and faculty and punitive suspensions of students, and invited extended police presence on campus. Soon I learned that President Schill had been targeted by a coalition of organizations that supported Israeli military policy: the Anti-Defamation League (ADL), the Louis D. Brandeis Center for Human Rights Under Law, and StandWithUs. And that they were calling for his resignation because he was negotiating. I and other faculty at Northwestern, from a wide range of perspectives, signed a letter of support for Schill's decisions to communicate and avoid violence, even though I also had doubts that these negotiations would lead to actual divestment, although they could.

In a constantly shifting situation like the popular protests against US complicity with Israeli violence, I practice big-tent politics. That means I look for places where I can stand with people in agreement, even temporarily, as part of a very diverse Palestine solidarity movement that includes many different kinds of people and different points of view. This means that my own precise opinions will not always be absolutely reflected by the people I generally stand with. And I have to accept that. There is an unease in coalition because we sacrifice the very specific personal politics that none of us can achieve alone, for a more compromised collective. But without that flexibility, no movement building would be able to take place. It is the change, the peace, and the justice we seek that are more important than being right in our living rooms. Probably the only thing we all agree on is the call for ceasefire. I think most of us want permanent ceasefire and support the Palestinian right to recovery of Gaza, instead of the stated Israeli intention to turn that strip of land into Jewish settlements. Then there are people who believe any combination of the following:

— The "two-state solution," which implies two independent nations. But this position is rarely accompanied by a map, so each person who claims it has a different concept of what territory each of these states would occupy. Do they mean two equal states with contiguous territory and water access? Or do they mean a tiny slip of the West Bank surrounded and filled by Jewish settlers to be called Palestine?

— Return all the land to historic Palestine with 1967 borders.

— Return to 1948 borders and end the entity known as Israel.

— Build "one state" of Israelis and Palestinians that is binational, where everyone who lives in the same area would have equal rights with both Jewish and Palestinian rights of return. This is a vision that—considering Israeli popular support for the war on Gaza—would probably require UN occupation to enforce, in the same way the UN occupied former Yugoslavian nations in order to end the ethnic cleansing and genocide of Muslims that was taking place.

But all these resolutions are far away from now. Now, multiple times a day, I shift positions to stand with people with whom I am usually in partial agreement. I sign open letters of support and condemnation, even if I don't agree with every word. If the letter is generally for peace and Palestinian autonomy, I sign it. I support leaders and organizations with whom I don't have complete agreement. I support candidates who are part of the congressional ceasefire caucus, even if I don't think the current governmental structure can do the right thing. I just decide that the collective power is more important than my individual perfectionist analysis. I worry about how to stop the violence, about being effective, and about the threat of complicity.

One of my heroes, the Palestinian novelist Susan Abulhawa, addressed these questions in her piece "Gaza Is Our Moment of Truth," published in *The Electronic Intifada* in spring 2024. Susan was the visionary behind the incredible Palestine Writes literature festival. I attended this global gathering of Palestinian writers at the University of Pennsylvania in September 2023, only a few weeks before the carpet-bombings began. Many of the writers who participated ended up murdered or in endless exile. As Susan said, because of this "celebration of Palestinian excellence and indigenous heritage—the billionaires Marc Rowan, Dick Wolf and the Lauder family conspired to remove the president of the University of Pennsylvania for her insufficient deference. . . ." Referring to the global student uprisings in the spring, she wrote:

> This time is different from the uprisings of the 1960s and 1970s. There is a new sense of global interconnection, an emerging class consciousness and foundational political analyses predicated on post-colonial studies and intersectionality. . . . [Administrations] will offer half-baked promises with no teeth, enough to quiet matters long enough to adopt new strategies and enact new laws. If we stop they will adapt, and they will do so with artificial intelligence,

against which we may well have no defenses, not for a long time to come. So beware of their concessions. Beware of victory that pulls us back into the lanes they made.

Similarly, a friend who teaches at Harvard texted me during the voluntary dismantling of their Gaza encampment: *Why did these students fold? I see it as being specific to Harvard in so many ways. Risk-averse. Conservative thinking. Scared of reputational damage. Not all of them but most of them see themselves as power brokers. "This was fun but not worth long term consequences." Many told me the end was a relief.*

Predictably, while the president was being threatened for negotiating, some students and faculty were also disappointed in the agreement to negotiate, for a number of reasons, including Susan Abulhawa's concern: that the "negotiation" might lead to nothing. But then again, what is gained by being assaulted? It is very hard to predict which road will lead somewhere.

When I returned to Chicago from Berlin, I met up for breakfast with my colleague in creative writing, Rachel Jamison Webster, the author of a family memoir, *Benjamin Banneker and Us*. I was not surprised to learn from Rachel that the US government's Committee on Education and the Workforce had sent a letter instructing President Schill to appear before them in Washington on May 28, 2024. This was the committee, dominated by right-wing extremist Elise Stefanik and chaired by religious fundamentalist Virginia Foxx, that had grilled previous university presidents, ultimately forcing the resignations at Harvard and the University of Pennsylvania and driving the president of Columbia to dramatic police action against demonstrating students. In fact, I had just signed a letter from Jewish professors supporting Rutgers president Jonathan Holloway, who had also been punitively summoned for, like President Schill, negotiating with students instead of beating them up and having them arrested.

But what really surprised me was the news that Rachel herself had been named in the congressional letter. Although I liked and respected my colleague, I had not experienced her to be a Palestine solidarity activist, nor to be outspoken on Palestine-related issues. As it turned out, she had been named in an official government document because she had preestablished in her syllabus for a section of her undergraduate poetry class to focus on protest poetry, including pieces by Israeli, Palestinian, and Native American poets. This previously announced week had coincided with the Gaza encampment, so she invited the students—if they wished—to observe the encampment in line with that week's readings. It was not obligatory, and there was at least one student who opted out. Apparently, someone had reported her to someone who had then reported her to the congressional committee.

As I read through the thirteen-page document written by Congresswoman Foxx, it became rapidly apparent that many of the ten professors named had been reported by students to some entity on campus, who had then forwarded these reports and names to the government. At first, I thought that Zionist Jewish students denouncing their teachers to fundamentalist Christian congresspeople was a new, gothic twist. But then I recalled my own experience with CUNY eight years before, when false and mangled allegations had been tunneled through Hillel to Zionist Organization of America and then to CUNY. And I started to wonder what role student organizations are now playing in bringing government charges against teachers. After all, someone is the go-between for students and the right-wing Christian fundamentalists in Congress. Otherwise, how would they get the names of teachers and these telephone-game mangled accusations? When I was in college in the 1970s Hillel was a place where all Jewish students could go for religious and cultural events. Jessica Winegar and Lara Deeb, writing in *Middle East Critique* in July 2024, point out that in 2009, Hillel International issued a "standards of partnership," which barred chapters from hosting anti-Zionist speakers or events. So, Hillel is actually a partisan pro-Israel political organization, not a haven for Jewish students. Making that connection let me realize that the ordeal I had been put through in 2016 was a rehearsal—within the limited sphere of the public university—for the tactics that were being played out now by the government.

As I read through the congressional document, "Kafkaesque" is too literal a description of the ludicrous, distorted, and simply false lists of accusations. But I think highlighting some of its absurdities is illuminating. The government's list of charges is framed as a response to the accusation of President Schill's "failure to protect Jewish students." From this pronouncement, essential lies are already put into position. "Jewish students" does not accurately describe the people who support Israeli military policies. The correct characterization would be "some Jewish students." This misuse of language obscures the inconvenient presence of large numbers of Jewish students, faculty, and staff who oppose the war on Gaza. According to an April 2024 Pew Research Center study—conducted before the Rafah bombing and Israeli-imposed starvation of Palestinians—33 percent of all American Jews opposed Israeli military policy in Gaza, with 5 percent being undecided. At least one third of the American constituency used by the government to justify persecuting students, faculty, and administration already opposed the killing by early spring. The presence of Jewish Voice for Peace, of Jewish students in SJP, and of Jewish students who were unaffiliated but opposed the war was completely erased. Later in the document Congresswoman Foxx admitted that the sample of students who were pro–Israeli military policy, which she labeled "many Jewish students," was actually only thirty-five individuals.

While falsely constructing Zionist Jews as all Jews, Foxx obliterated any consideration of the impact of the war on Palestinian, Arab, and Muslim students, as though they don't exist and don't count. She incorrectly characterized the encampment as "pro-terror" when it is the opposite, and as a source of "crime," "assault," and "threat"—none of which are documented. She called the encampment, which she had falsely constructed as not Jewish, "a hotspot for antisemitic harassment." But, to get to the heart of the matter, she called the president's decision to open negotiations on divestment "shameful," while remaining silent on the university presidents who actively invited police violence. She condemned the slogan "The people united will never be defeated." She attacked Northwestern's negotiated agreement to offer five scholarships to displaced Palestinian scholars at risk, whose universities had been destroyed by Israel, claiming this offer violates antidiscrimination laws. She condemned the administration for turning off the sprinkler where the encampment was. At every turn, actions for peace, equity, and safe harbor are misrepresented as assaults. She called for Schill's resignation "immediately" and demanded that Northwestern's board of directors remove him. She also singled out the Black woman Northwestern University Police supervisor, who calmed down a violent office, saying she had "prevent[ed] officers from arresting those resisting them."

It is the new normal for government committees to try to control elite higher education, which they mistakenly perceive as a hotbed of radicalism, when actually they are primarily status-quo corporations. A *Guardian* exposé by Will Craft and Tom Perkins in August 2024 revealed that the Elise Stefanik / Virginia Foxx campaign has been funded by one of the great rivals of elite education: for-profit colleges.

> The industry, which includes schools such as Keiser University, has drawn intense congressional and administrative scrutiny for predatory practices that frequently leave students with worthless degrees while enriching shareholders in recent decades. . . . A *Guardian* analysis of Federal Election Commission filings and Open Secrets data finds Stefanik and Foxx have received over $300,000 from the industry, including lobbying groups and those associated with for-profit schools, since 2019. Foxx, the chair of the House education and labor committee, is the largest recipient of for-profit education money in Congress, having received about $270,000.

Their ammunition is to seize on lies about endangered Jews, while millions of Gazans are displaced, traumatized, maimed, and murdered—in order for Christian fundamentalists to get more control of secular and marginally diverse educational institutions. The committee focused specifically on the vulnerable field of Middle Eastern and North African studies, while relying for information on student denunciation and unreliable sources. For example, they cite Canary Mission, an anonymous doxing service that lists unsubstantiated or misrepresented accusations against students and faculty, endangering them through photo identification to Israeli government intelligence and independent vigilante organizations, while also interfering with their employment.

By demanding all emails, videos, minutes, and records of communication between named administrators and faculty, the government has crossed every line of autonomy, free speech, privacy, right of association, and academic freedom. This is how intensely this sector of the US government is opposing Palestinian wishes for peace and self-determination and American expressions of solidarity that are necessary to move toward those goals.

On May 14, 2024, I listened to a talk by Omar Barghouti at the Palestine Festival of Literature. His subject, appropriately, was complicity.

In the face of the world's first televised genocide, Palestinians are not begging the world for charity. We are calling for meaningful, impactful solidarity and before both, we are demanding ending complicity as a profound ethical obligation.

Israel's current genocide against 2.3 million Palestinians in the besieged and occupied Gaza Strip is armed, funded, and shielded from accountability by a colonial, hypocritical Western establishment, governments, corporations, and institutions, creating a new paradigm where "might makes right" prevails, unmasked and uncontrolled by international law or moral principles. This establishment has actively amplified Israel's dehumanization and demonization of indigenous Palestinians, waging a wave of McCarthyite repression and silencing of voices defending Palestinian lives and rights.

This level of complicity, coupled with the fact that you live in this quasi-democracy, makes it ethically obligatory to act within one's community, organization, union, or other domain of relative influence to ensure accountability at two levels, in order to end complicity. Accountability from above, which is enacted by policymakers only when they must, due to a critical mass of pressure from below, of people power. And accountability from below, which is enacted by individuals and collectives, by ending all forms of complicity with the system of oppression. . . .

The unprecedented grassroots solidarity pressure globally has significantly increased the isolation of the US–Israel genocidal axis. Social, racial, climate, gender, LGBTQI+ justice movements, trade unions, progressive Jewish partners, academics, artists, students, writers have all mobilized like never before to stop the genocide but have yet to reach that critical mass of people power. But even when we do, and we force Israel to permanently stop bombing our people in Gaza, this would not end the genocide, it would deem it less visible. Israel's use of starvation as a weapon of war, as affirmed by Oxfam, the spread of infectious diseases, thirst, and deprivation of life-sustaining conditions will exacerbate Israel's ongoing Nakba. So what can be done?

To push for a ceasefire lifting the siege and ending oppression, we need to shift the narrative and end complicity. The former entails countering the lies and dehumanization of Palestinians. . . . If you fail to name the crime and shame the criminal, you perpetuate impunity.

And then he went on to quote Paulo Freire: "With the establishment of a relationship of oppression, violence has already begun. Never in history has violence been initiated by the oppressed. Violence is initiated by those who oppress, who exploit, who fail to recognize others as persons, not by those who are oppressed, exploited, and unrecognized." And then Barghouti details what Palestine is asking us to do to end the violence against them:

1. Pressure policymakers to endorse a comprehensive arms embargo on Israel. Ban the import of products of companies operating illegally in the occupied Palestinian territory, and withdraw all . . . investments from companies implicated in illegal settlements.
2. Support peaceful disruptions, sit-ins, occupations targeting government buildings, as well as corporate enablers of genocide and apartheid, especially arms manufacturers, investment firms, and institutions, media, universities, and cultural spaces that may be complicit.
3. Support declaring your community, union, cultural space an "apartheid-free zone," refusing to accept funding, institutional relations, or sponsorship from Israel or its complicit institutions.
4. Support trade unions blocking or disrupting arms shipments to Israel.
5. Escalate strategic boycotts and divestment campaigns targeting companies that are complicit in Israeli crimes. . . .
6. Help pressure city councils, universities, churches, cultural institutions to adopt procurement and investment guidelines that exclude companies implicated in grave human rights violations anywhere.

And he closed with:

When you feel overwhelmed by their McCarthyite repression, please remember, here they try to silence you with intimidation, antidemocratic legislation, and character assassination. In Palestine, Israel tries to silence us with bombs, bullets, and bulldozers. Yet, we are steadfast, we resist, and we insist on our full menu of rights. As Desmond Tutu once put it, "If you hate violence, end oppression. If you hate oppression, end complicity."

These US campus battles are filled with bravery and also with contradiction and threat—both the threat of retaliation and the threat of complicity. One of the hardest things in the world is to stand up for someone who not only cannot improve your material life, but whose mere association could keep you from your goals. As my friend, anthropologist Jacqueline Nassy Brown, quoted her minister, "It is about convenience versus commitment." Truth, after all, requires effort—to both find and hold on to. There is a reward in complicity. And no one can predict the future.

In August 2024, I received an update from Educators for Palestine at Northwestern: As feared, the campaign for divestment has seen mixed results. But the academic and cultural boycott, the *B* of BDS, seems more promising. Israeli universities have been fully complicit in the destruction of all of Gaza's schools. Not one is on record as opposing the genocide, let alone calling for ceasefire. As a result the campaign to dismantle study abroad programs in Israel is gaining steam. In most cases these programs are in clear violation of campus codes regarding nondiscrimination and equal opportunity because they are not accessible to all students and faculty. To quote from the Faculty for Justice in Palestine Network:

It is well-known that Israel routinely denies entry to persons of Arab, Middle-Eastern, or Muslim origin and subjects them to detention and harassment at borders, engaging unashamedly in racial profiling, which effectively declares such travelers to be suspect in advance. Those of Palestinian descent experience particular difficulties in entering. . . . Just as egregiously, a 2017 Israeli law prohibits entry for anyone who has publicly supported the BDS movement, on the basis of their political opinion alone. . . . No college should operate a program that contravenes its own campus policies by denying access to members of its community.

The summer after the hearings, I'd heard through the grapevine that a number of faculty members had been asked by Northwestern to hand over their personal cell phones so that the school could comply with the congressional *request*, not *subpoena*, for texts and emails. Another few were hit with a wide range of threats and accusations, including suspension, and in one case over a hundred pages of redacted emails but no articulated charges. Unfortunately, after doing the right thing by negotiating and avoiding violence, my school was doing the wrong thing by cooperating with government demands that were neither mandatory nor ethical. For the first time in my life I am employed by a corporate university, and as an institution situated in the private sector, in the face of government injustice it has an opportunity to not comply, and to teach *by example*.

By fall 2024, Northwestern joined a number of other universities by changing their policies about student protests. Expressions of ethical opposition to the US-funded war on Gaza were now extremely limited. Students could no longer build structures, stay overnight, or use amplification. By punishing students for expressing their deep emotional and political commitments to ending the war, the school would not succeed at stopping protest, instead they would simply criminalize more of their students. On October 16, 2024, the student group Jewish Voice for Peace decided to celebrate the holiday of Sukkot by building a sukkah, the traditional outdoor structure accompanying the harvest holiday. But the JVP students conceptualized it as a liberation sukkah, with statements about their solidarity with Gaza. After four hours of confrontation with school authorities, the campus security dismantled the structure and banned JVP from Northwestern campus student groups. The next day I became their faculty adviser.

Sami and Sireen's book talk for *My Brother, My Land* did eventually take place. But the context had dramatically changed. While the official death toll of murdered Palestinians was staying in the 40,000–50,000 range, it was clear that in addition to people who had been shot and exploded by bombs, thousands more were dead underneath rubble, while additional thousands faced death by intentional starvation and by the orchestrated weapon of thirst. Sophie Hurwitz, writing in *Mother Jones* on October 8, 2024, cited a Brown University report estimating the Gaza dead at over 100,000. So, when we were finally allowed to have our book talk in October 2024, emotions were at an all-time high. We were also joined by a Scholar at Risk, a university professor from Gaza whose school had been entirely demolished by bombs and whose colleagues, students, and family members had also been murdered. It was an honor to be with these colleagues and hear their testimony, and to witness their tears. We all sat together in shock that the mass killings had escalated to such heights, and that the US continued to feed money and arms to Israel, despite increasing international opposition and repeated world court and UN efforts. Yet we had our say.

By the time this book was sent to press, it was obvious that increased administrative restrictions on protest were not going to stop American students. Campus demonstrations started almost immediately across the nation. They were accompanied by a sober sense of separation from the universities themselves, as students now expected opposition from institutions fearful of government reprisals and from complicit media attacks. The self-presentation of universities as places of ethical investigation and personal development seemed to fade away. One exception was Wesleyan College in Connecticut. Its Jewish president, Michael Roth, wrote an opinion essay for *The New York Times* on September 2, 2024: "I'm a College President, and I Hope My Campus Is Even More Political This Year":

> The issue that matters most to many activists right now is the war in Gaza, and protesters will undoubtedly continue to make their voices heard. Last spring at Wesleyan, students built an encampment of up to about 100 tents to protest the war and to call for the university to divest from companies thought to be supporting it. Since the protest was nonviolent and the students in the encampment were careful not to disrupt normal university operations, we allowed it to continue because their right to nonviolent protest was more important than their modest violations of the rules.

President Roth went on to assert, "Education can prepare people for this kind of true political engagement, and true political engagement can prepare people for the highest goals of education." And here, I must agree. The point of school is not to create obedience by punishing students because administrations fear undemocratic congressional committees that are themselves lying. The point is to produce leaders who are brave enough to challenge these tactics and refuse the chilling effects of authoritarian behaviors. I am proud to support students who have emerged as the most ethical social sector of American life, most willing to risk punishment in order to stand up to our government's support of war crimes carried out by Israel and resulting in mass murder. If we hope for any kind of better future at all, we must have young people who find silence impossible.

7

Justification vs. Solidarity
in Arts and Entertainment

SOLIDARITY IN SHOW BUSINESS

The US entertainment industry is one of the last places a person can find solidarity.

Most corporate-produced culture is filled with terrible values, is blatantly retrograde or—at best—meaningless, which is its own politic. This product exists to make money for people who have fun solving intense but tightly focused problems. Its social function is to create individuals who can feed the need for fame, upon which American marketing depends. A friend once pointed out to me that America's greatest exports are film/TV and weapons, and most of the highest-grossing film and TV glorifies violence in a way that serves as advertisement for weapons.

I am not the only person who reads incredible reviews for plays or movies or TV shows that turn out to be banal, repetitive, reductive, or nonsensical. Part of the problem is that print and online critical publications are tied to the marketplace. Critics mostly write about books or actors or writers or filmmakers who have a new product on the market right now, rather than works that the critic feels illuminate our current moment.

It occurs to me that most (not all) of these institutions that drive me crazy have historically and consistently excluded, watered down, or marginalized the more interesting and necessary ideas in any given period. Risky and exciting movements of forward-thinking people were usually debased or ignored, while avoidant or repetitive work was elevated and glorified, and then given awards. This system of repetition is reinforced psychologically by the creation and strict maintenance of a scarcity-based concept of an elite. If an artist or intellectual or activist or any combination thereof is looking for non-market-based support adequate to live safely and comfortably while following their gifts full-time, it's literally a MacArthur or nothing. Repetitive ideas are selected by gatekeepers, elevated by critics, rewarded with prizes, and branded as good and important, when they are often actually stagnant. We have collectively underestimated the ultimate danger of that entrenched cycle. It turned out to be far more sinister than just boring, as corporate entertainment sells bad values about humans being expendable and worth destroying when compared to the risk of losing social status or influence with funders. Cultural producers should be joining the large numbers of people trying to stop this war on Gaza, but either being quiet or supporting the killing is actually consistent with the norm.

How can we have a culture industry that reflects real-world complexity and people's dreams of justice instead of repeating the glorification of weapons, simplistic ideas about relationships, and the primary centering of the white male experience and points of view that make them comfortable? I often hear publishers or producers say, proudly, that they choose work that speaks to them personally. It is the identification with this repetition that gets them in power in the first place. And there is an agreement among the people with the power of selection that their taste is objective. So, when artists who are not of the power players' demographics create work that is explicitly about confronting these power structures, articulating a politics of aesthetics in these industries, we are repeatedly told that our work is not art. That it doesn't meet the criteria.

There is nothing like having a male artistic director tell a lesbian writer that her work is "overwritten" when he is producing a four-hour play that should have been two. They search high and low for women or people of color creators whose characters don't notice the selectors' power. For example, New York theater loves plays about white southern "crackers" and how racist they are. But they rarely produce plays about white New Yorkers and our racism. Women or artists of color who are OK with the hierarchies or think they don't matter are considered good entertainment. This opinion, held by gatekeepers, is theorized as "artistic vision" instead of a cyclical manifestation of their power. As a result, huge swaths of experience are so unfamiliar that expressing these examples appears awkward, wrong, didactic. One of the most pressing questions in cultural production in this moment is how we get publics to grapple with their lack of information, with knowledge that has never made its way into commodified forms. How do we have solidarity in an age of ignorance?

THE ZONE OF INTEREST

I am reading my Twitter, now X. I have two frantic feeds, neither of which knows the other exists. One is a passionate, excited, and devoted multitude of posts about the Tony Awards of 2024, unfolding that evening on television. Beloved performers are showered with adoration. Grateful fans, theater professionals, and amateurs are cheering wildly for their favorite works and the high levels of skill and commitment that these artists display. Standouts include a play about a Fleetwood Mac–like band; a play that continues the American fascination with white southern families who lose their money; a devastating work about a mother dealing with the reality of her child's incurable illness; a new adaptation of a classic; a juke box musical; a few musical versions of movies—some bold, some comforting, and, of course, revivals.

Counterposed on my X that same evening is an international, multi-language, devastated, angry, desperate feed about ongoing shattering of lives and futures in Gaza, images of Israeli sadism included: people destroying food intended to aid the five hundred thousand starving Palestinians, soldiers playing sharpshooting games with live targets, mocking TikToks made by Israeli soldiers desecrating the ruins of people's lives that they have just deliberately destroyed.

These two conversations and experiences never seemed to meet.

I keep checking the posts about the Tony Awards to see if anyone says anything concerning the world, or even our own nation. Finally, there is one much retweeted quotation from a winner calling for more arts funding, how it is a requirement for "a civilized society." There is applause of appreciation and recognition; the quote and clip will be posted and reposted with gratitude for days to come. And of course, he is correct—it is absurd that we do not have arts funding in the United States of America.

A few months before at the Oscars, it was a little different. The winner in the category of International Feature Film was *The Zone of Interest*, a coproduction of the UK, Poland, and the United States. It had also been a finalist for Best Picture, which went instead to

Oppenheimer. On the surface, *The Zone of Interest* is a Holocaust film about the Nazi commandant of Auschwitz whose family home, where he raised his children, shared a wall with the extermination camp he oversaw. The film never enters the camp. We see the smoke, we hear some sounds, but the point of view lies strictly with the Nazi family on this side of the wall. On this side of the wall, they have a swimming pool, while the invisible people on the other side have no food. The people on this side have luxury items; they eat healthy, opulent meals; they give their children expensive presents; they tuck those children in and read them stories. Their servants clean their homes and change their sheets. We never see the others, but we know they are being exterminated. Had *The Zone of Interest* functioned only on the level of this story I just described, it would have been an exquisitely executed retread of information we already know and are, in some ways, comfortably familiar with. But there is a unique experience to watching this film: that wall! After a while, as we watch, the past and present resonate, and then they begin to merge—but all the transformation takes place inside us, the viewers. The film's narrative stays in the past, but its meaning engulfs the present. That wall becomes the Israeli separation wall, where one side fills swimming pools, while on the other side Palestinian villages have no water. One side controls the other, while tucking their children in to sleep in comfortable beds. And now that side is eliminating the other.

The winner, director and writer Jonathan Glazer, then takes this moment of personal recognition and, almost trembling—not with happiness but with fear—makes the following statement:

> All our choices were made to reflect and confront us in the present, not to say *Look what they did then*, rather *Look what we do now*. Our film shows where dehumanization

leads, at its worst. It's shaped all of our past and present. Right now we stand here as men who refute their Jewishness and the Holocaust being hijacked by an occupation which has led to conflict for so many innocent people. Whether the victims of October . . . whether the victims of October the seventh in Israel or the ongoing attack on Gaza, all the victims of this dehumanization—how do we resist?

In many ways this is a modest statement—that the intense violence, murder, and cultural destruction that Jews experienced historically by Nazis produced the violence against Palestinians that Israel is committing today is a well-known interpretation of the cycle of violence, a frequent explanation of the current cataclysm that equates Israeli and Palestinian suffering.

Glazer's work had already made this statement. He wasn't coming to the stage like many predecessors, winning for repetitive, familiar content, awkwardly squeezing in some unrelated political comment after thanking their agents. But I wondered if the people in the film industry who voted for him fully realized what the film was actually about—how intentional the dual meaning, which he confirmed in his acceptance speech, clearly was. I wonder how many of them thought it was only about the victimization of the Jews, and not also about the victimization by us. I wondered if there were people out there who thought *The Zone of Interest* was a sensitive, gorgeous, searing film only about bad Nazis and poor us.

Of course, he had to be punished for being one of the few public figures to speak the simple truth on American television, the truth that the entertainment and media industries had so studiously avoided that it sounded strange. That was March 10, 2024.

By March 18, over one thousand Jewish "creatives and professionals" signed their names to a public denunciation of Jonathan

Glazer's words that reiterated the meaning of his film, which had just won an Oscar. No one had denounced it before. Either they hadn't seen it, or they had not understood it. Signers included powerful and prominent actors, executives, creators, directors, producers, and agents. They wrote:

> The use of words like "occupation" to describe an indigenous Jewish people defending a homeland that dates back thousands of years and has been recognized as a state by the United Nations, distorts history.

The United Nations does recognize the state of Israel, and it also recognizes that Israel has occupied Palestinian land. To quote from the United Nations official document "The Question of Palestine":

> In the 1967 war, Israel occupied these territories (Gaza Strip and the West Bank) including East Jerusalem, which was subsequently annexed by Israel.

On May 28, 2024, days after this letter was published, the "state of Palestine" was also recognized by the vast majority of member states of the United Nations.

I was surprised that so many powerful and intelligent people's first objection was to Glazer stating the globally recognized and simple fact that Israel has militarily occupied land where Palestinians currently live or formerly lived before they were militarily displaced. Whether you count that from the creation of the Jewish state in 1948 or you date that from the military occupation of Palestinian land in the war of 1967, it is irrefutable that Palestinians' lives are controlled by Israel, and they are occupied. I would have expected the signers to justify that occupation, not to claim that it doesn't exist. This was so weird.

Equally peculiar is that so many worldly and, in many cases, secular people would use biblical justification for Jewish dominance of land that is inhabited by more than one people. Yes, it is certainly true that there have been Arab Jews coexisting with Arab Muslims, Arab Christians, and Druze throughout different empires and collective histories. Jews were an integrated part of the Arab world before the current created false binary of Jews versus Arabs; forty to fifty percent of Jews in Israel are of Arab origin from a range of nations including Iraq, Yemen, Egypt, Morocco, and Palestine. And so, Arab Jews were among the range of peoples indigenous to the region. But, for over one thousand people who have significant roles in the corporate creation of American arts and entertainment to think that Jews are the only indigenous people to that area, or that European Jews are indigenous to the Middle East, simply doesn't make any sense.

The letter further stated that these one thousand Jews believe that Glazer's statement

> gives credence to the modern blood libel that fuels a grow-
> ing anti-Jewish hatred around the world, in the United States,
> and in Hollywood.

"Blood libel" is an antisemitic claim, originating in the Middle Ages, falsely accusing Jews of vampirishly using the blood of Christian children to make Passover matzah. It is pretty crazy that so many people were willing to sign a letter interpreting Glazer's call for an end to using the Holocaust to justify murdering Palestinians as the same as him saying that Jews kill Christian children to make matzah. Medieval Jews, who were a vulnerable and often blamed minority, did not kill Christian children, but the thousand signers are betraying an unconscious association because Israelis, with American money, are killing children, daily and in large numbers. Save the Children estimates that twenty thousand missing Gazan children are "lost, disappeared, detained, buried under the rubble" by Israel since October 2023.

It is possible that Israel murdering children is contributing to anti-Jewish feelings "around the world, in the United States, and in Hollywood" and that this is growing. As long as the military and social policies of the state of Israel are seen as equivalent to world Jewry—Jews who do not live in Israel—this will continue to be the case. So, the people who keep insisting that criticizing Israel equals antisemitism are feeding this conflation.

I'm sitting in LA across the table from an old friend I love and respect. She is smart, kind, hardworking. From a modest Jewish background, she has earned millions of dollars working in corporate television. She is so upset about Israel's violence in Gaza. She is devastated. She looks around to make sure no one in the restaurant can hear her criticize Israel. She won't sign anything; she won't say anything in public. It could hurt her professionally. This is a common response that I have heard from many people in entertainment who I consider to be friends. They are afraid to say what they believe to be true because of the thousand people who signed their names and the thousands more who didn't sign but feel the same way. My feeling is that yes, doors will close—but those people don't control everything; other doors will open. In some strange way my silent friends believe the myth that the Zionist Jews who are punitive against other perspectives control all the entertainment industries. I, on the other hand, do not believe that. Let's face it, if my friend were correct, you would not be reading this book right now, and it wouldn't have been published by Penguin Random House.

It takes until April 5 to gather five hundred signatures to a new document, carefully and specifically titled "Jewish Creatives Supporting Jonathan Glazer's Oscars Speech."

We honor the Holocaust by saying: Never again for anyone. . . . We should be able to name Israel's apartheid and occupation—both recognized by leading human rights organization as such—without being accused of rewriting history.

Comparable to its predecessor, this letter includes signers who are composers, actors, writers, producers, showrunners, directors, and members of the Israeli film industry—but also visual artists. The names include Debra Winger, Todd Haynes, Chloe Fineman, Elliot Gould, Joaquin Phoenix, Joel Coen, Hari Nef, Tom Stoppard, James Schamus, Nicole Holofcener, Mike Leigh, Ira Sachs, Tavi Gevinson, Wallace Shawn, Emma Seligman, Lola Kirke, Ilana Glazer, Abbi Jacobson, Annie Baker, Molly Crabapple, Deborah Eisenberg, Nicole Eisenman, Naomi Foner, Noah Galvin, Sam Gold, Nan Goldin, Michael Greif, Miranda July, Naomi Klein, Jonathan Lethem, Kyle Lukoff, Alan Menken, Benjamin Moser, Laraine Newman, Francine Prose, Jeff Preiss, Mark Rappaport, Jacqueline Rose, Jane Schoenbrun, Amy Sillman, Gillian Slovo, Morgan Spector, Mattilda Bernstein Sycamore, Lynne Tillman, and many others—and me.

THREE CASE STUDIES OF ART WORLD SOLIDARITY (OR LACK THEREOF)

Joey Soloway, *Transparent*, and the Boycott of Israel

Television producer Joey Soloway started out as a writer on the TV classic *Six Feet Under*. After a Sundance directing win in 2013 for their feature *Afternoon Delight*, they made history with *Transparent*, an Amazon series about a dysfunctional family whose parent comes out as trans. In their book *She Wants It: Desire, Power, and Toppling the Patriarchy*, Joey opened the door to a public airing of how a BDS campaign influenced the Emmy-winning and paradigm-changing *Transparent*. The five-season show is about a Jewish family whose father starts transitioning to her life as a woman and the reactions of her wife and three adult children, all of whom have trouble taking responsibility for their own lives. While Joey and I have different lenses, focuses, and details in how we each tell the story, we both agree on the central fact: *Transparent* was profoundly affected by the Boycott, Divestment, Sanctions movement ultimately because of Joey's willingness to talk, listen, and rethink.

At some point Joey decided that season four of the highly successful series would be shot in Israel. A number of people among the writers and coproducers, almost all of whom got their professional starts with *Transparent*, objected, hesitantly. But because they were not tied to the BDS political movement, Joey proceeded with plans to bring actors and crew to Israel to film. I believe that Amazon higher-ups had approved the unusual proposal; in fact, I think location scouting had already begun. What made the specter of *Transparent* violating the boycott of Israel such a crisis was that it had the extra-special problem of pinkwashing: legitimizing the Israeli status quo through association with a major queer production. The potential nightmare of all the Israeli propaganda that would accompany these episodes was truly daunting. Israel would clearly use this intersection to advertise itself as "progressive" because trans and queer representation coded for modernity, despite the brutal occupation of the Palestinian territories and second-class citizenship of Palestinians living in Israel. Simultaneously, this would have been the most internationally visible representation of US trans people, and it would have associated them with Israeli apartheid.

I was made aware of this plan via an email from poet and cultural icon Eileen Myles, Joey's ex. I took it to Jewish Voice for Peace, and the then-director Rebecca Vilkomerson, whom I revered, advised me to write to Joey and ask them for a conversation. I also spoke to a trans producer inside the show who opposed the filming and had been bringing in information internally. For the next three months, a campaign of conversation was organized.

Now, as a person who does this kind of thing regularly, I have found that the people we are trying to talk to are usually very, very hostile. Especially in corporate settings, people feel that they are above uncomfortable conversations and should not be asked to have in-person meetings that could raise questions that are inconvenient to grapple with. No matter how much damage they do to cultural progress, these people think they are creating culture, not stopping it.

Not Joey Soloway.

They not only agreed to live conversation (not email) but also reached out to other BDS supporters to gather more information and points of view. In fact, Joey had a range of conversations with a variety of JVP members, as well as a number of Palestinians living in America, and they even reached out to Omar Barghouti in Ramallah, West Bank. Unfortunately that scheduled Skype had to be canceled when Omar was arrested by Israeli officials and held overnight as part of a regular intimidation campaign against him. Quickly, Joey listened to what people had to say and started to internalize the substance of the issues at hand. I think the real turning point was when Joey received a private letter signed by twenty-three trans activists, sent by law professor Dean Spade—who had been on that first LGBT delegation to Palestine a few years before. They asked Joey not to film *Transparent* in Israel.

As a result, despite all the original planning, Joey was not rigidly fixed and dramatically changed the conditions for *Transparent* season four. Instead of filming in Israel, they shot the whole season in Los Angeles, finding L.A. landscapes that looked like Israel and Palestine. Not a single actor was sent to Israel. As far as I understand, they constructed a fake Wailing Wall set on a lot at Paramount. Unfortunately, they did film cutaways in Israel, location shots without actors. I had suggested using archival footage instead, and I wish they had been fully consistent in honoring the Palestinian call, but shooting all the live scenes in L.A. was significant, historic, and a groundbreaking recognition.

When I watched season four, I saw many representations that I had never seen in a corporate American product before. The story and characters included queer Palestinians. They showed Black and Palestinian solidarity. They showed the insanity and danger of checkpoints. When I ran into Joey almost a year later, I said, "Thank you for changing your mind." It felt so rare and so good to be able to say that to a person with real power. My impression is that the thirty to thirty-five people I know of who were directly involved in this campaign also felt like it was a significant outcome. If more people with actual power were willing to listen and talk and go through an experience of exchange of ideas, change would come a lot faster and go further. And as my own experience of this movement always shows me, people needing solidarity are often available to talk.

Jeremy O. Harris and the Plight of Women Playwrights

Being a woman playwright is a nightmare. Men run the industry, so what you write must fit their criteria.

The degrading experiences are relentless. In a weird way we are treated in the traditional way unfamous actresses are treated: not as an equal, a dime a dozen, not as someone to be accountable to, but as a potential mascot.

Everything you could possibly imagine takes place, and a lot beyond your imagination. Recently a producer told me he has held one of my plays that he had agreed to read, without reading it, for over ten years. So, I said, "Why don't you read it now?" And he said, "Sarah, you took it like a man." How ironic. Actually, I took it like a woman playwright. There is one director who has promised to read a play of mine for twenty-one years; he still comments from time to time on my Facebook page, and occasionally emails me, asking me to resend the play, as he rises up the ladder. But he has never, ever read it. And so on, and so on, and so on.

Over four decades ago I emerged as a playwright into a world of all-white, all-male theatrical seasons, with white male artistic directors and white male critics. I don't have an MFA, so I didn't have a mentor or a brand. I'm included in a group photo hanging in the downstairs bathroom at Playwrights Horizons with a roomful of white men, a handful of women, and a few Black people. That's how it was. Over the decades I have watched support, invitations, and professional development be handed to multiple generations of men of a wide range of ability, constantly inaugurating the new darling. I have had two plays off-Broadway with Playwrights Horizons, one at the regional Wilma Theater in Philadelphia, and one at the Provincetown Theater on Cape Cod, which won a new play award, but they vetoed my next work, about *Roe v. Wade*, saying it was "too risky." They replaced it, first with *The Fantasticks* and then the second time with that old chestnut *Angels in America*. I have won a Guggenheim in playwrighting, have had workshops and readings everywhere: the Goodman Theatre, the Cleveland Play House, Vineyard Theatre,

Roundabout Theatre, and New York Theatre Workshop (where the male artistic director told me he wished my play about *Roe v. Wade* "had more from the man's perspective"). And I currently have three plays and one musical in the development/reading/workshop hamster wheel.

The problem of lesbian protagonists is particularly difficult. To date, there is no play with fully realized adult lesbian protagonists in the American theatrical canon—that is, in which women have sex with each other and don't die. I think we hoped the crossover of gay male plays would help, but those men were not interested in us. Then the hope that the increase in women getting productions would help, but that also did not translate. Then, I hoped the theater's burst of rhetoric about "diversity and inclusion" would include us, but it doesn't. But there is one man, in my many years of playwrighting, who actually tried and succeeded at helping women playwrights, and he is the only man I have ever encountered who actually risked his own play to help women get produced.

The second-tier status of women playwrights, especially those over fifty, who had emerged into highly segregated programming, got a moment in the spotlight in 2021 when L.A.'s Center Theatre Group announced a ten-play Mark Taper Forum season for 2020–21. Only one was by a woman, a revival of a play by Pearl Cleage. Many shouted out in anger and pain but to no avail. Then, Jeremy O. Harris responded by threatening to pull his transfer from Broadway, *Slave Play*, from the upcoming season.

If this has ever happened before, I've never heard of any man risking giving up anything so that women can get fair treatment. Especially in the buddy-buddy world that is the American theater. Harris had already taken chances to make his Tony-nominated play financially and socially accessible to Black audiences. He created "Black Out" nights for Black-only audiences so that theatergoers could see this highly provocative play about sex and race and relationships, without having to deal with white attitudes. He created very low-cost tickets. He invited Black people to the Broadway stage in clear and innovative ways. But then he stepped up to help women. Black women included, of course—but he actually stepped up to help all women. This bold threat was such a shock to the system that it actually worked. Center Theatre Group soon announced that Harris would remain in the lineup, but they committed to programming the following season with work written only by women and nonbinary playwrights.

The move was essential and the opportunity filled with promise. What would happen if one of the nation's most prestigious theaters did a season of new work by a wide range (race, age, sexuality, aesthetics, point of view) of underproduced women playwrights? It could change the tenor of the future of the American theater! It was so exciting. Who knew what could come of it? Maybe all the theaters in the country would realize that it was time to turn a corner, and for an entire season new works by underproduced woman would become the national culture. All those perspectives and ideas and stories that had never been seen on stage before! It would create a new audience, and new standards, and new aesthetic and political opportunities, and we'd finally have a public conversation instead of a secret one. It would all finally happen! And this thought was also sobering. Was that really all it took? For one successful man to put his foot down? It was actually that easy. Wow. Think about how different our lives would have been if someone else had tried this twenty-five years ago. But this was finally happening, and it was happening now.

At that point in history, fewer than one third of the plays produced in the US were by women, according to a survey by the Dramatists Guild. Women over fifty, especially women of color "who led the path to diversity we now enjoy," the guild reported in a follow-up email, "do not appear to have directly benefitted." Women did fight back. In 2018, playwright and television writer Jacquelyn Reingold—known for the series *In Treatment, Smash*, and *The Good Fight*—and some of her colleagues formed Honor Roll!, an organization that advocates with artistic directors for productions for women playwrights over fifty. The group has 1,300 members. Their goal is for theaters to create slots for women over fifty, in recognition of the deep-seated industry prejudice that has kept older women playwrights from the same kinds of theatrical development and opportunities that their male peers have had. But this twist of fate created by Jeremy O. Harris provided the opportunity for a paradigm shift. Jeremy had a fantasy. And so did we women playwrights. We might finally get our chance, because this time it was a man who was forcing our inclusion, instead of being the power stopping us at the door.

(Postscript: The all-women season promised to Jeremy O. Harris by the Mark Taper Forum was later revealed to consist of the following: a revival of Lily Tomlin and Jane Wagner's 1985 *The Search for Signs of Intelligent Life in the Universe*, a production of *Clyde's* by Lynn Nottage—the most produced play of that year—a revival of Anna Deavere Smith's *Twilight: Los Angeles, 1992*, and a musical stage adaptation of the television show *Transparent*.)

The Case of *Artforum*

I am having dinner with an old friend. He is a great guy who has spent his life on the right side of everything, as well as being an activist and educator. He's so excited about a new article he's been working on and it sounds great. Then, the punch line: "It's coming out in *Artforum*."

"*Artforum*? What about the boycott?"

"Is that still on?"

Yes, it is.

The day before our dinner, June 22, 2024, Israelis killed over one hundred Palestinians in Gaza, making it one of the deadliest dates since the mass killing began.

A month before, on May 24, *Hyperallergic*, a progressive art magazine, reported that both PACBI and the BDS movement had emphasized the importance of the ongoing boycott of *Artforum* since the sudden firing of editor David Velasco for publishing an open letter on October 19, 2023, from eight thousand artists opposing the Israeli assault on civilians in Gaza. Subsequently, seven hundred previous contributors, including me, Andrea Fraser, Dodie Bellamy, Rosalyn Deutsche, Jennifer Doyle, Rochelle Feinstein, Alex Fialho, Sasha Frere-Jones, Kay Gabriel, Nan Goldin, Ariel Goldberg, Bruce Hainley, Sharon Hayes, J. Hoberman, Hua Hsu, Barbara Kruger, Simon Leung, Tiona Nekkia McClodden, Tavia Nyong'o, Laura Poitras, Christina Sharpe, Helen Shaw, and hundreds of others committed to withdrawing our participation in the magazine and sister publication, *Art in America*.

PACBI's reinforcing announcement of the boycott called Velasco's firing "shameful repression" that reflects a broader "pervasive anti-Palestinian censorship." It urged others to respect "the picket line drawn by hundreds of previous contributors." "As things continue to get worse for the people of Palestine in Gaza and elsewhere, this moment is an essential one for reminding people of why it's important not just to speak, but to act," said Tobi Haslett, a former *Artforum* contributor.

What provoked this reminder to boycott was the hiring of a replacement editor, Tina Rivers Ryan, a former curator at the Buffalo AKG Art Museum, and her announcement that she would do an issue on two Palestinian artists.

Writers Against the War on Gaza responded with a public letter calling the magazine "Scabforum." "You were hired because he was fired for supporting Palestinian liberation," the letter said.

So, what about my friend? He had this look of terror in his eyes like we were going to have a fight or something. I just smiled, lowered my voice, and asked softly, "Why are you publishing there?" To be honest, I expected some kind of predictable answer, like "I don't believe in boycotts," or "I have family in Israel," or some kind of explanation or justification. But instead he explained, sincerely, "It is important." He felt his article was important, and the magazine was important, and the subject was important, and I concluded that he wanted to feel important. It was about success. Two days later *The New York Times* reported that five hundred thousand people faced starvation in Gaza.

What does it mean to be a success when we are funding a genocide?

One of the greatest obstacles to progress toward peace and justice is fear of disapproval and desire for status. Everywhere there are people who know that killing is wrong, and that mass killing and starvation are war crimes. But they are afraid of losing opportunities and falling out of favor. Facing the decision of whether to support a powerless person is a spotlight. Who are you really? Unfortunately, there is no relationship between justice and reward or quality and reward, and I say this as a person who has experienced both reward and derision. Most behavior that is rewarded in an unjust society reinforces its operative values. But not all. Occasionally something or someone who is actually making a real contribution to a more revealed and forward-moving world is rewarded. But it is crucial not to be fooled by the allure of acceptance, as much as we all want it and should have it, because people thrive with attachment and belonging. That is why we have to create communities of conscience of which we can be a part.

We all need places to talk, in real life, about what we experience and understand, even if it is contradicted by corporate news, arts, and entertainment. We need relationships of original thought, to be able to evaluate the power institutions that dictate opinion and frame the questions. I have come to understand that when *The New York Times* calls the assault on Gaza a "conflict"—implying two equal sides—this is the same machine that tells us which are the century's most notable books. The government that funds this slaughter regardless of public opinion is the same machine that provides National Endowment for the Arts grants. Approval and support are not separate from the sources of the powers that oppose us. Facing this is a lifelong process, because giving up crass patriotism may not mean weaning ourselves completely from the myth of the American dream of meritocracy, of being discovered and making it or "breaking out" and being the next big thing. These hopes are rooted in a pervasive branding and marketing that keeps us from fully penetrating the American facade.

In the end, many people are driven by a fear of losing opportunities. Many think of themselves as having good politics, but living what we believe is a different challenge. Solidarity helps us think of ourselves in close proximity to afflicted people whom the machine keeps outside consciousness. So, I am asking my friend to decide to place himself next to people he will never meet, who will probably never have power over his career. To give up what he feels he needs— publishing an "important" article in a boycotted magazine—in order to be part of something larger. A world of accountability and cross-identification.

Through many, many experiences of navigating these kinds of

waters, I believe that what a person wants more than anything, deep down, is to feel comfortable with themselves. What writers want more than fame, money, even more than approval, is to feel deep in our hearts that we are good writers. And that someone cares about what we are writing. That it means something to the people at the heart of the work. If we can each go through the process of acknowledging these larger stakes, we can say no to *Artforum*.

CARSON McCULLERS: WHITE WRITER AND HER ATTITUDE TOWARD LIFE

Throughout this volume I have shone the spotlight on individuals— Wilmette Brown, Alice Neel, Jean Genet—who practiced iconoclastic acts of solidarity from a multitude of motivations. They were far from saints, and their psychologies of solidarity and opposition were complex. But each was brilliant in their own way, and very creative. Their flawed individuality can inspire us to look for routes toward solidarity that are in line with our characters, inclinations, and talents. Into this mix, I want to add the example of my absolute favorite writer, Carson McCullers, who reached out in her own way to cross the color bar. And I want to show how her literary actions were meaningful in 1940 to her colleague Richard Wright, and then resonated for me more than seventy-five years later.

In 2016, there was an escalating public debate about the social role of the white writer, stimulated by the novelist Lionel Shriver's speech at a literary festival in early September of that year. It was a cultural moment that made white writers look in the mirror and wonder if we have been confusing it with a window. White writers are not used to being objectified in this way. One of our conceits has been to imagine ourselves as neutral, objective, and value-free.

Yet this sense of "objectivity" is itself constructed, organized, and enforced. And within the context of pervasive racism, with specifics of racist police violence, attacks on teaching about slavery, and obstruction to voting, it is particularly striking that the current incarnation of this old question has reemerged in the language of "rights." As Shriver told her audience:

> Taken to their logical conclusion, ideologies recently come into vogue challenge our right to write fiction at all. Meanwhile, the kind of fiction we are "allowed" to write is in danger of becoming so hedged, so circumscribed, so tippy-toe, that we'd indeed be better off not writing the anodyne drivel to begin with.

Shriver conveyed an image of white writers besieged by fierce and powerful forces that are leveraging punitive controls. Yet, despite her stance, many writers of color have generously responded to her talk instead of dismissing it with silence. The African American novelist Kaitlyn Greenidge wrote in *The New York Times*:

> It's the wish not so much to be able to write a character of another race, but to do so without criticism. And at the heart of that rather ludicrous request is a question of power.

The writer Viet Thanh Nguyen, in the *Los Angeles Times*, contextualized the debate in terms of material realities:

> It is possible to write about others not like oneself, if one understands that this is not simply an act of culture and free speech, but one that is enmeshed in a complicated, painful history of ownership and division.

But what of the white writer who wishes to be artistically engaged but simultaneously does not want to re-create cultural dominance in her work? Are there complex, nuanced representations by other white people that we might turn toward? I suggest that one answer may lie in the unlikely legacy of a pale, sickly woman from the midtwentieth century, who smoked and drank herself to death by the age of fifty, and whose own personal turmoil and self-destruction may be at the root of the enormous insights about difference found throughout her work, still inspiring and resonating in our own time.

In 1940, a white twenty-three-year-old novelist, slight and awkwardly charming, from segregated Georgia, published an extraordinary novel, *The Heart Is a Lonely Hunter*. Richard Wright, the Black author of *Native Son*, in his review in *The New Republic*, wrote:

> To me the most impressive aspect of "The Heart Is a Lonely Hunter" is the astonishing humanity that enables a white writer, for the first time in Southern fiction, to handle Negro characters with as much ease and justice as those of her own race. This cannot be accounted for stylistically or politically; it seems to stem from an attitude toward life which enables Miss McCullers to rise above the pressures of her environment and embrace white and black humanity in one sweep of apprehension and tenderness.

The writer in question was Lula Carson Smith, known to history as Carson McCullers. In her subsequent novels *Reflections in a Golden Eye*, *The Member of the Wedding*, and *Clock Without Hands* (typed with one finger after she was paralyzed from multiple strokes), in the novella and story collection *The Ballad of the Sad Café*, in the memoir *Illumination and Night Glare* (dictated from her sickbed), and in two plays, *The Member of the Wedding* and *The Square Root of Wonderful*, McCullers inhabits a startlingly broad range of characters: a Jewish gay deaf man, a dwarf, a Black Marxist doctor and his adult children, a gay Filipino man, and a number of role-defying white girls with great dreams. McCullers had an almost singular ability to humanize any kind of person, many of whom had never appeared in American literature before she created them.

For example, Dr. Benedict Mady Copeland, of *The Heart Is a Lonely Hunter*, defies most Black characters created by white authors, in any era. Middle-class and educated, Copeland is a physician, whose family life is emotionally complex; intellectually, he is a Marxist:

> All that we own is our bodies. And we sell our bodies every day we live. We sell them when we go out in the morning to our jobs and when we labor all the day. We are forced to sell at any price, at any time, for any purpose. We are forced to sell our bodies so that we can eat and live. And the price which is given us for this is only enough so that we will have the strength to labor longer for the profits of others.

In my experience, the only contemporary writer who approaches McCullers's breadth of characterization is Caryl Phillips, the novelist from St. Kitts, who can inhabit a white male slave owner so in love with a Black slave that he frees him and then reverses the crossing to chase him to Liberia; or a white woman in the 1820s, discovering the Caribbean for the first time; or other masterful illuminations of perspectives not his own. But McCullers remains the standard-bearer for white authors, and for almost twenty-five years now I have been on a journey to try to understand how she did it. Who does a white writer have to be in order to overcome the institutionalized ignorance in which we are trained and shrouded?

It would be easy to assume that someone with this gift had great empathy for others. But I think it's fair to say that this was not the source of McCullers's inspiration. I've had the opportunity to talk to a number of people who knew her before her early death, in 1967. One was the late writer Tobias Schneebaum, who was famed for having lived with "cannibals"—one of whom was his male lover, with whom he consumed human flesh. In his eighties, he told me about working as the secretary to the novelist Isabel Bolton in the 1940s, when she invited McCullers to lunch. McCullers showed up with three drunken sailors; chaos ensued. The late sculptor and diarist Anne Truitt, also in her eighties when we spoke, told me of the time she and her husband (an editor at *Time*) threw a party for McCullers in their Washington, D.C., home. McCullers showed up in a kimono and sat in a corner, refusing to mingle with the guests. The thing about these stories is that they were told with great glee, as though McCullers were still alive. And yet they were always about her making a scene or creating problems, usually having to do with drinking. A picture emerges of a vulnerable person, but not a hugely empathetic one. As I read her work over and over, and read other people's accounts and theories about her, I started to develop a picture of my own.

Years before Caitlyn Jenner or *Transparent*, I started to notice that McCullers had issues with her gender. The first evidence was the most superficial. Her given name was Lula, but she took on her middle name and mother's family name, Carson, reminiscent of the American cowboy Kit Carson. She wore men's clothes and was often photographed in a suit. Her main protagonists were young, boyish girls with men's names: Frankie and Mick. In fact, Carson invented this American prototype of the queerish tomboy girl, now a classic, later seen in *To Kill a Mockingbird*, *Harriet the Spy*, and eventually *Bastard Out of Carolina*. But there was more to it than that. As I met and spoke to more McCullers enthusiasts, it became apparent that what appeared to be her constant womanizing really came to nothing. Although she was married twice to the doomed Reeves McCullers, who had a brief relationship with the composer David Diamond, Carson notoriously chased women whom she never got, and actually never wanted.

On the surface, the story looked like a standard-issue lesbian trajectory, starting with a deep attachment to a music teacher, Mary Tucker, who helped McCullers attend Juilliard in classical piano. This was followed by a typical McCullers misadventure with a prostitute she met in New York who took all her money, forcing her back home to Columbus, Georgia. But then it became more overt. McCullers was deeply in love with a Swiss journalist, a lesbian drug addict named Annemarie Schwarzenbach, who in photographs appears to be a butch goddess—yet it was never consummated. At Yaddo, the artists' residency where she lived for two years and wrote *The Member of the Wedding*, McCullers was famously attached to Katherine Anne Porter, whose fame paralleled Philip Roth's in her time. Porter hated Carson and kept her protégée Eudora Welty seated at a separate table for dinner, far from the rowdy queers: Carson, Truman Capote, and Newton Arvin (later fired from Smith College for ordering muscle magazines in the mail). But I found it unusual that after all the years of loving and chasing women, many of whom were gay, Carson never slept with any of them. A fellow McCullers disciple, the late Dan Griffen, once told me that when McCullers and her best friend Tennessee Williams shared a summer house on Nantucket—where she wrote the stage version of *The Member of the Wedding* and he wrote *Summer and*

Smoke at the same table—she told him that she had slept with her housemate Gypsy Rose Lee, the celebrity stripper. But Dan found it odd that she told this to no one else, including her openly gay cousin, Jordan Massee. As Dan pointed out, "If you lived with Gypsy, wouldn't you say you'd slept with her, too?"

I started to realize that McCullers's gender trouble was not of the homosexual kind, and it slowly dawned on me that had she been alive today, not only would McCullers (and Williams and Capote) have probably been in AA and on antidepressants, but she might also have been living as a transgender man. She did once tell Capote, "I think I was born a boy," which doesn't, in and of itself, mean much—but how many of us, as little girls, have never had that thought? Most.

It may be that the "ease" with which Carson McCullers was able to inhabit any kind of person, in a manner that was recognizable to a reader as sophisticated as Richard Wright, did not come from empathy. No, perhaps this ease came from the simple fact of having an identity that history had not yet fully recognized. And because she didn't know who she was, she had no place to stand. So, she could stand with others who officially did not exist. That coincidence of experience, in combination with a hugely original natural talent, was aided by an unusually supportive mother who recognized her genius. Such maternal insistence was so rare, it might have been enough to let a person's genius come through. But, additionally, Carson held an organic understanding of the difference between justice and injustice, and with a writerly lens of a dreamlike surrealistic quality, much like the hanging heat of West Georgia, produced a model white writer for all of us to learn from. It gives us someone to aspire to, even if her experience is something that we can never reach. Amid her legacy is the revelation that profound solidarity with Black readers was accomplished at a level—so legible as to move a major Black writer—that could come not from consciousness, but from an unconsciousness, an undiscovered country, that lay within Carson's self.

What kind of solidarity is this? It functions on so many levels. McCullers, who was descended from Georgia enslavers, made the conscious decision to rebel against Southern norms. She publicly equated Southern racism with German Nazism and called her home of Georgia "a fascist state." "I must return to the South from time to time," she said, "to renew my sense of horror." So, the first identifiable solidarity in her work is the conscious resistance to white supremacy; she was what has been called "a race traitor."

But the second realization of her solidarity requires more than will. She was able, almost miraculously, to look so deeply into the human condition that she could depict scenes of Black people discussing their own differences in a way that Richard Wright, one of the most prominent Black writers of her time, could recognize a breakthrough in white anti-racist consciousness. Like the internal refugees in Gaza standing outside their tents acknowledging that they are being supported and seen by students on American campuses, Wright acknowledged a recognition that he described as occurring "for the first time in Southern fiction." The solidarity was so singular and therefore important that it reached him with enough significance to move him to say so publicly.

But even more particular is that Wright recognized this solidarity coming from a very individual place. He didn't attribute it to self-education or ideology, but rather to something more intimate and elusive that he called "an attitude towards life." It is only decades later, as we start to understand McCullers's complex and elusive sexual and gender identity, that this "attitude towards life" takes on content. Her difference, and her inability to understand fully that difference, opened the door to enable her to see others in a manner that transcended her training. This is a constitutional solidarity, a very specific kind of person, who is able to translate her own alienation into something of value to the most oppressed people of her time. This is a solidarity of both consciousness and the unconscious, of awareness and desire and instinct. And that it reached the person for whom the relationship of understanding was intended is a partial sign of its success. For one of the highest forms of solidarity is to let the intended recipient feel seen and supported.

8

When Solidarity Fails

"QUEER SUICIDALITY, CONFLICT,
AND REPAIR: THE DEATH OF BRYN KELLY"
(COWRITTEN WITH MORGAN M. PAGE)

(Presented at Le Cagibi in Montreal on October 10, 2016)

As you will learn by reading the transcript of this group conversation, the death of an artist, Bryn Kelly, and the response of her community created a tension that writer and historian Morgan M. Page and I decided to address in a public event. This story is filled with both failed and partial solidarities, and then a constituted attempt at repair: teacher-student, cis-trans, sister intellectuals, and generational divides within expanded communities.

Morgan M. Page is a trans writer, historian, and artist based in London. She is the cowriter of the Sundance award-winning film *Framing Agnes* and the book *Boys Don't Cry*.

MORGAN M. PAGE (MMP): I'm Morgan. I'll more fully introduce myself in a minute. I just wanted to, like, say hello and get the attention of the room and let you all know that this event is Queer Conversations: Suicidality, Conflict, and Repair. Obviously, this is a very emotionally loaded subject for probably most of us, right? So, if you feel like you need to leave at any point, don't feel bad, just, you know, do what you need to do to take care of yourself. We've also posted, albeit not a comprehensive list, a small list of resources for follow-up afterwards, if you feel like you need counseling or anything like that.

I also wanted to begin . . . by acknowledging the fact that not only is it Indigenous Peoples' Day today, we're also, obviously—I hope obviously—on occupied Indigenous land, the traditional territories, I believe but I may be wrong, of the Haudenosaunee and Algonquin, and any conversation that is about conflict on occupied territories really shouldn't ignore the fact that these conflicts are happening on conflicted land, right? That makes sense to everybody? So, I want to make sure that that was kind of the first thing we broached and hopefully it will also continue to be part of the conversation that we have later this evening. So, should we begin? Are we, are we good?

SARAH SCHULMAN (SS): Hi, everyone. I just want to say I'm really, really happy to be here with all of you. Morgan and I met in an airport and we clicked like crazy with a beautiful conversation and the beginning of a really authentic friendship that I'm really honored to be part of and I'm so happy that we're doing this together today. Thank you.

TOM NAKAYAMA (TN): Hi, my name is Tom Nakayama. I'm at Northeastern University in Boston, and, with Chuck Morris who is at Syracuse University in New York, we coedit a journal called *QED*. I'll pass around some information about the journal. One of the regular features of the journal—the journal aims to bring together academics and activists on issues of GLBTQ worldmaking—has been what we call Queer Conversations, which pairs diverse queer worldmakers for an exchange of ideas. This evening, we are pleased to stage this queer conversation with Sarah Schulman and Morgan Page. And so, to begin this queer conversation, I wanted to ask them about their experiences at Bryn's funeral. Do you want to introduce yourselves first?

ss: I'm Sarah Schulman and that's Morgan Page *[laughter]*.

MMP: So, if you don't know us already *[laughter]*.

ss: So, I thought that I would tell a little bit about—a little background—to the eulogy that I wrote and maybe Morgan would like to do the same and let you in on what was happening for each of us, and then we're gonna share our eulogies with you. And just to let you know, mine is seventeen minutes long, so just keep that in mind. So, let me just start.

After Bryn Kelly killed herself, a group of her close friends—closest friends—who were in New York organized the funeral for her. This group included her partner Gaines, myself, and Kelli Dunham, Anna, Alice—a little bunch of us that organized the event and the decision was made to have it at St. John the Divine cathedral, which is an iconic enormous cathedral in New York City, because Bryn was a church person. We had gone to some other churches that were more in her religious tradition but they wanted to charge us, and St. John the Divine felt that they weren't doing enough to support the trans community and so they gave us the space.

So, the decision was made that I would give the central—a large—eulogy and so I wrote the draft and I submitted to the other people who were organizing the event. And we had about three rounds of corrections and comments on the phone and through email and then we met as a group in person to go over the text one more time, and at that point we read the guidelines for people dealing with public events related to suicide and particularly the guidelines for describing the way that people killed themselves, and what we felt that the guidelines said was not to give people instructions on how to kill themselves, that the guidelines said do not say, you know, *Take this number of this drug and mix it with this amount of that*. But that saying the way that the person killed themselves was not the same as telling people how to kill themselves, and the way that she had killed herself was such a big part of the experience. After all, a number of us spent a long time in her house with her body directly after she died.

So, the group went through and changed a lot of things, we all agreed on the text, then a few other people vetted the text. Morgan read the text and also the minister at St. John's, which is an Episcopal church. So, then we had the service and about seven hundred people showed up, many of whom did not know Bryn, and when I gave the eulogy—sitting in the front it was mostly women and then Ted Kerr sitting up in the front. So, there was Ted, there was me, there was Naomi who had been Bryn's roommate, Eva, her girlfriend whose name I don't remember, Morgan, and then Red Durkin. Those were the speakers and we were all seated together in the front. So, when I went up to give my talk—like I said, it was seventeen minutes long—and I really couldn't tell, I really couldn't see the audience, but I could hear Red crying while I was talking. And when I came down from the podium I passed her and she was going to the bathroom and I could see that she was crying. Then I went back and sat next to Naomi and when the service was over Naomi turned to me and hugged me and said, *Thank you for your words*. Eva and her girlfriend hugged me. Morgan, I knew, had already read it and told me that that was exactly what she wanted from the service. So as far as I was concerned, the people that were closest to Bryn, this was something that they could feel good about.

There was one person who felt that it wouldn't be good for Bryn's family to hear the way that she killed herself, and he was opposed to me describing that. However, after the service, Bryn's sister said that it was the most powerful thing she had ever heard, so it turned out that that was something that was meaningful to them. (Editor's note: The family member later denied that she said that.) Anyway, I got about ten messages from people telling me that they appreciated the honesty, and a few people telling me that they had recommitted to staying alive. But the next day there were people online and on Facebook, who were not close to Bryn but who really objected to my eulogy, and very, very, very much so objected. So, I just wanted to say how I understand the objections, what I understood them to be, and how I processed them or understood them.

So, one of the biggest objections was that people said that they had come to the funeral to feel better, and for me, one of the things I realized, what I should have realized before, is that I come from the AIDS generation, I come from the ACT UP generation, and I have been to many, many political funerals. And the concept of the political funeral is present in my mind. It never occurred to me that there are one or two generations that had never experienced a political funeral, and didn't recognize it for what it was. Now I realize that I should have contextualized that at the top. This was a misunderstanding on my part.

The other thing was that I think there were a lot of people who are not used to being live in a room with seven hundred queer people. I think there's a generation of people who have not had that experience before and that's very overwhelming. And I also think that there were people who were so young—and also that because they haven't had the AIDS experience—even with the level of suicide that is present in our community, there were quite a few people there who had either never been to a funeral at all, or had only been to, like, an elder relative or something like that and they were used to a kind of nicety of a formal, traditional funeral, so that thing that for me is very natural, which is to use the funeral as a gathering place to talk about the things that are really going on in our lives, some people felt that that was inappropriate. So that, I would say, was the major arena of objection.

Another arena of objection was the assumption that some people made that I had just gone rogue, that I had just gone up there and just said all this shit. People didn't realize that we had all vetted it, that it had been discussed, that the minister had read it in advance. It was interesting that this assumption was made. Not one person asked me, *What was the discussion, what was the prep?* Nothing. So, there was just this assumption that I had done something terrible on my own and all of that, which is also something that—this has to do with the book I've just written [*Conflict Is Not Abuse*], which is, *How come people don't ask questions?* Why do we just assume the worst? Why don't we just ask the person? You know, and part of it has to do with us not being in person with each other and I think that's one of the reasons we don't ask.

The final objection had to do, I think, with religion. So, I'm Jewish, and I'm very culturally Jewish, but I'm not religious. This was in an Episcopal church and there's this concept of ascension. Bryn was religious. And so, one of the criticisms was, *Why did you have to say her death was a waste? Why couldn't you say: "Bryn, you did the best you could"*? And the reason I couldn't say that is because, for me, Bryn is not addressable. Because, for me, her death means that she's gone. I do not have a religious concept of her looking down on us or hearing me. And this is something that is really—and this is something that I didn't understand until I heard the objection— and it's just a cultural, religious framework that we each come from. Some of us have rejected them, some of us haven't, and for some people that was very offensive on those terms.

So, that's what happened there. But in the end I felt like our community of people who were closest to Bryn were united by the service, and I do feel good about my participation, so that was my experience there.

MMP: Just to back up a little, before I go into my little spiel, for those of you who don't know, Bryn Kelly was a prominent trans woman artist living and working in Brooklyn, New York. She was thirty-five years old. She was a theater maker, she was a fantastic writer. You may have read some of her blogs without even knowing it because she often used anonymity and constructed characters as an online form of writing, so she's "The Hussy" online, which if you've ever gotten to read is incredible, one of my favorite pieces of writing ever. She also wrote about her experiences as an HIV-positive trans woman accessing social services through another blog called *Party Bottom*, which was also wildly popular. You may have seen posts from it a couple years ago called "How to Be a Good Roommate to Someone with HIV" that went viral; it was quite large.

I guess I'll start by acknowledging that we are in the middle of a suicide epidemic within queer and trans communities that reaches across all segments of our community and has very disproportionate impacts on the most marginalized in our community, particularly Indigenous people who often cross over with our communities and in Canada have the highest suicide rates of any group as well as Black and other people of color. It is a large and extremely sensitive topic that we can't possibly hope to unravel in one evening, but we're hoping that through discussing one person's suicide this can be fruitful as we move forward to future events which, hopefully, there won't be too many of.

I've been very active within the trans community within the past ten years and Bryn's suicide was not the first suicide of someone close to me that I've seen. Suicides happen very regularly within the close community around me. Whether they're friends I have, coworkers, or community members I've shared space with, they happen with an astounding regularity that contributes to many of us who see this happening, feeling hopeless and ourselves feeling suicidal ideation, right? So on January fourteenth, when I heard about Bryn's death, I was actually on the tail end of one of my deepest periods of depression and suicidality that I've ever gone through in my life, which was about four months long and was the cumulative effect of grief and trauma including seeing many of the bright and incredible people that I know take their own lives through suicide, and also including the sudden death of my boyfriend, Jack, in 2013, and the deaths of about half a dozen people since then that I've been close with. Bryn's death and the pain caused for so many, particularly her close friends and partner, were a wake-up call to me about my own suicidal ideation and escalating behaviors. In fact, when I read Sarah's eulogy for the first time—I was part of the organizing committee for the memorial, but I was living up here in Montreal and Gaines, Bryn's partner, emailed it to me and said, "What do you think of this?"—I didn't know that there were conversations happening about this piece. I was just like, *Oh, what do I think of this?* So, I read it and the effect on me was very immediate, that I felt that it dissuaded all of the suicidal ideation that I'd been feeling for me personally and I really respected what a bold statement it was, as you all will hear shortly. I did have some objections whereas, you know, like, while I think this is great and I support you on this with going forward on this, however *[laughter]* there are, like, one or two little things that I think may be not appropriate for this space and this time so let's, you know, edit *[laughter]*. And that's when I was told about the conversations that were happening and contacted by all the other people in the organizing committee that was doing this and we had a lot of intense discussions about the purpose of what Gaines, Bryn's partner, called a "political sermon." He kept referring to us to stop calling it a eulogy and to start calling it a political sermon because that's what it is, which is, I think, a really smart way of summing it up.

Anyway, through all of this process, I was traveling down practically every couple of weeks to help with the organizing and just be supportive and I was asked by other people in the organizing committee if I would write a eulogy myself so that there would be a more "traditional" eulogy that would happen, and so that's what I did, and I'm gonna read it to you in a little bit.

I think the—I also want to say about the event, so for those of you who haven't been there, the cathedral of St. John the Divine is the third-largest Christian church in the world. It's gigantic. If you look up at the ceiling there's practically clouds, like, it's so big and it was full, as Sarah said, with seven hundred people, many of whom didn't know Bryn, which was a very interesting thing to negotiate emotionally to be in a place of mourning and to have to interact with people who were mourning someone that they didn't know. But something that was very . . . that wasn't new to me because in 2012 I was also involved in the organizing for the funeral of trans activist Kyle Scanlon in Toronto, who, I don't know if any of you are familiar with his work, but basically if you're a trans person in Canada, you owe him so much in terms of how you're able to access hormones, how you're able to access shelters, very basic things that, in some ways, we're still fighting over today. We wouldn't be as far without Kyle, and I felt that the situations were very similar.

Anyway, it was a big, weirdly alienating, large event that was very anxiety-producing in the ways that queer and trans events often are anxiety-producing. I'm sure there are some of you today who are having internal freak-outs because someone you had an argument with on the internet two years ago is sitting in the back of the room, and you can just feel their presence. I know I feel that way *[laughter]*. Just me? OK.

But um, anyway, I think one of the things I found really interesting to the response to Sarah's piece—and we'll probably get more into it after we actually go into the pieces—was that those who were reacting to the piece online who had not seen it being read in person had missed an incredible amount of nuance and tone to how the piece was actually delivered. In person, when I walked up to Sarah in the cathedral, there were tears in her eyes from the moment that I walked up and throughout the entire eulogy, or as Gaines called it, political sermon; it was very emotional. And to me that—I really felt like those emotions were hard to discount and that they were important to the experience of the eulogy. Of course, the words are very important and words matter but also an idea of where it was coming from felt very important and really affected me. My speech went off without a hitch. People loved it *[laughter]*. People still share it on the internet *[laughter]*. Not to rub it in *[laughter]*. But I guess those are my introductory thoughts on this exciting topic that we have to share with you in a moment.

TN: OK, so why don't both of you read your eulogies.

ss: OK, and then we can open it up.

mmp: Would you like to go first?

ss: Sure. Relax. *[laughter]*

I had the honor of being Bryn's creative writing teacher at the Lambda Literary Retreat. As a writer, she was an organic intellectual, funny, deep, and her work grappled with things that matter. Our relationship evolved into a loving, enriching friendship—I called on her a number of times and she was always there for me. She knew that I loved and respected her.

I am not a religious person and I do not believe in an afterlife. Instead, it has been my experience that heaven and hell take place on earth. And so, our lives provide us with opportunities for depth of meaning and understanding—*if* we face and deal with difficulties honestly. It is that uncomfortable, sad, and overwhelming work that can bring us to the revelations we need to survive, thrive, and be accountable to others. For this reason, I approach this earthly catastrophe with openness. This tragic waste of our beloved friend, Bryn, is a challenge we have to face. Many people today will tell the story of her life. Bryn Kelly's warmth, her genius, her deep, soft beauty, and kindness. But I want to take this time to talk, in detail, about Bryn Kelly's death. I want to make a contribution to this ongoing conversation about how to end the terrible idealized fantasy of suicide that has overtaken our community. A falsity of distorted thinking that has become not only an option, but in fact an expectation.

Several suicide attempts ago, Bryn ended up in a terrible Brooklyn hospital where she was told that they only had room for her on the men's ward. They also confused her HIV medications, endangering her ability to continue her regimen. And instead of administering her hormones, they gave her Depo-Provera, a long-lasting form of birth control. These kinds of cruelties, and acts of hostile, dehumanizing indifference do not make a person want to ask for help. In fact, like all forms of shunning, they exclude people from help. Then, about a year and a half ago, Kelli Dunham called and told me that Bryn had taken an intentional overdose, and that Gaines and Nogga—ever loving and vigilant—had found her checked into a fleabag hotel in Bushwick. Arguably a better choice than a men's ward at a bad hospital.

Gaines and Nogga and I agreed that they would take her in a car and meet me at the NYU emergency room. I stood outside with a wheelchair, they pulled up, and we swooped into the ER with Bryn groggy and hovering on unconsciousness. In addition to the pills, she had drunk a lot of beer. NYU triaged her in eight minutes. She was treated with kindness, decency, and care. Her friends and partner were respected and engaged with support and care. They brought her to a beautiful private room, placed a full-time nurse in the room. And we—her community—started the process of repair.

A few events: Gaines wisely asked the doctor if NYU had a trans patient advocate. Bryn became very upset. "Gaines," she admonished, as though he had done something wrong, when actually he did exactly the right thing. She was angry that she had been revealed as trans—even though she had just tried to kill herself— because she'd already learned the hard way, many times over, that this exposure, in an institutional setting, could lead to more pain than she could bear. The doctor, with recognition and responsibility, acknowledged that NYU did not have a trans advocate, but that they should have one.

I then tried to phone her therapist. The public clinic she attended for therapy was a disorganized bureaucracy with no provision for emergency contacts. I was given an endless runaround, for hours. Finally, Kelli googled the whole staff list until she found someone's home phone, and in that manner, I got to talk to the therapist directly. It did not take long for me to realize that she was completely inadequate to the task. She was young, inexperienced, had never had a suicidal patient before, and didn't even bother to come to the hospital. The situation was clear. Despite all the love in the world from her friends and partner, Bryn Kelly had not been getting the quality of professional care that she needed in order to solve the pain of her life enough to fully live it.

Some hours later, Bryn beckoned me to her bedside. She was soft, vulnerable, and open. She held my hand. "Why did I do this?" she asked. "Why did this happen?" We started talking. She told me that she had become so angry that she couldn't think of anything but hurting the people close to her. As she described it, she experienced small events—normative conflict or normative frustrations in close relationships—as these hugely threatening, catastrophic assaults. This anger was not focused on hostile institutions, inadequate services, or incompetent and indifferent practitioners. It was tunneled into anger at the people who loved her and a desire to punish them. I would call this process "cumulative pain"—a combination of anxiety and oppression. Where the pain of one's life becomes focused onto the person or people right in front of you, the ones who are there to be blamed because they love you. And therefore, the pain gets expressed by destroying these people, these relationships, and ultimately one's own life, thereby leaving the exterior structures of oppression fully intact, unburdened, and unaddressed.

After recovering medically, Bryn spent some time on the psychiatric service at NYU. I visited her there and she seemed to feel it was a beneficial experience. But when she was discharged, I was concerned. Bryn's doctors wanted her to go into a program to deal with her substance use and she did not want to go. That is when I knew, truly, that this cycle was not over.

This time, when Bryn finally took her own life, the path to destruction engaged these same unresolved issues. She had been doing very, very well. The last time I saw her she was energetic, engaged, caring, fun. We danced outside St. Mark's Church to a Christmas band. Just two days before her death we planned a group dinner at my house. Friends were commenting on how happy she seemed, that her medication seemed to be working. How well she was doing.

Then, as in every person's life, Bryn had a normative conflict with her partner. But the pattern of trauma combined with anxiety, and long experience with depression, of course kicked in. And because no method had been developed in her life of what to do when it kicked in—she became very distressed and began to destroy. She drank a bottle of vodka. And I want to say here, that no one I know has ever killed themselves sober. She wrote an extremely angry and punitive suicide note that expressed a kind of tunnel vision of rage at the people closest to her. And the note was so focused on hurting other people that it contained no real recognition that she was actually ending her own life. Her note showed an interior logic, way out of sync with what events were actually occurring in the exterior world. Many times I have wished that she could have spent the day in 12-step meetings, called her sponsor, and asked her friends and doctors for support to hospitalize herself back to the positive environment at NYU. But, because of alcohol and depression, the fact that these conflicts were entirely resolvable eluded her completely. That there were many options eluded her. While she did invoke the many suicides and deaths of trans and queer women in recent years, listing their names in her letter, it was only to momentarily claim in her rage and pain that ultimately these deaths had no impact—which is the opposite of the truth. These deaths have devastated us and, clearly, they contributed to Bryn taking her own life.

No, the drunken, anxious tunnel vision of her letter was a singular, one-note, designed to hurt a few people. The ones who loved her the most. In fact, the note assumed that when Gaines came home from work, and found the door barricaded, and discovered her dead, he would call the police, who would be the ones to deal with her body and the death scene. But in fact, Gaines forced the door open, saw that she had hung herself, and then he and Nogga cut down the body, cut off the noose, and tried to resuscitate her through chest compressions and mouth-to-mouth. But she was dead. Then they called the paramedics, who laid her out on the floor of the front room.

For the rest of the night, those of us who came over were confronted by Bryn's corpse on the floor of the apartment, her arms extended and her hands open. I sat with her body for hours, dealing with the police, the detectives, the medical examiner, and then the transport workers. Identifying the body. At each interview level, to the officer, to the homicide detective, to the medical examiner, I said that same sentence. "She was a wonderful person, with a beautiful partner and many caring friends." "So, what happened here?" the police would ask. "She didn't have a system for tolerating frustration," I said. I signed the body identification form. And in that time, I spent most of the night looking at her lying dead on the floor. This was not her suicide fantasy—lying on the floor with a police detective Scotch-taping her noose to her leg, her loved ones crushed, her sisters and community threatened by her example. The policeman stepping on her bed with his shoes.

There were many acts of kindness that night. I particularly remember Elias volunteering to call Bryn's mother, and tell her what had happened. He had a deep, caring sense of responsibility, kindness in the way he communicated this terrible information. I saw Nogga and Jax gently clean up after Bryn's body had been removed by the police transport workers. Nogga's loving mother and sister, making tea. Dr. Zil Goldstein, who Bryn called "the only doctor who ever listened to me," giving her history, privately, to the medical examiner. And all the friends who came to love Gaines, to hold him, to be truly with him and to give him all the love that he well deserves. This is what we do when our friends take their own lives. These are the details of those consequences. This is what suicide really does. It causes nothing but despair. It does not get revenge. It ends a life filled with love and promise. It deprives the world, and it causes more death. Just as the suicides of queer and trans women before contributed to Bryn's death, we must make sure that Bryn's suicide does not continue to cause the deaths of others. Please stop this idealized fantasy that suicide will satisfy any need, when all it does is cause more pain. We must stop killing ourselves. It is an act of violence, helping to create a violent future.

After her body was finally removed, we started the well-worn, modern ritual—now habitual—of calling people around the world so that they would understand what had happened, before they saw it on Facebook. We all spent the next day taking care of people, letting them know gently, and in person, that Bryn had taken her own life. As I had this multitude of conversations, each one causing pain, I kept thinking back to that time in NYU, Bryn in her hospital bed, holding my hand, asking, "Why did this happen?" Finally, late in the day, I talked to Morgan Page on the phone, and she illuminated something very important for me. Morgan pointed out that Bryn had never stopped seeking a solution. That she had repeatedly attempted to find treatment. She went to many different kinds of clinics and engaged a wide range of therapists and doctors.

She tried enrolling in many different kinds of classes. She constantly tried to find a way out of the problem and into her own real and rich life. And then I realized the obvious. Bryn Kelly died not because of a lack of community—she had a wealth of community. She died because she was poor and could not afford the sophisticated level of treatment and support that someone so intelligent and complex needed in order to fully live her life.

I now believe that Bryn Kelly died of poverty, of lack of services. That had she been able to be sure of secure housing, had she been able to enter an immersive, individuated, full-service environment that recognized and valued her, as we here all recognize and value her, perhaps her life could have been saved. But without it, she could not get to a place where the frustration provoked by normative difficulty did not become an emblem of all the grotesque institutional oppression and erasure and burden that she had been asked to bear.

I do not view Bryn's death as a failure of our community, but rather as a wound on our loving, caring, yet fragile community assaulted regularly by a punitive and indifferent system. We must stop destroying ourselves, while letting the institutions that are hurting us stand unopposed. In this case, our love could not overwhelm that institutional cruelty and abandonment. But that does not diminish how much we all give each other, and the beauty and the power and the wealth of how much we all love and care. We have to stay alive, and fight like hell for the living.

MMP: So here's my eulogy. Much easier to get through, I promise.

Of all the hussies in this whole rotten, hussified world, this hussy was my favorite. Even before I knew her personally, I was obsessed with Bryn. Her pseudonymous writing struck a chord of recognition in me that I'd never felt before. It was as though she were writing directly to me, a feeling I think many of us here shared in one way or another.

Bryn and I were, in her words, "pretend rivals/frenemies or whatever."

I've never met anyone else I felt so directly in competition with, not only artistically but also often for the attentions of the very same transmascs. The first time we dated the same man, I was green with envy. I thought, in horror, "She's prettier than me." In a short, two-year fit of jealousy I even grew out my undercut to compete with her voluptuous locks. And by her own admission the jealousy was a two-way street. I was the Eve Harrington nipping at her heels. But for all of this, our friendship never turned sour, as it so easily could have.

Bryn's wit was a rapid-fire mixture of high- and lowbrow—a complex bricolage seamlessly pairing Dolly Parton with Preciado, Halberstam with Stevie Nicks. Around her more than anyone else I felt like I needed to keep on my toes—to step up my game as an artist, as an activist, and as a fellow MTF4FTM masc hunter.

Many knew her as a party girl, as a performer, as a hairstylist, and as a writer—an aloof and sometimes capricious social butterfly. But to some of the luckiest of us, Bryn meant so much more. Her presence in the world, as the first trans woman I've ever met whose whole thing was so close to my whole thing, made me feel like it was possible for me to exist in the world uncompromising.

To those who were close to her, Bryn was not just the brilliant raconteur and beautiful artist. She was a keen listener and emotional support. In 2013, when my boyfriend died suddenly, it was Bryn who called the ambulance and stayed up for hours dealing with both the cops, who didn't want to take the call, and my own shell-shocked reaction. Throughout the most painful thing I have

ever experienced, she showed me incredible kindness. It takes a lot
of hurt to make high-riding bitches like us, but that same hurt endowed her with a deep well of compassion.

When all was said and done that night, she wrote these words
to me, which I think are relevant for all of us here this evening: "So,
this is going to be hell, I can assure you. But you will get through it,
because you are strong. End Oprah talk." Thank you.

TN: What we would like to do next is to open the conversation to
all of you, if you have questions or comments you want to ask either
or both of them.

MMP: Or just want to say.

TN: Or just comments you want to say.

Q1: This is for Sarah. It's Sarah, right? There's a couple of things that
you mention in your political sermon that I understand your point
of view. I understand what you wrote—from your position or from
the other side, like, as a friend so close from Bryn and for so long,
and I've been helping her for so long, I can understand what you
went through yourself and what brought you to write all of that.

I've been suicidal for twenty-five years—actually right now I'm
going through a crisis, with the help of some friends. And I think
it's interesting what you said, but if I may, I think there's a misunderstanding about what being suicidal means. Some people have it
as an obsession, some people it's revenge, some people it's sickness,
but it is more than—you said she didn't have a system to deal with
frustration. It's true if we see it at a binary level, but it's so much
more complex for some people, like myself. It's an obsession. It's
like I live with it every day. Every day if you give me the choice

between death and life, I will choose death. But I stand up and live because that's the option that I think is relevant, because it's the good thing to do. But this doesn't mean that this is something that my soul is torn about. Sometimes it can also be physical, it can be cognitive. It can be something that I'm missing from the youth that I cannot even . . . ah, my English is not perfect so I don't have all the words to say so. I think it's way more than that for Bryn. I understand the revenge that Bryn had, that somewhere it was just a way to yell this suffering that she couldn't explain or express and that the only way that she found was to hurt because she was so hurt, but I don't think it was just because of the system. And I understand the goal is to discourage youth to kill themselves, and it's true it's a violence process, but I do think that the love—I really, really think that Bryn could not make it to thirty-five years old if she did not have all that love. I already told a best friend before a suicide attempt I wanted to do, "If I did please cry, but remember I'd been successful to get through that until that time." Because for me, I didn't even know I could get to that point. And since that day, I'm still alive, and I'm like, "Oh, I'm alive—whoa, that's awesome." But for a suicidal person it's like a sickness, it's like cancer. Every day you make it, it's wild. So, I don't feel like it's a waste—it's not a giving up. It's the end of a battle, yes, and it's hurtful for everyone around, but that person had fought for so many years, that person had failed and succeeded—but that thirty-five years? She made it. And that, for me, it's awesome. So, every time someone dies from suicide, I cry because it's like, "Man, this is the end of a battle," but me, I'm still standing up, so I'm going to continue to battle until I fall myself. But we continue fighting, and that love that you've all given to her? That's what made her get to there. That's the way I see it.

SS: Thank you.

MMP: Yeah, thank you for that. I really agree with you that it's not a failure of a person, that it's the end of a very long struggle, generally, and that it is the community around a person that enables that person to continue going on. I think that's very, very true, and I think one of the things that I think a lot about because so many of the people that I know have committed suicide is the responsibility we have to each other to provide that kind of love and that kind of support, even, and especially, when, as Sarah speaks about in the eulogy, or political sermon, even when there are no services available or when the only available services are transphobic or racist and inaccessible because they're expensive and all these things I think that's why I think as a community we need to be showing people love and helping people through extremely difficult times, you know? And I think this is one of the things we wanted to get to, that part of that responsibility is not just when someone comes to you and is like, "I'm feeling suicidal." It's a responsibility that carries through all of our interactions with each other where we, I feel, you may not feel this way. Your mileage may vary. But I feel we have a responsibility to each other all the time to de-escalate all kinds of conflicts that a person is having. When someone is having obsessive thoughts or suicidal ideation, for example, to be that sounding board, to help bring that person back into a way of looking at the reality of their life, or the reality of whatever situation is going on, and making responses that are equal to that reality, you know? And this goes beyond when someone is having suicidal ideation, when we're having community conflict. Queers love—we love yelling on the internet and we love going on Tumblr and tearing each other apart. One of the things—I have this friend who is a poet. His name is Stephen Ira; he's a trans guy poet, he's super brilliant, you should follow him on Twitter. He's @supermattachine on Twitter. And he says that—I'm loosely quoting him—because we're in a suicide epidemic, it's irresponsible of us to, essentially, try to destroy each other. The responsible choice for all of us, since we're all at risk, is to actually have the difficult conversations, where we sit down with people and try to de-escalate conflicts and try to respond with responsibility and accountability to each other in ways that are fair and equitable for all parties involved, you know? That's some of the things that came up when you were speaking, so thank you.

Any other thoughts people want to dive into? I can talk all night. I have, like, pages of things I can talk about. Been makin' notes for days *[laughter]*. Yes.

Q2: My question's for Morgan. I just wanted to dig in a little bit more to your initial reaction to the draft that you first read. I've known Sarah for a while. I've always known her to be a considerate person who is about the conversation, so I guess the most disturbing thing that came out of this for me, as someone who didn't know Bryn but who did know a lot of the people who were very much affected by this suicide, was that somehow she was using this as a political line to centralize herself within a situation that no one would want to center themselves in. And so when you guys talked about the difference between political sermon and eulogy, that was really striking to me because perhaps there's an irreconcilable chasm between those two concepts, like, would it be more appropriate for Sarah to talk at someone's funeral if she were trans and that was the political sermon and would it be more appropriate as someone who was very close to Bryn to only talk about what was good about her as a person rather than as a part of the larger sociocultural matrix. And so, I guess my question is for you because you're central within those matrices as someone who really cared about this person and as someone who hews so closely to that identity politic, that sense of who can speak for whom. I guess I wanted to know what were the things you thought were inappropriate and, like, what was your take? If you don't mind sharing them.

MMP: Totally. Um, so when I first read Sarah's speech, I read it and my eyes just, like, opened, like, "Whoa, that's a lot." I thought it was a very, very powerful piece of writing, which is unsurprising because I've been a follower of Sarah's writing; I generally find it to be quite powerful. There was only one thing—well, two things, really—that I objected to that I asked to be changed. And one of them was—it was just one sentence. It was kind of a gruesome sentence about the state of Bryn's body, and I understand why Sarah would include this because the point of this is to dissuade suicide. One of the conversations we were having as the organizers were going back and forth about whether or not this is appropriate and who should be saying what was the idea of suicide contagion and suicide clusters. So as some of you may know, but perhaps some of you don't, when a person commits suicide—particularly a prominent person—it tends to trigger suicidal ideation in many, many, many people around them, and because Bryn was so prominent we, in particular, wanted to take pains to make sure that a suicide cluster (as it's referred to in the literature) did not occur, and I felt like the rest of Sarah's speech without this one line that was kind of gruesome could adequately convey that. That was kind of the consensus we had as organizers. I mean, I can't speak for everyone else but this is the impression that I got. You know, we asked Sarah to change it and she did.

The only other thing I asked her—I didn't ask her to change, but I talked to Gaines about—was the mention of Bryn and Gaines having what Sarah calls a normative conflict, essentially a big argument. Because I had a really tricky experience when my boyfriend died and the reactions I received particularly from people who didn't know him, of, like, blame in these weird ways, which makes no sense. He died of an unexpected medical condition. You know, it was a very weird experience. So, I was like, "Just as your friend who wants to protect you, Gaines. Have you thought about the reaction people could have to hearing that you had a fight with Bryn?" Because as we all know, sometimes queer community is a really intense game of broken telephone, where one phrase can suddenly be drawn out of proportion and suddenly two weeks later we can hear, like, "Gaines hit her! And the police were called!" and all this, which none of this happened and none of which is at all the root. So, it was more of a, like, "Let's think carefully about this." But to me, one of the reasons I—it was Gaines and I who were so fiercely and strongly advocating amongst the others for the inclusion of this. One of the reasons of this was that Bryn and Sarah were close— closer, I think, than I was to Bryn—and Bryn held Sarah's, what I've called her steel core of moral fiber and her insight, really, on a very high pedestal in her life. And Bryn was not a person to mince words if she had something to say, and I felt in reading the speech that this was something Bryn would defend if she heard this being read at somebody else's funeral. I felt like it was something in line with her own thoughts. So, I felt like that was good.

Some of the reactions that happened centered around the fact that Sarah is not trans. And I found that really interesting because they all came from people who were not close to Bryn, which is always interesting to watch, when you're close to a situation and then you see people who you don't even know reacting to a situation that you're actually a part of. And, for us, Bryn's whole life wasn't just being trans. She was a very active member of the queer femme community in Brooklyn. She was—even though she did not identify as a lesbian—very active in the lesbian community. In fact, she once judged lesbian fiction at the Lambda Literary Awards, and she posted about it on her blog. She was like, "My favorite activity is judging lesbians" *[laughter]*. And so, to me, I think sometimes we fall down a bit of a rabbit hole where we think that only a person who is exactly like this person can talk about this person, and I think that doesn't talk about the truth of who that person's community was. You know, it doesn't talk about the many different communities that a person can be part of. You know, God forbid I ever succumb to my various thoughts, but I don't think that it would only be trans people saying interesting things or difficult things at my funeral if that happens, God forbid. In fact, one of the things that I posted in response to Sarah is that, well, I hope when I go, Sarah has something really intense to say about it *[laughter]*! But that's my punishing impulse deep inside my head, and the fact that I think her insight is so valuable. I don't know, does that answer your question?

Q3: Sarah, so I wanted to thank you for posting your eulogy online, because that's where I read it. And it really, and fairly dramatically, changed the rhetorical relationship I have with rhetoric of suicide. Like, it really helped shift the frame for me. And one thing that was really quite powerful and awesome about hearing about your conversations with Bryn's partner was that it really felt to me that the act of that eulogy and the way you built the service was that you really wrapped love around Gaines at a really crucial moment. So, I wanted to hear you talk a bit more about that, the community act of caring for someone in such a difficult position.

SS: I don't think I can say anything as articulate as what Morgan just said. I mean, you know, queer people, our culture, we're locked in blame. We're locked into finding out who is the bad person, finding out who they are and making sure that they get punished. And I wish we could change that to trying to understand what's happening. I just think that trying to understand what's happening will help us a lot more because I'm old—I'm fifty-eight years old—and I've never seen punishment do anything positive. I just don't think punishment works, and I don't even understand what the goal of it is, to be honest. And also, Gaines is very, very young and it's very traumatizing, and we just wanted him to feel the love that is there for him.

MMP: To piggyback off that a little bit, right before we jump into you. Actually, no, I'll just let it go.

Q4: Actually, it's kind of along the lines of the last question, but kind of, and I guess it's for both of you. There's just been a lot of talk, like, outside this talk there was a panel on Black Lives Matter and one of the speakers was talking about how we should be shifting from a space of self-care to a space of collective care. And I guess in talking about this, especially from your positionality, being so close to this person, but also having to do this work in thinking about it as a political sermon rather than maybe as something for yourselves as the people who were close—maybe my question's getting a little bit off—but just in talking about the idea of self-care versus the idea of collective care and what that means to you.

SS: I haven't gotten to the self-care part yet. I've never gotten there. No, you know, it's because I'm coming from AIDS. That's influencing everything, and, you know, I do experience Bryn as an HIV-positive person and I think that is part of her death. This was my instinct, was to do it this way because this was the way everyone I knew in ACT UP or whoever who died of AIDS, that was how we handled their death. When a person dies for reasons that are social as well as personal, and you're talking about an oppressed community, it's my natural impulse to articulate both of those moments.

MMP: I think, in terms of self-care versus community care, I think it's really difficult for people in my age group, not that I can speak for all of us, but I think it's very difficult for us to understand generationally what the AIDS crisis was like and the very different way that people were interacting with each other in care relationships. One of the things that a lot of people don't know is that the lesbian community in particular stepped up to be in-person caregivers for so many people before better medications were available. And I think this is something we can learn from, in terms of suicide and in terms of so many other things going on in our community, that we can step up for each other in ways that can affect the outcome. And that stepping up doesn't just mean—though it does mean—showing up to the hospital. It also means being a patient advocate, and it means taking that advocacy even further to ensure that someone like Bryn isn't put on the men's ward ever again, not just in her case, but in all cases, you know? I think, to me, that's what collective care looks like, when we not only show up on the actual day, we don't just show up on the night Bryn dies to take care of Gaines, we also continue to show up to make sure that the social conditions that Sarah outlines so eloquently are not reproduced, that we do everything in our power to stop them.

I think one of the other things about Sarah's political sermon that I so valued and also found shocking was how political it was. You know, I've been to so many funerals. I'm twenty-nine years old and I've been to fourteen funerals and that's not all the people I know who have died. That's just the funerals I could get to. And I've never seen something like this happen before, where people were willing to stand up and say what actually happened. Espe-cially for, I don't know how it is in other communities, but I feel like in white communities we have a very delicate way of speaking about tragic events that have happened so that no one gets upset anymore and we can slide it back under the rug where we keep the racism and all the other things we don't want to talk about, and I feel that what Sarah did is to take away the rug and make us not look away, you know? She describes the scene that night so that you're not idly imagining it, so that you have a concrete idea of the effects that your loss, in my case—I'll just speak for me—I had a very strong idea, then, of what would happen if I did the same thing, which in the four months preceding Bryn's death I had been thinking about every day, you know? And to me, that made me stop and think, as much as sometimes life feels unbearable to me, I can't bear to put the people that I love, even if I'm in a mood where I'm like, "I want them to feel pain and I want them to know how bad they hurt me." Even in that moment, I can't imagine putting those people through that. Like, knowing the details of that takes the wind out of the sails of that for me personally. Again, I can only speak for my own experience, but that's what comes to mind.

Q5: So, I just wanted to echo back the brutal honesty of describing suicide attempts and suicide and how much that helps the commu-nity to talk about what's happened. And the next thing that I want to say is that I feel that I'm hearing two conversations here. I'm hearing a main conversation about suicide and what that looks like and how that affects our community and another conversation is sort of like one that we're all laughing at about conflict and how everybody at one point in their life has had a conflict with someone in this room. And I want to know if you two can connect those two. I know that when I came to this event, I did a lot of thinking on that, and I realized that every suicide and suicide attempt that I've ever witnessed has involved alcohol and also a normative conflict while somebody's in a mental health crisis. So, my question is specifically for both of you: How can people in the framework of knowing that everybody is possibly suicidal and trans or oppressed or anxious or just bad at conflict support each other in a collective way that prevents suicide, that prevents eviction from housing, that prevents all these things going on in the community every single day?

ss: Well, I mean, you can't fix all those things, right? A lot of people here know that you can't control people's alcoholism and their addictions, right? However, we can make things worse for each other by, I'm gonna quote myself here, *overstating harm*, which is the subtitle of my new book; by acting as though things that are difficult, uncomfortable, and upsetting are cataclysms and crimes of the highest order, when they are not. And if we can take down the accusations, and the condemnations, and all of that, we can make each other's lives a little easier. We have control over that.

mmp: I see it as the critical importance of de-escalation in our lives. Again, I'm very influenced by this book Sarah keeps referring to, which just came out. It's called *Conflict Is Not Abuse*, and if you want copies, we have copies you can buy later. But I feel like we have these conflicts, and this is very true of my own suicidal ideation: I have what I would describe as normative conflict—like, someone disagrees with me, or someone yells at me on the internet, or a boy broke up with me and was a dick about it. I have these normative conflicts and then my mind spirals out of all reasonable scale of what has happened. So, for example, someone dumps me for a cis woman, and I lose it. And I'm calling my friends and I'm like, "He's the worst person who ever lived, I hate him, I'm so mad." And I'm just, like, freaking out to everyone I know, when in reality it's just a breakup. It's not the end of the world; it's not like we have children together. Which even then would not necessarily be the end of the world but might be a heightened thing compared to two people around thirty who don't have children and don't live together who, you know, were just seeing each other for a few months. But I think that it's really important for all of us to step in and de-escalate these conflicts, including when we see people blowing up at each other and when we see ourselves blowing up at each other, we need to able to step in and be like, "What is the actual problem here?"

Like, if a person made some political faux pas which no one is saying is a great thing—does that justify socially isolating them? I think this is one of the big problems we have in queer community. We pay a lot of lip service to prison abolition, but we don't actually internalize that in our lives and how we interact with each other. The logic of the prison is isolation, and the number one danger to queer and trans lives, other than outside violence, is social isolation. I work in the social services, I've provided services for trans people for many years, and in every one of my funding applications the number one thing we're trying to reduce is social isolation, because when you're isolated you become hopeless, and you despair, and you also have no access to resources and people who care about you. In the queer and trans community unfortunately right now in this moment we have a tendency to, as Sarah says, catastrophize small conflicts, which, again, no one is saying there's no bad things happening, but often we're taking very small conflicts and catastrophizing them and calling for the removal of this person from community spaces and saying, "Oh, you can't come to this queer space anymore because you said something transmisogynistic and that was hurtful to us, so you're not allowed to come."

Often, this isolationist move comes without terms, so there's no terms for repair, there's no room for nuance about what each party thinks is happening. So, for example, recently someone didn't know I was a trans woman and exploded at me on Twitter for making a joke about trans woman stuff because they thought I was being transmisogynist and they, like, blocked me and made all these horrible jokes about me and photoshopped pictures of me. It went completely berserk and there were all these other people feeding into it, and I was like, "I'm sorry to disappoint you, but I'm not cisgender. I am in fact transgender, and I'm pretty sure that means I can say whatever I want about my own body." And I feel like this is one particularly ridiculous example, but there are examples where there are genuine conflicts going on where a person has done something shitty or has been accused of doing something shitty whether or not they understand it as something that's shitty, and things just spiral out of control. I think, again, I would just call it the importance of de-escalation. We need to be able to step in and say to our friends, "I see that you're having a huge blowup with this person. How are you? Can we talk about this? Can we meet in person and talk about this? Can I help the two of you sit down and talk about this?" I don't know what we can do, but we all have to deal with each other. I don't know if you've noticed, but Montreal is a small island. It is a very small island and you're going to run into these people at events like this for the rest of your life.

ss: Morgan, you recently wrote on Twitter, and you suggested that we reintroduce the word *heartache* and I think that's right, you know, instead of saying, "That person did this terrible thing," just say, like, "My heart is broken. I feel really sad. I feel really upset. I feel really frustrated."

MMP: Before we get to another, I just want to talk about this specific one. What I was thinking about when I tweeted that was what I see every day, especially on Tumblr, people who are having normative conflict with their partner—again, abuse is very real and that is not what I'm talking about. I'm talking about people who have break-ups, and I'm implicating myself in this because I feel the same way when I go through a breakup sometimes, where you break up with someone and the only terms we have to talk about it are that this person has done something to me, when in reality it's just a breakup. Sometimes, I'm like, "What would straight people call this?" Oh, right, it's breaking up. That's what it is. I feel like there's a resistance to talking about our own psychology when talking about conflict in queer community, because we are very, very invested in only looking at things on the kind of identity politics or sociopolitical levels. We're not often willing to talk about thoughts and feelings and how they influence situations, because everything is so politically clear-cut and is only political—including our breakups, which are always political—that we can't really talk about, *Oh, I'm really upset* or, *This really hurt my feelings, I am mad at this person, I feel disrespected by this person.* We can't ever talk about that, so we always— it's almost like a distancing technique where we step outside of it so that we can just deal with the anger part of it and the punishment part of it, by being like, "This is the biggest political crime that has ever happened! This trans man dumped me for a cis woman and he's clearly being the biggest transmisogynist who ever existed, and he should never have friends ever again!" Which is not really a reasonable expectation when you step back and look at it a little more objectively. And I think it's the role of friends of community members to sit us down and be like, "OK, let's look at the order of events. Let's look at what happened and figure out a response that's in scale to those events," you know? That's just my thought.

Q6: If we're talking about the distinction between political and personal stuff, I feel like I've heard you talk somewhere, Sarah, about how we talk about it in terms of personal rather than the structures that exist. I feel like it's almost too personalized or detached from structures that suck. But then on the other hand, I agree with what you just said about how when we talk about our personal conflicts we make it very political. I don't know, I feel like you get what I'm saying.

MMP: Small question! Sarah, do you have any immediate thoughts? Well, sometimes I think we displace what's going on in our lives and I think this is part of the root of this catastrophizing of normative conflict where we walk through the world, especially those of us of particularly marginalized identities, where we are dealing with so much garbage 24-7—we're dealing with it from people on the street, we're dealing with it trying to access medical institutions, from trying to deal with the government on any level in any way, and we have basically zero power to change that, or at least we feel that way, most of the time.

And then in our personal relationships, and this is part of what Sarah talks about in her speech, is about how we move all the pain and anxiety of that onto the people closest to us because we know we have an effect on them, because you can see the hurt in someone's eyes when you tear into them, and there is some part of our lizard brain that finds that very satisfying in a way that we will never find trying to deal with an institution satisfying, because you can't hurt an institution. You can't get an institution to understand that you felt pain. You can't get an institution to empathize with you. And you rarely can get an institution to apologize to you, and when you do it's always like [right-wing Canadian prime minister] Stephen Harper trying to apologize to Indigenous people. It just comes off real awkward and does not address the real problems and does not come up with real solutions, you know?

So I feel like sometimes our politics can be very vague in terms of what to do because we honestly don't know most of the time, especially people on campus who are, like, eighteen to twenty-two who are very smart and very earnest but who do not have access to an older generation and a legacy of activist tactics that could be used to change these situations, right? Like, it takes a long time to meet the Sarahs of the world who tell you, "OK, now this is what we're going to do," or, like, "Let's brainstorm about what we're going to do to change this bwaaah horrible thing" or whatever, you know? When you're, like, eighteen to twenty-two and you're, like, a first-year university student who's just become politicized, you don't have access to those tools yet. It takes a while to make those connections and get those tools.

[audience deciding who will ask a question next, and in what order the questions will be asked]

Q7: Yeah, what I wanted to say was, going off of what you were saying, Morgan, about how we're socialized into a prison-industrial-complex culture where punishment and punitive measures are the go-to, and that for me means that these aren't really skills we're born with, and, in fact, our human compassion toward each other and our lovingness and our kindness get sort of clouded over by all of the trauma and exploitation and oppression that we're experiencing.

I live and work in Ottawa, and one of the things I've been trying to do and a bunch of us are now starting to do are gaining skills around conflict mediation and conflict coaching and affirmative listening, getting to what's actually going on underneath the content and conflicts, and then we are bringing them into the queer community, so we've paired up with a conflict community, conflict-mediation organization that is now doing a training for just queer and trans people and that will give us access to practice nights with them, and long-term we have a goal of building a queer conflict-mediation team.

A bunch of us are going to do respectful confrontation training. It's actually really hard to put these de-escalation skills into practice, especially because there's so much personal involvement. Like, when people that I know and love are in conflict, I'm really stressed out. Sometimes, the skills that I do have just go right out the window because I'm in my feelings and not able. Basically, I'm encouraging people to say, "I don't have these skills and that's OK," because none of us are born with them, and as part of a community practice of strengthening our community and strengthening our relationships with each other, that should be something we intentionally invest in.

MMP: I completely agree. This is part of why I'm trying to shove Sarah's book down everybody's throat in my personal life. Everybody who's been around me has heard about Sarah's book nonstop, because I've been like, "We have to talk about this!" Not because I think you have to agree with everything that's in it, but because we need to have this conversation desperately, and I think the things that you're doing in your community in Ottawa are incredible and exactly the direction we need to take, and it takes a lot of deprogramming to take out these ideas we have that the only conflict resolution we have is punishment, you know?

And that's really hard! We've been taught that for hundreds of years, you know? And it's reinforced on every level every day and it's a really difficult but really, I think, a fruitful thing to do. I have said on Twitter several times that I have this rule now—several of my friends have started referring to it as the Morgan Page rule, which makes me feel like such a jerk—where I will not talk shit about trans women in public. Period. Because it's not helpful. It's not helpful to anyone. If I have a problem with someone, I'm going to go to them and have a conversation with them, and if it's not worth having that really difficult and awkward conversation, then it's not worth freaking out about. But also, part of the reason I say I will go to that person is because I do not think it is useful to try to mediate conflicts on social media in front of eight million other people who are not on the same page about conflict resolution. That doesn't end well. I've never seen that end well. So that's what I have to say about that.

Q8: I just wanna say thanks to you guys. I feel a lot wiser but I also think it's really brave to bring forward political eulogies that are contentious, and I thought it was also a really brave intervention for you because we don't always agree in our communities and I feel like I really learned a lot from the discussion. But I guess I'm just curious because I'm personally very scared of making political errors when I'm speaking, and I wondered how you folks weather when people disagree with you and how you continue to be courageous in bringing forward interventions that speak to when we disagree with each other and hanging in there when we don't, understanding that folks have been really gentle and kind tonight, but it still kind of feels hard even in those situations. I myself hate to make political errors, or just to say things that people politically don't agree with, and that makes it really hard to have difficult conversations in our communities.

SS: I have no fear of in-person conversations. But some stuff online is way too much for me. It's just very overwhelming. But you can get to a point; for example, I'm a very strong pro-Palestine activist and I get in discussions with other Jewish people who don't agree with me all the time. At a certain point it's not worth pursuing. You don't have to keep going until you're screaming at each other. You can see right away that it's not gonna go, so you can let it go, like, I made my point clear. So, I know in person when to stop trying to convince the other person, or when I'm not listening anymore. Online it's just so much harder. For me, part of it is, again, this generational thing. My relationship to technology is very different to someone in their twenties, and I find it really dehumanizing sometimes.

Q9: Just on the topic of internet conflicts, you were talking about how, for you, conflict on the internet is harder than conflict in person. I just wanted to talk about another chasm that exists between people is that for many people because of things like political status or social capital or race or reputation or body of work, it's really hard, if not impossible, to address people in person. I think the internet is amazing in how it bridges that gap and allows, like, a person of color with comparatively little or no social capital to address maybe the most politically significant and well-known person in rad queer circles right now, and I think that's something to be celebrated and is really amazing, so, yeah.

MMP: I think it can have that power. Where it can have problems, for me personally—where it kind of breaks down—is the kind of "dogpile" effect that happens, where one person has a critique and has something they want to challenge another person, and then eighteen million other people who aren't involved in the situation come and escalate. Where suddenly it goes from *This person said and did something that hurt me or was politically fucked up*, to now, five people coming on in increasingly catastrophic language saying that this person is the worst person who ever lived, or on Tumblr saying that this is a trash person, this is a garbage person, these people should not exist anymore in community. This is why I definitely think the internet can be—I'm from a different generation than Sarah; I'm obsessed with social media even though it gives me total anxiety all the time, but I'm totally addicted to it. I'm surprised I haven't been tweeting right now. It's because I'm concentrated on being present with you all today *[laughter]*. But I think a problem for me is that these conversations are done for the public, sometimes, more than they're done for resolution, that there are instances where people are trying to make a point to other people uninvolved in the situation rather than trying to resolve a conflict with the other person. I don't blame people for that because sometimes I feel that way too, and I feel we are very encouraged to do that all the time, but I think that this is maybe not the most helpful way to de-escalate and resolve a situation is basically my hot take on that. But I do agree with you that it can be a very democratizing force, by ensuring that those who feel voiceless have a less anxiety-producing way of getting their voice heard. I think that's really important. I just think it's complicated and difficult.

Q10: You were talking about institutionalization, and you were talking about the health care that Bryn was seeking, and you were talking about collective care. Do you think that there's a way that what you're doing tonight could be a beginning of the renaissance of collective care? Because the truth is we have been fighting for legal rights, and we do have enormous progress socially, and when you come to helping each other, we are not that strong. That conversation right there is a start on a subject we should discuss more often as a whole community. Do you think something can be done?

Because we cannot change the institution, you know? We are the victims of it. So, what can we do?

MMP: I think collectively, over time, we can change institutions, but I do think that this often begins with changing our personal relationships, the ways that we react to interpersonal conflict and the ways that we move through the world. I think that's very real. I feel like my head would get very large if I thought that this night was the beginning of a renaissance in the trans and queer community to change all of our ways of interacting. But I do hope that it's the beginning of a conversation here in Montreal for all the people in this room (and our fabulous friends from Ottawa and Toronto) to take these conversations back and try to engage people with them, I guess, to try to continue this conversation.

QIIA: I wasn't sure what to expect by coming tonight, but I'm really appreciating how I'm hearing a lot of different things coinciding, because for me, the presence of suicidal ideation in my life and the lives of people around who we're mutually trying to keep alive— it's a lot of things that coincide all at the same time. And it just feels like you're just sitting in this wind tunnel that is life all the time. I really appreciate bringing up the role of alcohol and addiction, particularly in a community where you feel like you have to participate in consumption to be anybody or in order to go to anything that happens you need to drink and if you don't drink, then you're alone or you feel like you can't go to things. And I appreciate talking about how we create or escalate conflict.

I guess that what I'm having all these realizations about as I'm sitting here that the number one thing that leads me to those dark places where I consider suicide is two feelings. One is feeling isolation and when it's combined with feeling overwhelmed. It's like I feel super isolated, and I don't know what to do because everything feels like it's too much. And it's not just that my problems are too much. It's that the solutions are too much. It's that everybody's throwing a million solutions at me, fucking online memes about self-care twenty-four hours a day, or, like, fucking start a Wicca practice and that might make you feel better. And it's, like, I can't handle the enormous amount of work it would take to solve the problems in my goddamn life and I think that the thing that sometimes makes me feel better is realizing that I'm not really gonna solve the problem that is my life. I guess that's the number one thing that makes me feel better is when I realize that my feelings of isolation combined with being overwhelmed are primarily a symptom of larger systems. For example, I think self-care is a product of austerity, really. I think this moment of self-care comes from austerity, because there's no social services to gain access to any fuckin' shit that's gonna help me and so they're like, "Here's a scented candle" *[laughter]*.

MMP: Take a bath about it!

QIIB: Yeah! Meditate and shit like that! And I'm not saying that none of these things help. I don't mean to tease. If a candle really helps you, then more power to you, but my point is that every time I feel super overwhelmed, when somebody makes that connection to the larger thing, I feel a little bit lighter. Because I realize that I often feel like I'm shouldering everything personally.

And having that moment that actually I'm not shouldering it personally, that I'm shouldering it collectively with everybody else who has to deal with life under austerity, with everybody else who has to deal with this world of postcolonial, Christian separation— like, all these things. That it comes back from somewhere, I think, helps me, and that's why the thing I'm taking away from tonight is that I'm very glad that you did take the risk of doing a political sermon. I know it's a personal risk that you take to stand up in front of people and do something like that. And I think that's valuable, because I think that sometimes being able to connect our personal suffering to larger political frameworks reduces isolation and makes something overwhelming maybe a little more clear. I don't have to agree with everything you say, but I really like that you're saying it.

Q12: I just wanted to thank you so much for the generosity you have about this issue, and for me I didn't really know what to expect today as someone living with HIV and actively involved in HIV activism, I've known ten-plus people who have killed themselves in the HIV movement and know more people who have died of killing themselves than have died of AIDS since I've been alive, so connecting that to the structural and political issues, as you did in the political sermon, is really important and has given me some things to contend with, to think through how to connect those dots to a political system, which is a lack of care and a lack of support for people. I'm also wondering, because a lot of the people I've known who have taken their own lives have been in these leadership positions, they're stars in the community. Kyle, who was like a mentor to me, and taught me how to be an HIV activist and claim rights for people with HIV, was a major person in the trans community in Toronto. And we assumed he has this network of support and care because he was a leader, and he didn't. I just wanted to thank you first of all for this and I was just wondering what you think about this idea, this gap in support for leaders in our community.

MMP: I think I can best express this through what happened with Kyle. So, Kyle Scanlon—I think I mentioned this earlier—was a huge activist in the community for over a decade. He was a gay trans man in Toronto who did an astounding amount of work to make sure that we had the few social services that trans people have today across the country. He was my coworker. We worked directly beside each other, and we talked all day, every day, for three years about suicide. We talked about it all the time because we both dealt with it like many, many people in the trans community do, and we had a unique position because we were both in leadership roles. And one of things Kyle talked about that was relevant to him and, I think, relevant also to Bryn was that people in leadership positions and artists and well-known personages are assumed to have access to supports that they don't actually have.

In Kyle's case, he couldn't go to any social services because he ran all the social services! There were no counselors for him because every single one of them were his friends and colleagues he knew and had to maintain a work relationship with—he didn't have access to the FTM support group that he used to run because he used to run it. He didn't have that access, and additionally, because he was a leader, he was subject to repeated acts of cruelty because we believe that people in leadership positions within the queer and trans community are open season. If you have a problem with someone who is in a leadership position—if they didn't acknowledge you at a party, if they hold a position that you disagree with, or they've legitimately politically fucked up or something like that—we believe that because they are a leader, they must be made an example of. I've had this happen to me. There are a lot of people in this world who don't like me, who have a lot of really mean and nasty things to say about me, some of which are true, and I'm totally willing to take accountability for those things, and I try to move through the world doing my best to not repeat those issues. But that doesn't stop those people from doing cruelty toward me, because they really, really want to see punishment. We kind of put our leaders up on a pedestal. We're like, "Where's the leader? Where's the leader? Where's the leader?" Then we elect someone leader, basically, or someone gets a job—this is the Canadian model—where suddenly they're a leader and then everything about their life is open season. This is literally why when I quit my job—I used to run the trans services at the 519 Church Street community center in Toronto, which is the LGBT community center—when I quit my job, I, the very next day, moved to Montreal because I knew that I would never not be seen as the person running that job, which means I'd just be doing that work for free for now, which happens. I get called on all the time to do this work, support work, all kinds of work for people in Toronto. And I'm just like, "There are other people who can do this work for you." Also, having had that leadership position, I was always going to have my personal life and everything I touched be examined with a fine-tooth comb. Through that leadership position, I had people file complaints about or go on Tumblr and write long posts because I was dating someone they had a problem with, like, three years ago. And I'm like, "I don't even know what's happening. Why are you coming after me?" you know? This is all just to say that leaders are in a particularly tricky position because we're often the ones who are running the services, who are being the supportive people, and so we don't have access to those services. And at the same we justify any act of cruelty against leaders in our community because they're an example of how everyone else should live. I don't know. Sarah, do you want . . . ?

SS: We need to consult about how late we can go. *[talks to Morgan]* Two more!

MMP: Two more questions.

Q13A: Should I do, like, a turkey thing and talk up to the . . . ?

MMP: It's OK *[inaudible]*. Let's light a candle about it *[laughter]*.

Q13B: Just to reiterate what you are talking about and what Alex brings up, there are two documents called "Living and Serving 1 and 2" that talk about the problematics of trying to access services as an HIV person when you're part of the HIV response. So, you get a job, and you get put in a leadership role, and specifically if your work is around social support, then to have social and emotional stuff that you need to work through seems like a particularly personalized emotional failing. That prevents folks from accessing services. I know that it's prevented other people, but I will name that it's prevented me as well.

I work for a community health center and I run a street outreach center for people that are homeless and use drugs—and one of the ongoing conversations that we're having that I feel like has become apparent tonight is about grief and loss. We're talking about how we deal with complex and elevated emotional states. So, I've been hurt and/or I've been pissed off and/or I'm mourning a loss, so the harm reduction movement is, unfortunately, expert at dealing with grief and loss and multiple loss because everybody fucking dies all the time. So, seeking out training—this is the other thing too. There are just no available mental and emotional health services in Canada, like, it's just not a thing that exists, so we find other ways of coping. But there's also tools that we can learn, and we can share with each other about how to unpack and process some of complex stuff that we're handed just by existing.

SS: Thank you! Last one?

Q14: Super, super psyched about your book. These thoughts have been trailing around for a while. So, I guess I really appreciate the conversations surrounding differentiating conflict from abuse, and also kind of owning your trauma and subsequent reactions. I'm just sort of wondering, because of the conversations around care and healing that are often happening in Montreal. We often have these circles, particularly queers, that are looking to heal, and we can do so together. And because of the way that trauma functions, and the way that we're re-creating our trauma reality, you've got these queers that are basically in the process of retraumatizing each other. And so I guess I'm wondering how to kind of deal and mitigate that while this conversation about community care and accountability is happening, and when I'm talking about this I do mean abuse and not conflict. I'm gonna read your book; I'm super psyched about it, so if you can answer *[inaudible]*.

ss: It's such a complex construction. I'm having my book launch tomorrow at the Concordia bookstore. It's a three-hundred-page book and I haven't learned how to say "duddle duddle duh," you know what I mean? But tomorrow I'm going to really lay out a lot of tropes and ideas, so that might help. I just don't have a sound-bite answer for something like that.

TN: On behalf of QED, I just wanted to thank Sarah and Morgan. Let's all thank them for a wonderful time. *[applause]*

ss: I just wanted to say that I've heard a lot of things tonight that I've never heard before, and I really, really appreciate it and I'm definitely gonna think about it. This was very enriching for me. So thank you.

Conclusion

Confronting Repetitive Thinking Makes Solidarity a Way of Life

T THE SAME TIME THAT fascists have been elected in the US and around the world, a global generation has woken up to the cause of the Palestinian people, and this is an introduction to being in opposition, yet one that remains a protest from below. Those in power stay hostile to the actual needs of people from whom they extract every dollar and natural resource. The killing escalates at the same time as we help each other rise in understanding and purpose. As enraging as it is for so many people to be unheard while the suffering continues, solidarity is about getting ready for the change that we need right now. It does not deliver when we want it or need it, but there is nothing else that can bring us closer to a justifiable future.

Why do American politicians continually sell weapons to Israel, despite its violation of every international law and tenet of human decency? In a way, we can imagine the answer: Historian

Ilan Pappe's 2024 six-hundred-page study, *Lobbying for Zionism on Both Sides of the Atlantic*, details the nuts-and-bolts history of building Zionist influence on governments. But the bigger lesson is that for the most part, politicians don't make change, we do. And long after, they sometimes follow suit when doing so is necessary for their maintenance of power. The futility of seeking progress through elections often ends up with us having no one to vote for, and then threatening to withhold our votes from Democrats as a pressure strategy—as many had to do with Kamala Harris during her campaign. Sometimes this works or moves the discourse forward, at least. Completely withholding a vote usually disappears into the vapor, mixing with the large percentage of Americans who never vote for reasons ranging from sexism to apathy to confusion to disgust. So, pressuring politicians from where we assuredly stand in tandem with building communities in honest discourse becomes our best action in a skewed and unrepresentative electoral system.

Since most actual social change takes place in countercultures of opposition, where the real creation of new culture lives, we are continually working to articulate the literal mechanics of why so many esteemed cultural institutions, sophisticated national publications, and American universities are completely failing to respond to the moral crisis of this bloody slaughter of people in Gaza. It is more than finances; there is a stagnant mindset at play. After all, when university professors were called before the Republican-dominated congressional subcommittee and heard their students and themselves (Jewish or not) called "antisemitic," a number of them lost their jobs, but none overtly defied this false accusation. Not one of them spoke against US funding of the war on Gaza, and not one supported their students for being the most coherent national voice against the genocide. They were going down anyway, but it was an identification with the censorious decorum of power systems, and bureaucrats' acculturated fear of rebellion, that kept them all from telling the truth.

It occurs to me that most of these corporate information industries—universities, magazines and newspapers, cultural organizations, entertainment conglomerates, publishers, theatrical and screen producers—have long histories of excluding the most interesting and necessary ideas that circle around them. In a sense, their refusal of complexity defines them and is their power base. The inability of the media to grapple with what the country actually needs is lethal. The lack of housing in America, the lack of living wage, these topics disappeared from pundits and debates. In the election of 2024, the Democrats used the word *economy* to mean the stock market, while for people it meant prices.

What makes it so confusing is their embedded accompanying system of self-praise telling us repeatedly that the repetitive, banal ideas in mass circulation are special and deserve reward. Year after year we are told through many selections at elections, through promotions or even the Oscars, Tonys, Pulitzers, and the full range of intellectual and citizenship awards in corporate marketing venues, that irrelevant products deserve to be the focus of our attention and should be replicated. This reinforces the idea that the way things are is not only *great*, but the *best*. This merry-go-round debases and marginalizes risky, exciting movements of forward-thinking people while elevating and glorifying avoidant work that pretends away the most important questions of our time: Who has the power, and why?

As a result, there exists an imposed immobility and punishment of dissent as an inherent component of the norm of American culture branding. Understanding this process helps, in a sense, to comprehend why the smart and successful individuals who signed the letter against Jonathan Glazer have such an ignorant and, in fact, false understanding of world events and their moral implications. After all, if you spend your entire life in a bubble of wealth, devoting all your time to creating, financing, and marketing commercial projects that relentlessly denigrate change and glamorize hierarchy, and then you are told that these objects are *great* and the *best*, you end up spending your existence within protected subcultures of a tiny, cyclical range of thought.

This world of non-ideas shows up in the most established places. I watched a Zionist right-wing journalist claim at the 92nd St Y (after they canceled Pulitzer Prize winner Viet Thanh Nguyen for signing a letter) that she is protested because she is Jewish, and not because she is supporting mass murder. I read a writer in *The Atlantic* proclaim the "new antisemitism" while being unable to grasp Israeli fascism. I followed a student from a campus group called Bears for Israel claiming that her classmates are upset with her because they are antisemitic, not because her actions endorse genocide. What all these people have in common is a strange childishness—an inability to imagine that they could be part of anything wrong. A total refusal to be self-critical. Repeatedly each of them makes a specious claim that they are being "called out"—that is, criticized—by groups, and that the only reason this could be happening is because they are Jewish. The only thing they can imagine that would make someone contest them is antisemitism, because they cannot conceptualize themselves as doing anything justifying criticism.

I mean, I am just as Jewish as they are. The people who are yelling at them are not yelling at me. So the anger is not about us being Jewish, but about our actions. Yes, I do get messages constantly on social media from other Jews calling me a Nazi and a "kapo," but that is because I name and oppose Jewish supremacy, and they can't stand that. The issues at stake are politics and values. What I want to say back to these people is:

Let me tell you something, you are not being persecuted. That is made up and pretend. What is actually happening is that you are supporting a genocide, and history will understand this as a genocide, and your selfish, shallow self-conception, your refusal to see yourself realistically, your endless agreement with brutality—these crimes will follow you for the rest of your lives. You are lying to yourself. It is too bad that magazines and cultural institutions and companies, governments, and universities are supporting the distortions in your self-perceptions, but what they are doing is unethical and cruel and absolutely wrong. And history will ask you about what you have said and done today. So, look in the mirror and see the pain you have created and justified, and you will see yourself.

This is why people are in the streets, this is why campuses are demanding divestment, this is why writers boycotted PEN, this is why our organizations must make public statements of solidarity: *to end complicity with genocide.* This moment is a huge spotlight on every one of us. And I am actually surprised by some individuals' unpredictable integrity and others' unpredictable greed. We are each showing our true selves.

Within this process, there are many challenges, including the most personal one: to strive to be coherent. This involves being willing to be thought of as strange or annoying and being outside other people's approval systems. It is a risk to undertake the imposed loss of credibility that brings with it a loss of influence, when we challenge power directly. But being in solidarity means giving each other the approval and support, the insight and strength, the love—if you will—to continue to transform our relationships to status, safety, institutions, and the machinery of approval, whether from our families, our professions, the state, or the standards constantly fed us from corporate entertainment, which includes media. There is a kind of happiness that comes from trying to be a consistent person, and sometimes that is the only obtainable goal, to try. After all, there is a pleasure in thinking for yourself that, once it finds its home, becomes rejuvenating, fascinating, and life-giving.

No power structure is stagnant. Healing takes place in relationship, and that is personal and also social. New approaches, understanding, and conversations are needed now and will always be needed. Solidarity is our way of life, and to keep it breathing, innovation is our friend. My motto for these coming years is: "Don't stop yourself from doing what you think is right. Make them stop you." And I hope to keep to that in solidarity with many of you.

Acknowledgments

Some material in this volume previously appeared in whole or different formats in: *The New Yorker*, *New York*, *The New York Review of Books*, *WomaNews*, *Los Angeles Times*, *Harper's Bazaar*, *The New Republic*, *QED: A Journal in GLBTQ Worldmaking*, *Mondoweiss*, and the following books: *Crashing Cathedrals: Edmund White by the Book*, edited by Tom Cardamone (Itna Press), *Saturation: Race, Art, and the Circulation of Value*, edited by C. Riley Snorton and Hentyle Yapp (MIT Press), *Extraordinary Rendition: (American) Writers on Palestine*, edited by Ru Freeman (OR Books), and *Letters to Palestine: Writers Respond to War and Occupation*, edited by Vijay Prashad (Verso Books).

Grateful appreciation to Niki Papadopoulos for taking the time to sit down in person so we could grapple with these ideas. After forty years in publishing, it is clear to me that only through in-person conversations can artists and publishers or producers develop mutual understanding about complex and unfamiliar ideas and how to share them with the public. Thanks to everyone at Thesis Books and Penguin and to Michael Bourret, who shares all the frustrations with kindness.

Special thanks to Kristen Morgenstern for research, and Mac-Dowell for a lifetime of support. And thank you to my colleagues at CUNY College of Staten Island and at Northwestern University.

Thanks to Claudia Rankine, Rochelle Feinstein, Matt Brim, Marcia Cohen-Zakai, Jack Waters, Peter Cramer, Jim Hubbard, Jacqueline Reingold, Gina Gionfriddo, Nuar Alsadir, Jacqueline Woodson, Lydia Polgreen, Kaitlyn Greenidge, Candace Feit, Dudley Saunders, Linda Villarosa, Jana Welch, Rachel Harris, Heidi Schmid, Ava Chin, Morgan M. Page, Brad Taylor, Susan Brown, Sur Rodney (Sur), Harriet Clarke, Amelia Evans, Lisa Balthazar, Jacqueline Nassy Brown, Zab Hobart, and in Chicago: Natasha Trethewey, Brett Gadsen, Kate Masur, Peter Slevin, Daisy Hernández, Steven Thrasher, Jane Rhodes, Lynn Hudson, Jennie Brier, Lynette Jackson, and all my colleagues for their insights, support, friendship, and conversation. Thank you to Sa'ed Atshan and Ghadir Shafie for your everlasting integrity, example, and friendship. Special thanks to Leslie M. Harris and Ella, a great dog.

Notes

1. SOLIDARITY: FANTASY AND NECESSITY

6 **Americans in the 1930s who opposed:** Jeremy Scahill, "The 3,000 Americans Who Fought Fascism Before World War II," *Intercept*, September 30, 2017, https://theintercept.com/2017/09/30/the -americans-who-fought-fascism-before-wwii/#:~:text=In%201936% 2C%20young%20Americans,in%20the%20Spanish%20Civil%20War.

7 **The Spanish Civil War veterans:** Fraser Raeburn, "The 'Premature Anti-fascists'? International Brigade Veterans' Participation in the British War Effort, 1939–45," *War in History* 27, no. 3 (2020): 408–32.

9 **deliberate slaughter of over forty thousand:** AJLabs, "Israel-Gaza War in Maps and Charts: Live Tracker," Al Jazeera, July 31, 2024, https://www.aljazeera.com/news/longform/2023/10/9/israel-hamas -war-in-maps-and-charts-live-tracker; Rasha Khatib, Martin McKee, and Salim Yusuf, "Counting the Dead in Gaza: Difficult but Essential," *Lancet* 404, no. 10449 (2024): 237–8, https://www.thelancet.com /journals/lancet/article/PIIS0140-6736(24)01169-3/fulltext.

10 **protesting the complicity of their institutions:** Kenichi Serino, "Tens of Thousands Have Joined Pro-Palestinian Protests Across the

United States. Experts Say They Are Growing," *PBS News*, January 16, 2024, https://www.pbs.org/newshour/politics/tens-of-thousands-have -joined-pro-palestinian-protests-across-the-united-states-experts-say -they-are-growing.

2. AN AMERICAN JEW IN SOLIDARITY WITH GAZA

13 **the Nakba—the Palestinian name:** "About the Nakba," United Nations, https://www.un.org/unispal/about-the-nakba/.

15 **town square of their city of Rohatyn:** "The Shoah in Rohatyn," Rohatyn Jewish Heritage, https://rohatynjewishheritage.org/en /history/timeline-shoah/.

16 **murdered poets like Refaat Alareer:** Zeena Saifi et al., "Daughter of Prominent Palestinian Poet Killed in Israeli Airstrike in Gaza," CNN, April 27, 2024, https://www.cnn.com/2024/04/27/middleeast /shaima-refaat-alareer-death-intl/index.html.

16 **Even mainstream NBC News:** Chantal Da Silva, "Mass Graves Found at Gaza Hospitals Raided by Israel Prompt Demands for Independent Investigation," NBC News, April 27, 2024, https:// www.nbcnews.com/news/world/mass-graves-found-gaza-hospitals -raided-israel-prompt-demands-independ-rcna149110.

16 **American journalists like Jazmine Hughes:** Katie Robertson, "New York Times Writer Resigns After Signing Letter Protesting the Israel-Gaza War," *New York Times*, November 3, 2023, https://www .nytimes.com/2023/11/03/business/media/new-york-times-writer -resign-israel-gaza-war.html; Zachary Small, "Artforum Fires Top Editor After Its Open Letter on Israel-Hamas War," *New York Times*, October 26, 2023, https://www.nytimes.com/2023/10/26/arts /artforum-editor-fired-david-velasco-palestine-gaza.html.

16 **Mehdi Hasan was pushed out:** Al Jazeera Staff, "Palestine Advocates Decry MSNBC's Cancellation of Mehdi Hasan News Show," Al Jazeera, November 30, 2023, https://www.aljazeera.com/news/2023 /11/30/palestine-advocates-decry-msnbcs-cancellation-of-mehdi -hasan-news-show.

16 **eighty are currently imprisoned:** Steven W. Thrasher, "Why American Journalists Should Be Outraged About the Dozens of

Palestinian Journalists Jailed in Israel," *Literary Hub*, June 21, 2024, https://lithub.com/why-american-journalists-should-be-outraged -about-the-dozens-of-palestinian-journalists-jailed-in-israel/.

20 **US Congress voted in 2023:** Strongly Condemning and Denouncing the Drastic Rise of Antisemitism in the United States and Around the World, H.R. 894, 118th Cong. (2023–2024).

23 **"There is nothing Jewish":** "Omar Barghouti: 'BDS: Ending Complicity in Genocide and Apartheid,'" YouTube video, 13:39, posted by the Palestine Festival of Literature, March 14, 2024, https:// www.youtube.com/watch?v=0WowN9nHknY.

24 **Arendt and Einstein signed a letter:** "Einstein Statement Assails Begin Party," *New York Times*, December 3, 1948.

24 **there would be thirty-two million Jews:** Ofri Ilany, "How Many Jews Would There Be If Not for the Holocaust?," *Haaretz*, April 19, 2009, https://www.haaretz.com/2009-04-19/ty-article/how-many -jews-would-there-be-if-not-for-the-holocaust/0000017f-e76e-dea7 -adff-f7ffe8900000.

24 **only fifteen million Jews:** Judy Maltz, "World Jewish Population Totals 15.2 Million—with Nearly Half in Israel," *Haaretz*, April 26, 2022, https://www.haaretz.com/israel-news/2022-04-26/ty-article /world-jewish-population-totals-15-2-million-with-nearly-half-in -israel/00000180-66f6-d5ca-a986-7eff58900000.

25 **Austrian journalist Theodor Herzl:** Theodor Herzl, *The Jewish State* (1896; Project Gutenberg, 2008), https://www.gutenberg.org/files /25282/25282-h/25282-h.htm.

25 **there are now more refugees:** "Global Appeal 2024," UNHCR, https://reporting.unhcr.org/global-appeal-2024#:~:text=The %20Global%20Appeal%20provides%20information,find %20solutions%20to%20their%20situations.

25 **One of Herzl's ideas:** Herzl, *Jewish State*, 96.

25 **part of a larger rhetoric:** "Statement from Gerald Rosberg, Chair of the Special Committee on Campus Safety," *Columbia News*, November 10, 2023, https://news.columbia.edu/news/statement -gerald-rosberg-chair-special-committee-campus-safety.

26 **Students from Columbia and Barnard College:** "Where Protesters on U.S. Campuses Have Been Arrested or Detained," *New York*

Times, July 22, 2024, https://www.nytimes.com/interactive/2024/us
/pro-palestinian-college-protests-encampments.html.

26 **over three thousand student and faculty arrests:** Ava Thompson
and Alexandra Marquez, "Hundreds of Pro-Palestinian Protesters
Arrested on Capitol Hill Ahead of Netanyahu Visit," NBC News,
July 23, 2024, https://www.nbcnews.com/politics/congress
/hundreds-palestinian-protesters-arrested-capitol-hill-ahead
-netanyahu-rcna163368; Aya Elamroussi and Rob Frehse, "Pro-
Palestinian Protesters Snarl Manhattan Traffic and Limit Grand
Central Access as They Call for Ceasefire Friday," CNN, November
11, 2023, https://www.cnn.com/2023/11/11/us/pro-palestine
-protesters-new-york-city/index.html; Derick Waller, "Protesters
Arrested After Blocking Traffic on Manhattan Bridge," CBS News,
May 12, 2024, https://www.cbsnews.com/newyork/news/manhattan
-bridge-protesters-arrested/; Eyewitness News, "More Than 200
Arrests During Protest at Grand Army Plaza in Brooklyn," ABC7,
April 24, 2024, https://abc7ny.com/more-than-200-people-were
-arrested-during-a-protest-at-grand-army-plaza-in-brooklyn
/14725687/; Selina Wang, Quinn Owen, and Tesfaye Negussie,
"Dozens Arrested at White House as Protesters Call for End to
Israel's Response to Hamas Attack," ABC News, October 16, 2023,
https://abcnews.go.com/Politics/dozens-arrested-white-house
-protesters-call-end-israels/story?id=104023675.

28 **holding signs thanking students:** "Palestinians in Rafah Express
Thanks to US University Protesters," Al Jazeera, April 28, 2024,
https://www.aljazeera.com/program/newsfeed/2024/4/28
/palestinians-in-rafah-express-thanks-to-us-university
-protesters#:~:text=Displaced%20Palestinians%20in%20Gaza
%20are,on%20their%20tents%20in%20Rafah.

28 **despite all the false reporting:** Jennifer Schuessler, "92NY Pulls
Event with Acclaimed Writer Who Criticized Israel," *New York
Times*, October 22, 2023, https://www.nytimes.com/2023/10/21
/arts/92ny-viet-thanh-nguyen-israel.html; Ian Ward, "We Sat Down
with the Conservative Mastermind Behind Claudine Gay's Ouster,"
Politico, January 3, 2024, https://www.politico.com/news/magazine
/2024/01/03/christopher-rufo-claudine-gay-harvard-resignation

-00133618; Howard Monroe, "Penn Donor Ross Stevens Threatens to Pull $100 Million Donation After Liz Magill's Testimony in Congress," CBS News, December 8, 2023, https://www.cbsnews.com /philadelphia/news/liz-magill-university-of-pennsylvania-ross-stevens -wharton-donation/; Michaela Zee, "CAA Agent Maha Dakhil Resigns from Board After Controversial Social Media Posts on Israel," *Variety*, October 22, 2023, https://variety.com/2023/film/news/caa -maha-dakhil-resigns-board-israel-social-media-posts-controversy -1235764577/; Adrian Horton, "Susan Sarandon Dropped by Talent Agency After Remarks at Pro-Palestine Rally," *Guardian*, November 21, 2023, https://www.theguardian.com/film/2023/nov/21/susan -sarandon-pro-palestinian-remarks-uta-dropped.

29 **Writers have pulled out of lucrative:** Zoe Guy, "PEN Awards Facing Disaster After Many Withdraw in Solidarity with Palestine," *Vulture*, April 17, 2024, https://www.vulture.com/article/pen-awards-authors -withdraw-palestine.html.

29 **not to publish in *Artforum*:** Zachary Small, "Artists Call for Boycott After Artforum Fires Its Top Editor," *New York Times*, October 27, 2023, https://www.nytimes.com/2023/10/27/arts/design/artforum -boycott-goldin-eisenman.html.

29 **coalition of Black clergy:** Audra D. S. Burch and Maya King, "Prominent Black Church Leaders Call for End of U.S. Aid to Israel," *New York Times*, February 16, 2024, https://www.nytimes.com/2024 /02/16/us/ame-church-us-israel-aid.html.

29 **United Auto Workers union have opposed:** Rishikesh Rajagopalan, "United Auto Workers Union Calls for 'Immediate, Permanent Cease-Fire' in Israel-Hamas War, Becoming Largest Labor Union to Do So," CBS News, December 2, 2023, https://www.cbsnews.com /news/israel-gaza-war-united-auto-workers-cease-fire/.

29 **ruled in July 2024:** Case 186— Legal Consequences Arising from the Policies and Practices of Israel in the Occupied Palestinian Territory, Including East Jerusalem, International Court of Justice, July 19, 2024.

30 **Jewish Voice for Peace, founded in 1996:** "FAQ," Jewish Voice for Peace, https://www.jewishvoiceforpeace.org/faq/.

30 **murder of over two thousand civilians:** "Gaza Crisis: Toll of

Operations in Gaza," BBC News, September 1, 2014, https://www
.bbc.com/news/world-middle-east-28439404.

30   **"I was born in 1958":** Sarah Schulman, "Explanations Are Not Excuses,"
New York, October 16, 2023, https://nymag.com/intelligencer/2023
/10/israel-gaza-war-manufactured-consent.html.

36   **Congresswoman Alexandria Ocasio-Cortez:** Nick Reisman,
"AOC Knocks 'Bigotry and Callousness' of Times Square Rally
for Palestinians," *Politico*, October 10, 2023, https://subscriber
.politicopro.com/article/2023/10/aoc-times-square-rally-israel
-palestine-00120684.

36   **Times Square to support these civilians:** Chelsia Rose Marcius
et al., "Pro-Israel and Pro-Palestinian Demonstrators Stage Impassioned
Protests in New York," *New York Times*, October 8, 2023, https://
www.nytimes.com/live/2023/10/08/world/israel-gaza-attack-hamas
-news?smid=url-share#pro-israel-and-pro-palestinian-demonstrators
-stage-impassioned-protests-in-new-york; Sarah Schulman, *Ayman*,
aired October 30, 2023, on MSNBC, https://www.instagram.com
/aymanm/reel/CzBwixYuwoq/. See also: Karen Bekker, "MSNBC:
Four Months of Disinformation," Committee for Accuracy in Middle
East Reporting and Analysis (CAMERA), January 28, 2024, https://
www.camera.org/article/msnbc-four-months-of-disinformation/.

37   **broken up by the police:** Thomas Escritt, "Police Shut Down
Pro-Palestinian Gathering in Germany over Hate Speech Fears,"
Reuters, April 12, 2024, https://www.reuters.com/world/europe
/police-shut-down-pro-palestinian-gathering-germany-over-hate
-speech-fears-2024-04-12/.

37   **Palestinian doctor, Ghassan Abu-Sitta:** Jack Jeffery and Geir
Moulson, "Prominent Surgeon Says He Was Denied Entry to
Germany for a Pro-Palestinian Conference," AP, April 12, 2024,
https://apnews.com/article/germany-gaza-doctor-conference-entry
-refused-e82252cb9bc5e010e8bfd0689f816e53; Sal Ahmed, "Meet
the Jewish Activist Germany Arrested for Being Pro-Palestinian,"
Middle East Eye, April 18, 2024, https://www.middleeasteye.net
/news/germany-crackdown-israel-gaza-jewish-activist.

38   **Butler sitting quietly:** Tessa Solomon, "Judith Butler Withdraws
from Centre Pompidou Lectures over Hamas Statements," *ARTnews*,

April 4, 2024, https://www.artnews.com/art-news/news/judith-butler
-withdraws-from-centre-pompidou-lectures-over-hamas-statements
-1234701774.

3. SOLIDARITY IN ACTION

41 **campus solidarity encampments:** "An Interactive Map of Gaza
Solidarity Encampments Around the World," Palestine Is Everywhere,
2024, https://www.palestineiseverywhere.com/.

43 **three hundred in one day:** Ayana Archie, "New York Police Arrest
300 People as They Clear Hamilton Hall at Columbia University,"
NPR, May 1, 2024, https://www.npr.org/2024/05/01/1248401802
/columbia-university-protests-new-york.

43 **six-year-old Hind Rajab:** "The Killing of Hind Rajab," Forensic
Architecture, June 6, 2024, https://forensic-architecture.org
/investigation/the-killing-of-hind-rajab.

43 **students later refused:** The Hind's Hall 46, "Columbia University
Hind's Hall Defendants Reject Deals in Solidarity with the CUNY
22," *Mondoweiss*, June 28, 2024, https://mondoweiss.net/2024/06
/columbia-university-hinds-hall-defendants-reject-deals-in-solidarity
-with-the-cuny-22/.

43 **the school stood by:** "UCLA Clashes: Pro-Palestinian Protesters
Attacked by Israel Supporters," Al Jazeera, May 1, 2024, https://www
.aljazeera.com/news/2024/5/1/ucla-clashes-pro-palestinian-protesters
-attacked-by-israel-supporters.

43 **police beat and arrested:** Timothy Pratt, "'Like a War Zone': Emory
University Grapples with Fallout from Police Response to Protest,"
Guardian, April 27, 2024, https://www.theguardian.com/us-news
/2024/apr/27/emory-university-georgia-police-campus-protests.

43 **sixty-five-year-old professor, Annelise Orleck:** Dartmouth Senior
Staff, "College Clarifies Stance on Professor Annelise Orleck's Arrest,"
Dartmouth, May 2, 2024, https://www.thedartmouth.com/article
/2024/05/college-clarifies-stance-on-professor-annelise-orlecks-arrest.

43 **faculty started their own encampment:** Anni Irish, "First-of-Its-
Kind Pro-Palestine Faculty Encampment Continues at New York's
New School University," *Art Newspaper*, May 13, 2024, https://www

.theartnewspaper.com/2024/05/13/pro-palestine-faculty
-encampment-new-school.

43 **number of faculty stopped teaching:** Gloria Oladipo and Erum
Salam, "Columbia Faculty Members Walk Out After Pro-Palestinian
Protesters Arrested," *Guardian*, April 22, 2024, https://www
.theguardian.com/us-news/2024/apr/22/columbia-university-protests
-shutdown.

44 **Columbia's divestment in South Africa:** "Let Us Remember the
Last Time Students Occupied Columbia University: Omar Barghouti,
Tanaquil Jones and Barbara Ransby," *Guardian*, May 3, 2024, https://
www.theguardian.com/commentisfree/article/2024/may/03
/columbia-pro-palestinian-protest-south-africa-divestment.

45 **2.3 million Gazans:** "UN Agency Says 40 Percent of Gaza's Population
'At Risk of Famine,'" Al Jazeera, December 28, 2023, https://www
.aljazeera.com/news/2023/12/28/un-agency-says-40-percent-of-gazas
-population-at-risk-of-famine#:~:text=The%20United%20Nations
%20agency%20for,trucks%20to%20enter%20the%20enclave.

45 **50 million deaths globally:** "HIV," World Health Organization, https://
www.who.int/data/gho/data/themes/hiv-aids#:~:text=Since%20the
%20beginning%20of%20the,at%20the%20end%20of%202023.

46 **registered with the UN as refugees:** "Figures at a Glance," UNHCR,
June 13, 2024, https://www.unhcr.org/us/about-unhcr/who-we-are
/figures-glance.

53 **She had previously been:** "The U.S. and the United Nations Human
Rights Council: Principled Engagement," US Department of State, May
24, 2011, https://2009-2017.state.gov/p/io/rm/2011/166802.htm.

53 **Novelist Randa Jarrar:** New Arab and Global Voices MENA,
"Palestinian Writer Randa Jarrar Dragged Out of PEN America Event
for Protesting," Global Voices, February 8, 2024, https://globalvoices
.org/2024/02/08/palestinian-writer-randa-jarrar-dragged-out-of-pen
-america-event-for-protesting/.

54 **opposing an award:** Andrew Patner, "McNamara Awarded Tonight;
Noon Picnic Leads Off Protest," *Chicago Maroon*, May 22, 1979,
https://campub.lib.uchicago.edu/view/?docId=mvol-0004-1979-0522
#page/1/mode/1up.

58 **rule of dictator Jorge Videla:** *Encyclopedia Britannica*, s.v. "Jorge

Rafael Videla," July 29, 2024, https://www.britannica.com/biography
/Jorge-Rafael-Videla.

62 **one in four American women:** Becca, "1 in 4 American Women Will
    Have an Abortion by Age 45," Planned Parenthood, February 15, 2018,
    https://www.plannedparenthood.org/planned-parenthood-pacific
    -southwest/blog/1-in-4-american-women-will-have-an-abortion-by
    -age-45.

63 **Lizzo did an event:** Taylor Mims, "Lizzo, Beck and Sara Bareilles Join
    SXSW Speakers Roster," *Billboard*, February 15, 2022, https://www
    .billboard.com/business/touring/sxsw-keynote-speakers-lizzo-beck
    -1235031993/.

64 **"Madame Bovary, c'est moi":** Rebecca A. Demarest, "C'est Moi:
    Gustave Flaubert's 'Madame Bovary,'" *Inquiries Journal* 3, no. 3 (2011),
    http://www.inquiriesjournal.com/articles/405/cest-moi-gustave
    -flauberts-madame-bovary.

65 **Audre Lorde warned us:** Audre Lorde, *Your Silence Will Not Protect
    You* (Silver Press, 2017).

67 **Wilmette Brown, a Black gay woman:** Sophia Mirviss and Sarah
    Schulman, "Housewives and Prostitutes Unite—with Wilmette
    Brown," *WomaNews* 1, no. 10 (1980): 3, 4.

67 **"prostitutes would be raising":** Mirviss and Schulman, 3.

68 **"There is a lot of sex appeal":** Mirviss and Schulman, 3.

68 **"We can reach the broadest number":** Mirviss and Schulman, 3.

69 **"Everything is going up":** Mirviss and Schulman, 3.

69 **"The way you deal":** Mirviss and Schulman, 3.

70 **"that was the place to go":** Mirviss and Schulman, 3.

70 ***"Oh yes, we have a Black":*** Mirviss and Schulman, 3.

70 **"I was living a double life":** Mirviss and Schulman, 3.

71 **"All during this time":** Mirviss and Schulman, 3.

72 **"I was fed up with CR":** Mirviss and Schulman, 4.

4. SOLIDARITY AND THE PROBLEM OF CRITERIA

77 **openly gay performer Olly Alexander:** Nadeem Badshah, "Queer
    Artists Call on Olly Alexander to Boycott Eurovision over Israel
    Participation," *Guardian*, March 28, 2024, https://www.theguardian

.com/tv-and-radio/2024/mar/28/queer-artists-call-on-olly-alexander
-to-boycott-eurovision-over-israel-participation.

77 **"We firmly believe in the unifying power":** Max Pilley, "Olly
Alexander Responds to Eurovision Boycott Calls: 'We firmly believe
in the unifying power of music,'" NME.com, March 29, 2024, https://
www.nme.com/news/music/olly-alexander-among-eurovision-acts
-responding-to-boycott-calls-we-firmly-believe-in-the-unifying-power
-of-music-3610915.

78 **"By participating in Eurovision":** PACBI – BDS Movement
(@PACBI), X, March 29, 2024, https://x.com/PACBI/status
/1773664170937868781.

78 **who booed the Israeli performers:** "Boos for Israel's Entry at Eurovision
Rehearsal," YouTube video, 0:30, posted by Al Jazeera English, May 9,
2024, https://www.youtube.com/watch?v=bnDBzf9Jiog.

79 **sentenced a poet to five months:** "Dareen Tatour," PEN America,
https://pen.org/individual-case/dareen-tatour/.

82 **The year before Dareen's arrest:** Sarah Schulman, "Why Israel
Imprisoned a Poet," Jewish Voice for Peace, https://www
.jewishvoiceforpeace.org/2018/08/07/whyisraelimprisionedapoet
/#:~:text=Annual%20reports%20from%20Hamleh%2C%
20The,2017%20alone%20for%20posting%20online.

82 **best known perhaps is Martin Niemöller:** "Martin Niemöller: 'First
They Came For . . . ,'" United States Holocaust Memorial Museum,
April 11, 2023, https://encyclopedia.ushmm.org/content/en/article
/martin-niemoeller-first-they-came-for-the-socialists.

82 **canceled concerts in Israel:** Peter Beaumont, "Lorde Cancels Israel
Concert After Pro-Palestinian Campaign," *Guardian*, December 25,
2017, https://www.theguardian.com/music/2017/dec/25/lorde
-cancels-israel-concert-after-pro-palestinian-campaign?CMP=share
_btn_url; Michael Bachner, "Pussy Riot Cancels Israel Show Without
Explanation," *Times of Israel*, April 8, 2018, https://www.timesofisrael
.com/pussy-riot-cancels-israel-show-without-explanation/.

82 **In Britain, the High Court ruled:** Susanna Rust, "UK Government
Divestment Rules 'Unlawful,' Court Rules," *IPE*, June 26, 2017, https://
www.ipe.com/uk-government-divestment-rules-unlawful-court-rules
/10019585.article.

82 **international filmmakers pulled out:** Amy Spiro, "Tel Aviv LGBT Film Festival Targeted by Anti-Israel Boycotters," *Jerusalem Post*, May 29, 2017, https://www.jpost.com/israel-news/tel-aviv-lgbt-film-festival -targeted-by-bds-494215.

82 **Following appeals from 250 writers:** Charlotte Silver, "PEN America Drops Israel Sponsorship," *Electronic Intifada*, February 23, 2017, https://electronicintifada.net/blogs/charlotte-silver/pen-america -drops-israel-sponsorship.

83 **Great March of Return reached its sixth week:** Huthifa Fayyad, "Gaza's Great March of Return Protests Explained," Al Jazeera, March 30, 2019, https://www.aljazeera.com/news/2019/3/30/gazas-great -march-of-return-protests-explained.

83 **"The soul asks who am I?":** Schulman, "Why Israel Imprisoned a Poet."

85 **public system of five hundred thousand:** "New Study Confirms CUNY's Power as National Engine of Economic Mobility," CUNY, June 17, 2020, https://www.cuny.edu/news/new-study-confirms-cunys -power-as-national-engine-of-economic-mobility/.

85 **undocumented students could not qualify:** "Tuition and Fees," College of Staten Island, https://csi-undergraduate.catalog.cuny.edu/financial-aid -and-tuition/tuition-and-fees; "The Percentage of Full-Time Entering Undergraduates Who Received Grant Aid," CUNY, https://www.cuny .edu/financial-aid/information-resources/ft-undergrad-grant-aid/.

86 **graduation rate of 34 percent:** "College of Staten Island CUNY," College Factual, https://www.collegefactual.com/colleges/cuny -college-of-staten-island/academic-life/graduation-and-retention/.

98 **Black women are only 4.4 percent:** Marybeth Gasman, "Hand in Hand: Black Women in Pursuit of the Ph.D.," *Forbes*, August 9, 2021, https://www.forbes.com/sites/marybethgasman/2021/08/09/hand -in-hand-black-women-in-pursuit-of-the-phd/.

100 **she attributed her communism:** Ben Davis, "Alice Neel's Communism Is Essential to Her Art. You Can See It in the 'Battlefield' of Her Paintings, and Her Ruthless Portrait of Her Son," Artnet, April 15, 2021, https://news.artnet.com/art-world-archives /alice-neel-was-a-commie-a-battlefield-of-humanism-1958503.

101 **her subsequent single-motherness:** Lauren O'Neill-Butler, "Futility of Effort: Alice Neel and Motherhood, 1930–46," Pioneer Works,

May 27, 2021, https://pioneerworks.org/broadcast/futility-of-effort
-alice-neel-lauren-oneill-butler.

101 **moved into a poor building:** Lydia Figes, "Alice Neel: A Radical Painter
and 'Collector of Souls,'" Art UK, February 22, 2023, https://artuk.org
/discover/stories/alice-neel-a-radical-painter-and-collector-of-souls.

102 **"which had dominion over me":** Matthew Holman, "One Plus One,"
Sidecar (blog), New Left Review, May 12, 2023, https://newleftreview
.org/sidecar/posts/one-plus-one.

104 **sat for a portrait:** Ethan Brown, "Geoffrey Hendricks, Brian Buczak
& Sur Rodney (Sur) Residence & Studio," NYC LGBT Historic Sites
Project, 2023, https://www.nyclgbtsites
.org/site/geoffrey-hendricks-brian-buczak-sur-rodney-sur-residence
-studio/; Alice Neel, *Geoffrey Hendricks and Brian*, 1978, oil on canvas,
The Metropolitan Museum of Art, https://www.metmuseum.org/art
/collection/search/827194.

104 **most influential of Neel's subjects:** "Discovering Rose Fried's
Nephew by Alice Neel," Wadsworth Atheneum Museum of Art,
https://www.thewadsworth.org/focus-alice-neel/.

105 **Neel had only six solo shows:** "Alice Neel," Art Story, https://www
.theartstory.org/artist/neel-alice/.

105 **even on *The Tonight Show*:** "Artist Alice Neel Makes Her Classic
Appearance," YouTube video, 10:56, posted by Johnny Carson on June
6, 2022, https://www.youtube.com/watch?v=xoP3aNU4m8c.

105 **She was on the Works Progress Administration:** Jordan Casteel,
Jasmin Wahi, and Miguel Luciano, "Alice Neel: People Come First,"
The Met, March 22, 2021, https://www.metmuseum.org/perspectives
/articles/2021/3/alice-neel-people-come-first.

106 **annual stipend for life:** Karen Chernick, "Two Exhibitions Spotlight
Muriel Gardiner Buttinger, Alice Neel's Benefactor of 20 Years," *Art
Newspaper*, January 25, 2022, https://www.theartnewspaper.com/2022
/01/25/alice-neel-muriel-gardiner-buttinger-freud-museum-brussels.

106 **When Neel talks to Barbaralee Diamonstein:** "Inside New
York's Art World: Alice Neel," YouTube video, 33:20, posted by
DukeLibDigitalColl, October 2, 2015, https://www.youtube.com
/watch?v=2icegblNSI0.

106 **contrasts the "sophisticated painting":** "Inside New York's Art World."

106 **As Vivian Gornick reminded me:** Vivian Gornick, "Outside Looking In," *Women's Review of Books* 13, no. 5 (1996): 9.

107 **Neel had been reviewed by him:** Phoebe Hoban, "A 'Desperate Beauty,'" *ARTnews*, March 1, 2010, https://www.artnews.com/art -news/news/a-desperate-beauty-286/.

108 **John was a Jewish Holocaust survivor:** Margalit Fox, "John Gruen, Cultural Renaissance Man, Dies at 89," *New York Times*, July 19, 2016, https://www.nytimes.com/2016/07/20/books/john-gruen-cultural -renaissance-man-dies-at-89.html.

108 **Alice Neel famously painted Warhol:** Alice Neel, *Andy Warhol*, 1970, oil and acrylic on linen, Whitney Museum of American Art, https://whitney.org/collection/works/2887.

110 **Alice Neel did paint some women:** Alice Neel, *Adrienne Rich*, 1973, ink on paper, The Metropolitan Museum of Art, https://www.metmuseum. org/art/collection/search/835039; Alice Neel, *Kate Millett*, 1970, acrylic on canvas, National Portrait Gallery, https://npg.si.edu/object /npg_NPG.78.TC588; Alice Neel, *Annie Sprinkle*, 1982, oil on canvas, David Zwirner, https://www.davidzwirner.com/artworks/alice-neel -annie-sprinkle-aa8a4.

110 **had wisely cast Neel:** Luther W. Brady Art Gallery, "The Other 90%: Alice Neel," *Found in [GW] Collection* (blog), March 27, 2024, https://blogs.gwu.edu/foundingwcollection/2024/03/27/the-other -90-alice-neel/.

5. FROM FANTASY TO NECESSITY: THE CASE FOR STRATEGIC RADICALISM

116 **Campus Uprisings for Palestine:** Palestinian Campaign for the Academic and Cultural Boycott of Israel (PACBI), "Campus Uprisings for Palestine: Strategic Radicalism, Ethical Principles, and Incremental Wins," BDS, https://bdsmovement.net/news/campus-uprisings-for -palestine-strategic-radicalism-ethical-principles-and-incremental-wins.

119 **made me think of ACT UP:** "ACT UP," ACT UP, https://actupny.org/.

119 **ACT UP developed many of these:** "ACTUP Capsule History 1989," ACT UP, https://actupny.org/documents/cron-89.html.

124 **Lebanese Psychiatric Society announced:** "Statement from the

Lebanese Psychiatric Society (LPS)— 2013," LebMASH, May 11, 2016, https://lebmash.org/2016/05/11/statement-from-the-lebanese -psychiatric-society-lps/.

124 **Arab and Muslim queer groups:** "Over 1,000 People and 39 Organizations Signed the Statement," Black for Palestine, 2015, https://www.blackforpalestine.com/view-the-signatories.html.

125 **Omar Barghouti and I:** "GRITtv: Omar Barghouti: Equality Now, Not After Liberation," YouTube video, 1:11, posted by Laura Flanders & Friends, April 11, 2011, https://www.youtube.com/watch?v =qKu87nBQpTM.

125 **When Haneen Maikey:** "Rabih Alameddine and Haneen Maikey— Keynote from the Homonationalism and Pinkwashing Conference," YouTube video, 1:16:55, posted by CLAGS: The Center for LGBTQ Studies, July 19, 2013, https://www.youtube.com/watch?v=FRRTH 81MoFs&list=PLjVC7odFrjQDiR4OCnHsDWlxJ5Eu7SDUe& index=3.

125 **several key actions were taken:** Claire Fahy, Julian Roberts-Grmela, and Sean Piccoli, "'Let Gaza Live': Calls for Cease-Fire Fill Grand Central Terminal," *New York Times*, October 27, 2023, https://www .nytimes.com/2023/10/27/world/middleeast/grand-central-protest -nyc-israel-hamas-gaza.html

126 **stopped traffic on the Golden Gate Bridge:** Dan Levy, "A Decade of AIDS Activism Changed America—and ACT-UP," *SFGate*, March 22, 1997, https://www.sfgate.com/news/article/A-Decade-of-AIDS -Activism-Changed-America-and-2849161.php.

126 **ACT UP's affinity group creation:** "The New York Crimes," New York Public Library Digital Collections, https://digitalcollections .nypl.org/items/510d47e3-53a4-a3d9-e040-e00a18064a99.

126 *The New York War Crimes*: *New York War Crimes*, Writers Against the War on Gaza, https://newyorkwarcrimes.com/.

126 **resuscitated "Money for Healthcare, Not Warfare":** ACT UP NY (@actupny), "ACT UP and HIV/AIDS veterans stood in coalition . . ." X, December 1, 2023, https://x.com/actupny/status/173074275600 6318573.

126 **ACT UP's most iconic T-shirt:** "ACTUP NY, Silence=Death Watermelon T-Shirt to Benefit Palestine, Black," ACT UP, https://

give.actupny.com/product/act-up-ny-silence-death-watermelon-t-shirt
-to-benefit-palestine-black/.

127 **NYU professor Lisa Duggan called "homonormativity":** Lisa
Duggan, "The New Homonormativity: The Sexual Politics of
Neoliberalism," in *Materializing Democracy*, ed. Russ Castronovo and
Dana D. Nelson (Duke University Press, 2002), 175–94.

127 **Jasbir Puar named this "homonationalism":** Jasbir K. Puar,
Terrorist Assemblages: Homonationalism in Queer Times (Duke
University Press, 2007).

128 *The New York Times* **on "pinkwashing":** Sarah Schulman, "Israel
and 'Pinkwashing,'" *New York Times*, November 22, 2011, https://
www.nytimes.com/2011/11/23/opinion/pinkwashing-and-israels
-use-of-gays-as-a-messaging-tool.html.

128 **"If you are gay in Gaza":** "Jake Sherman Interviews Benjamin
Netanyahu: Full Transcript," *Punchbowl News*, June 21, 2024, https://
punchbowl.news/article/foreign-policy/jake-sherman-benjamin
-netanyahu-full-transcript/.

129 **campaign to rebrand the country's image:** Nathaniel Popper, "Israel
Aims to Improve Its Public Image," *Forward*, October 14, 2005, https://
forward.com/news/2070/israel-aims-to-improve-its-public-image/.

129 **"Americans don't see Israel":** Gary Rosenblatt, "Jewish Week:
Marketing a New Image," *Israel21c*, January 20, 2005, https://www
.israel21c.org/jewish-week-marketing-a-new-image/.

130 **foreign ministry organized a Brand Israel conference:** Popper,
"Israel Aims to Improve Its Public Image."

130 **appointed Ido Aharoni:** Herb Keinon, "Veteran Diplomat to Be
Livni Spokesman," *Jerusalem Post*, June 5, 2006, https://www.jpost
.com/israel/veteran-diplomat-to-be-livni-spokesman-pg-3.

130 **Saatchi and Saatchi was also working:** Bill Berkowitz, "Israel
Looking for an Extreme Makeover," *Electronic Intifada*, January 12,
2007, https://electronicintifada.net/content/israel-looking-extreme
-makeover/6676.

130 **David Saranga told PRWeek:** Ted McKenna, "Israel Branding Effort
Aims to Humanize Nation's Image," *PRWeek*, December 14, 2006,
https://www.prweek.com/article/1259503/israel-branding-effort-aims
-humanize-nations-image.

130 **he would "rather have a Style section":** Berkowitz, "Israel Looking for an Extreme Makeover."

130 **Aharoni's office hired TNS:** Ilan Pappé, "Brand Israel 2013," Artists for Palestine UK, https://artistsforpalestine.org.uk/2017/09/04/the -naked-face-of-israel-ilan-pappe-on-rebranding-zionism/.

131 **funded a pilot program:** Pappé, "Brand Israel 2013."

131 **In 2008, PACBI published:** Yitzhak Laor, "Putting Out a Contract on Art," *Haaretz*, July 25, 2008, https://www.haaretz.com/2008-07 -25/ty-article/putting-out-a-contract-on-art/0000017f-defd-df9c-a17f -fefdf0c50000?v=1723243110659.

131 **"The service provider is aware":** Laor, "Putting Out a Contract on Art."

131 **challenge facing Brand Israel:** "Brand Israel Should Integrate Conflict and Adversity, Says Advisor," Nation-Branding, February 24, 2010, https://nation-branding.info/2010/02/24/brand-israel/.

133 **campaign to "improve Israel's image":** Mel Bezalel, "Gay Pride Being Used to Promote Israel Abroad," *Jerusalem Post*, June 7, 2009, https:// www.jpost.com/israel/gay-pride-being-used-to-promote-israel-abroad.

133 **January 2010 conference:** Program, Tenth Annual Herzliya Conference, January 31, 2010, IDC Herzliya, https://www.runi.ac.il /media/203ikaty/3019agenda10.pdf.

133 **conference had some very interesting findings:** Vera Michlin, "Winning the Battle of the Narrative," working paper (Herzliya 2010, IDC Herzliya, January 31–February 3), https://www.runi.ac.il/media /xdbgdccw/3051winning2010.pdf.

134 **Also in 2010, Scott Piro:** Noah Rayman, "TA's 'Gay Vibe' Aims to Set Tourism Records," *Jerusalem Post*, July 21, 2010, https://www.jpost .com/israel/tas-gay-vibe-aims-to-set-tourism-records#google_vignette.

135 **"Rising from the global shores":** Danny Sadeh, "Campaign Branding Tel Aviv Gay Destination Underway," *Ynetnews*, July 21, 2010, https://www.ynetnews.com/articles/0,7340,L-3922524,00.html.

136 **The phrase was coined in 1985:** Kim Elsesser, "Pinkwashing, Greenwashing and Momwashing Explained," *Forbes*, May 31, 2024, https://www.forbes.com/sites/kimelsesser/2024/05/30/pinkwashing -greenwashing-and-momwashing-explained/.

136 **Brand Israel launched Israeli Pride Month:** E. B. Solomont, "San Francisco Festival to Showcase Israel's Gay Culture," *Jerusalem Post*,

April 17, 2010, https://www.jpost.com/international/san-francisco
-festival-to-showcase-israels-gay-culture#google_vignette.

137 **"Foreign Ministry is promoting"**: Tovah Lazaroff, "Foreign
Ministry Promoting Gay Israel," *Jerusalem Post*, October 26, 2006,
https://www.jpost.com/Israel/Foreign-Ministry-promoting-Gay-Israel.

138 **on condition of anonymity**: Lazaroff, "Foreign Ministry Promoting
Gay Israel."

138 **But David Saranga**: Lazaroff, "Foreign Ministry Promoting Gay Israel."

138 **One soldier had a photo**: David Propper, "Gay Israeli Soldier Proudly
Displays LGBTQ Flag on Gaza Soil in War Against Hamas," *New
York Post*, November 13, 2023, https://nypost.com/2023/11/13/news
/gay-israeli-solder-yoav-atzmoni-proudly-displays-lgbtq-flag-on-gaza
-soil-in-war-against-hamas/.

139 **"While Palestinians in Israel"**: Haneen Maikey, "Rainbow over
Palestine," *Guardian*, March 10, 2008, https://www.theguardian.com
/commentisfree/2008/mar/10/rainbowoverpalestine.

141 **wrote three iconic plays**: Edmund White, *Genet: A Biography*
(Alfred A. Knopf, 1993), xiv.

141 **his lover, Abdallah**: White, *Genet*, xvi.

141 **"apostle of the wretched of the earth"**: White, *Genet*, xvi.

141 **was an atheist**: White, *Genet*, xvii.

142 **Palestine and to the Black Panthers**: White, *Genet*, xvi.

143 **"He traversed the space"**: Edward Said, "On Jean Genet's Late Works,"
Grand Street, http://www.grandstreet.com/gsissues/gs36/gs36c.html.

145 **Edmund White himself helped me**: Edmund White, "A Witness to
Her Time," *New York Times*, January 28, 1996, https://www.nytimes
.com/1996/01/28/books/a-witness-to-her-time.html.

145 **He was visited by Marc Barbezat**: White, *Genet*, 249.

145 **Cocteau famously attended a party**: Adam Kirsch, "Couldn't Resist:
French Artists and Nazi rule," *Tablet*, January 12, 2009, https://www
.tabletmag.com/sections/arts-letters/articles/couldnt-resist.

146 **"Since Genet wants his lovers"**: White, *Genet*, 275.

146 **He met Sartre**: White, *Genet*, 275.

148 **"Maybe a homosexual"**: Blackpast, "(1970) Huey P. Newton,
'The Women's Liberation and Gay Liberation Movements,'" Blackpast
.org, April 17, 2018, https://www.blackpast.org/african-american

-history/speeches-african-american-history/huey-p-newton-women-s
-liberation-and-gay-liberation-movements/; Susan Faludi, "Death of a
Revolutionary," *New Yorker*, April 8, 2013, https://www.newyorker
.com/magazine/2013/04/15/death-of-a-revolutionary.

151 **he started to write *Prisoner of Love*:** Jean Genet, *Prisoner of Love*
(New York Review Books, 2003), 50.

6. THREATS OF PUNISHMENT AND OF COMPLICITY

153 **letter to the CUNY chancellor:** Rebecca Downs, "Pro-Palestine
Groups Oppose Bill to Fight Anti-Semitism on Campus," *Red Alert*,
March 14, 2016, https://www1.cuny.edu/portal_ur/news/in_news
/2016/March_15_2016.pdf, 13.

154 **movement leaders like Nerdeen Kiswani:** Sharon Otterman,
"Pro-Palestinian Group Is Relentless in Its Criticism of Israel, and It
Isn't Backing Down," *New York Times*, October 5, 2024, https://
www.nytimes.com/2024/10/05/us/within-our-lifetime-pro
-palestinian-activism.html.

154 **Paul Shechtman, was not present:** Alan Feuer, "If Police Stairwell
Shooting Was Accidental, Circumstances Around It Were Not," *New
York Times*, April 21, 2016, https://www.nytimes.com/2016/04/22
/nyregion/if-police-stairwell-shooting-was-accidental-circumstances
-around-it-were-not.html; "Zuckerman Spaeder LLP Named to the
National Law Journal's Midsize Hot List for Fourth Consecutive
Year," Zuckerman Spaeder, April 11, 2013, https://www.zuckerman
.com/news/press-release/zuckerman-spaeder-llp-named-national-law
-journals-midsize-hot-list-fourth-consecutive-year.

155 **a press campaign calling me antisemitic:** Kenneth Lovett,
"EXCLUSIVE: Pro-Israel Group Accuses CUNY Professor of Anti
-Semitic Behavior," *New York Daily News*, April 9, 2018, https://www
.nydailynews.com/2016/03/21/exclusive-pro-israel-group-accuses
-cuny-professor-of-anti-semitic-behavior/.

165 **Preexisting student organizations:** "Statement from Gerald
Rosberg, Chair of the Special Committee on Campus Safety,"
Columbia News, November 10, 2023, https://news.columbia.edu
/news/statement-gerald-rosberg-chair-special-committee-campus

-safety; Ron Liebowitz, "A Space for Free Speech, Not Hate Speech," Brandeis University, November 8, 2023, https://www.brandeis.edu /president/letters/2023-11-08-free-speech-not-hate-speech.html #:~:text=Dear%20Brandeis%20Community%2C,Justice%20in %20Palestine%20(SJP).

165 **new national US organization:** Faculty for Justice in Palestine Network, https://www.fjp-network.org/.

171 **President Schill had been targeted:** David Samson and Beatrice Villaflor, "ADL Midwest, StandWithUs, Brandeis Center Call for NU President Michael Schill's Resignation," *Daily Northwestern*, May 2, 2024, https://dailynorthwestern.com/2024/05/02/campus/adl -midwest-standwithus-brandeis-center-call-for-nu-president-michael -schills-resignation/.

173 **Palestinian novelist Susan Abulhawa:** Susan Abulhawa, "Gaza Is Our Moment of Truth," *Electronic Intifada*, May 14, 2024, https:// electronicintifada.net/content/gaza-our-moment-truth/46401.

173 **"This time is different":** Abulhawa, "Gaza Is Our Moment of Truth."

176 **33 percent of all American Jews:** Becka A. Alper, "How U.S. Jews Are Experiencing the Israel-Hamas War," Pew Research Center, April 2, 2024, https://www.pewresearch.org/short-reads/2024/04/02/how -us-jews-are-experiencing-the-israel-hamas-war/.

178 **"The industry which includes schools":** Tom Perkins and Will Craft, "For-Profit Colleges Fund Lawmakers Who Led Attack on Top Universities Over Campus Protests," *Guardian*, August 2, 2024, https://www.theguardian.com/us-news/article/2024/aug/02/elise -stefanik-virginia-foxx-funding.

179 **talk by Omar Barghouti:** "Omar Barghouti: 'BDS: Ending Complicity in Genocide and Apartheid,'" YouTube video, 13:19, posted by the Palestine Festival of Literature, March 14, 2024, https:// www.youtube.com/watch?v=0WowN9nHknY.

182 **"It is well-known that Israel":** "Study Abroad in Israel Violates Your Campus Policies," Faculty for Justice in Palestine Network, https:// www.fjp-network.org/study-abroad.

184 **Sofie Hurwitz, writing in *Mother Jones*:** Sophie Hurwitz, " Report: In One Year, More Than 100,000 Deaths in Gaza—Aided by $17.9

Billion From the US," *Mother Jones*, October 8, 2024, https://www
.motherjones.com/politics/2024/10/us-israel-funding-gaza-palestine
-deaths-october-100000-17-billion.

185 **"The issue that matters most":** Michael S. Roth, "I'm a College
President, and I Hope My Campus Is Even More Political This Year,"
New York Times, September 2, 2024, https://www.nytimes.com
/2024/09/02/opinion/college-president-campus-political.html.

7. JUSTIFICATION VS. SOLIDARITY IN ARTS AND ENTERTAINMENT

191 **"All our choices were made to reflect":** Jonathan Glazer, acceptance
speech, 96th Academy Awards, March 10, 2024, Academy of Motion
Picture Arts and Sciences, Dolby Theatre, Hollywood, CA.

192 **over one thousand Jewish "creatives and professionals":** Tatiana
Siegel, "Over 1,000 Jewish Creatives and Professionals Have Now
Denounced Jonathan Glazer's 'Zone of Interest' Oscars Speech in
Open Letter (EXCLUSIVE)," *Variety*, March 18, 2024, https://
variety.com/2024/film/news/jonathan-glazer-oscar-speech-zone-of
-interest-open-letter-1235944880/.

193 **document "The Question of Palestine":** "History of the Question of
Palestine," United Nations, https://www.un.org/unispal/history/.

193 **Ten days after this letter:** United Nations, "UN Experts Urge All
States to Recognise State of Palestine," news release, June 3, 2024,
https://www.un.org/unispal/document/un-experts-pr-ohchr-3jun24/.

194 **Jews believe that Glazer's statement:** Siegel, "Over 1,000 Jewish
Creatives and Professionals."

194 **"Blood libel" is an antisemitic claim:** "Blood Libel," United States
Holocaust Memorial Museum, https://encyclopedia.ushmm.org
/content/en/article/blood-libel.

195 **Save the Children estimates:** "Gaza's Missing Children: Over 20,000
Children Estimated to Be Lost, Disappeared, Detained, Buried Under
the Rubble or in Mass Graves," Save the Children, June 24, 2024, https://
www.savethechildren.net/news/gazas-missing-children-over-20000
-children-estimated-be-lost-disappeared-detained-buried-under.

196 **five hundred signatures to a new document:** Ellise Shafer and Alex

Ritman, "Alan Menken, Sarah Sherman, Alex Winter and Larry Charles Join Jewish Creatives Supporting Jonathan Glazer's Oscars Speech in Open Letter (EXCLUSIVE)," *Variety*, April 10, 2024, https://variety.com/2024/film/global/jonathan-glazer-oscars-speech -support-jewish-creatives-open-letter-1235960158/.

196 **signers who are composers:** Shafer and Ritman, "Alan Menken, Sarah Sherman."

201 **ten-play Mark Taper Forum season:** "CTG Leadership Update on Upcoming Taper/Douglas Seasons," Center Theatre Group, October 12, 2021, https://www.centertheatregroup.org/about/social -accountability/taper-douglas-leadership-update/; Sarah Schulman, "Op-Ed: Sure, Resolve to Stage More Plays by Women. It Still Won't Make Up for All We've Lost," *Los Angeles Times*, October 20, 2021, https://www.yahoo.com/news/op-ed-sure-resolve-stage-101021373.html.

201 **Jeremy O. Harris responded:** Charles McNulty, "'Stupid and Enraging': Lack of Women in L.A. Theater Lineup Sparks Protest," *Los Angeles Times*, October 5, 2021, https://www.latimes.com /entertainment-arts/story/2021-10-05/center-theatre-group-slave-play -jeremy-o-harris.

203 **The all-women season:** "2022/2023 Season," Center Theatre Group, https://www.centertheatregroup.org/about/press-room/press-releases -and-photos/mark-taper-forum/202223-season/.

204 **one of the deadliest dates:** Mersiha Gadzo and Urooba Jamal, "Israel War on Gaza Updates: Israel Kills 101 Palestinians in 24 Hours," *Al Jazeera*, June 22, 2024, https://www.aljazeera.com/news/liveblog/2024 /6/22/israel-war-on-gaza-live-hospital-overwhelmed-with-victims-from -camp-attack.

204 **hundreds of others committed:** "An Attestation for Editorial Independence," October 27, 2023, https://docs.google.com/document /d/15VS0P4Io4IKX3C0gX3__otazDhnxDitFwwPzS3UENEM/edit.

204 **"shameful repression" that reflects:** Maya Pontone, "Calls to Boycott *Artforum* Resurface Amid Rumored Palestine Edition," *Hyperallergic*, May 24, 2024, https://hyperallergic.com/918890/calls-to-boycott -artforum-resurface-amid-rumored-palestine-edition/.

204 **"As things continue to get worse":** Pontone, "Calls to Boycott *Artforum*."

205 **"You were hired because":** Pontone, "Calls to Boycott *Artforum*."
208 **"Taken to their logical conclusion":** Lionel Shriver, "Lionel Shriver's Full Speech: 'I Hope the Concept of Cultural Appropriation Is a Passing Fad,'" *Guardian*, September 13, 2016, https://www.theguardian .com/commentisfree/2016/sep/13/lionel-shrivers-full-speech-i-hope -the-concept-of-cultural-appropriation-is-a-passing-fad.
208 **novelist Kaitlyn Greenidge:** Kaitlyn Greenidge, "Who Gets to Write What?," *New York Times*, September 24, 2016, https://www.nytimes .com/2016/09/25/opinion/sunday/who-gets-to-write-what.html.
208 **writer Viet Thanh Nguyen:** Viet Thanh Nguyen, "Arguments over the Appropriation of Culture Have Deep Roots," *Los Angeles Times*, September 26, 2016, https://www.latimes.com/books/jacketcopy /la-ca-jc-appropriation-culture-20160926-snap-story.html.
209 **"most impressive aspect":** Richard Wright, "Carson McCullers Understood Human Nature," *New Republic*, February 19, 2014, https://newrepublic.com/article/116651/carson-mccullers-understood -human-nature.
210 **defies most Black characters:** Carson McCullers, *The Heart Is a Lonely Hunter* (Modern Library, 1993).
211 **Her given name was Lula:** Mary V. Dearborn, *Carson McCullers: A Life* (Alfred A. Knopf, 2024), 417.
212 **the late Dan Griffen:** "Tennessee Williams Scholars Conference Panel: Exotic Birds of a Feather: Carson McCullers and Tennessee Williams," *Tennessee Williams Annual Review*, 2000, https://www .tennesseewilliamsstudies.org/journal/work.php?ID=31.

8. WHEN SOLIDARITY FAILS

217 **"Queer Suicidality, Conflict, and Repair":** Sarah Schulman and Morgan M. Page, "Queer Suicidality, Conflict, and Repair: The Death of Bryn Kelly," transcript from presentation at Le Cagibi, Montreal, October 10, 2016.

Index

Brim, Matt, 18
Brooklyn College, 92
Brown, Jacqueline Nassy, 182
Brown, Wilmette, 11, 65–73
Brown University, 171, 184
Brutus, Dennis, 82
Buczak, Brian, 104
Burns, Ken, 15
Butler, Judith, 38, 52–53

Call Off Your Old Tired Ethics
    (COYOTE), 68
*Capitalist Patriarchy and the Case for
    Socialist Feminism* (Eisenstein), 99
Capote, Truman, 212, 213
Center for Constitutional Rights, 154
Center Theatre Group, 201, 202
Chomsky, Noam, 32
Christians, 21, 23, 36, 63, 127, 175
    and antisemitism, 23
    and anti-Palestinian activism, 175
    Christians and abortion rights, 63
    Christian homophobia, 127
    Christian Palestinians, 36
    Christian replacement theory, 21
    Christian right, 21
    Christians United for Israel, 21
    Christian Zionists, 21
Circle Repertory Company, 108
Citizen (Rankine), 94
City University of New York, 43, 85–86,
    90, 93, 125, 153–58, 169, 175
class divisions and consciousness
    and abortion rights activism, 65
    and antisemitism charges against
        author, 158
    and campus protests against Gaza
        War, 173
    and criteria for access to rights, 76, 79
    and cultural boycott of Israel, 197
    and Gaza War campus activism, 28
    and historical context of Gaza War, 36
    and McCullers's characters, 210
    and Neel's portraiture, 102
    and open admissions system, 88, 91–92,
        95, 98–99

and pinkwashing, 128
and policing of virtual space, 81
and solidarity rooted in inequality, 2
and strategic radicalism in BDS
    movement, 117
Cleage, Pearl, 201
Clyde's (Nottage), 203
Coalition of African Lesbians, 124
Cocteau, Jean, 144–45
collective care, 254–55
College of Staten Island, 85–94,
    153–54, 156
colonialism, 7, 32, 50, 78, 140–43, 147,
    150–52, 179
Columbia University, 25–26, 28, 43, 49,
    165, 170–71, 174
Committee for Abortion Rights and
    Against Sterilization Abuse, 61
Committee on Education and the
    Workforce, 174
Committee to Protect Journalists, 39
communism, 25, 100–101, 111, 123, 141
complicity, 158–59, 171, 173, 179–82,
    184, 267
Conflict Is Not Abuse (Schulman), 30, 221
Congress of Racial Equality, 70
consciousness-raising (CR) groups, 71–72
"context sensitivity" principle of effective
    activism, 116
Copelon, Rhonda, 60–61
corporate media
    and abortion rights activism, 64
    and activism of lesbians of color, 66
    coverage of Gaza War campus
        activism, 26
    and pressure on media professionals, 195
    and punishment of dissent, 265
    and responsibility to listen/hear, 48,
        50–51
    and shortcomings of culture industry,
        187–89
    and Wilmette Brown's activism, 69, 73
Council on American-Islamic Relations, 29
counterculture, 3, 15, 44, 264
*A Coupla White Faggots Sitting Around
    Talking* (film), 110

INDEX

wealth inequality, 100–101, 266. *See also* class divisions and consciousness; poverty
Webb, Marilyn, 148
Webster, Rachel Jamison, 174–75
We Could Have Been Friends, My Father and I (Shehadeh), 48
Wegmann, Phil, 33
Weimar, Germany, 168–69
Weiss, Jeff, 95
Weizman, Yaniv, 137
Welty, Eudora, 212
Wesleyan College, 171, 185
West Bank, 36, 124, 139, 150, 153, 172, 193
West Village, 109
White, Edmund, 141–42, 145–47, 149
white supremacy, 21, 214
Whitney Museum of American Art, 111
Wiley, Kehinde, 112
Williams, Tennessee, 212
Wilma Theater, 200
Wilson, Jane, 107
Winegar, Jessica, 176
Winter, Stephen, 18
Within Our Lifetime, 29, 154, 165
Wolf, Dick, 173
Wolfe, Maxine, 121
WomaNews, 66, 67, 72–73
Women for Wages for Housework, 71

women of color, 86, 99, 202–3
women playwrights, 199–203
Women's House of Detention, 107, 109
Woodson, Jacqueline, 112
Works Progress Administration, 105
World Court, 78
World Herald Tribune, 107
World Pride, 137
World Voices Festival, 52, 83
World War Two, 7, 45
Wright, Richard, 207, 213, 214
Writers Against the War on Gaza, 39, 126, 165, 205
Wunderman, 129

Yaddo, 212
Yale University, 28
Yevish, Charles, 15
Yevish, Dora, 14
Ynet, 133, 135, 137
Young and Rubicam, 129
Youth Council (of the NAACP), 70

Zambia, 71
Zionism, 21, 24–26, 43, 117, 133, 149, 156–57, 168, 175, 177
Zionist Organization of America, 153, 155, 157, 175
The Zone of Interest (film), 190–92